THE MCDONALDS

OF
SUGAR CREEK TOWNSHIP,
STARK COUNTY, OHIO

Robert Alan McDonald,
Kathie Eileen McDonald Courtney,
Richard Edwin McDonald,
Mary Jo McDonald Helfrich

ROBERT ALAN MCDONALD, KATHIE EILEEN MCDONALD COURTNEY, RICHARD EDWIN MCDONALD, MARY JO MCDONALD HELFRICH

The McDonalds of Sugar Creek Township, Stark County, Ohio
Copyright © 2025 by Robert Alan McDonald, Kathie Eileen McDonald Courtney, Richard Edwin McDonald, Mary Jo McDonald Helfrich

ISBN: 978-1-959700-64-7

All rights reserved. No part of this book may be reproduced or transmitted in any form or by any means without written permission from the authors.

Dedication

This is our attempt to say thank you to our parents, Marian and Mack McDonald, for the knowledge they gave us and the effort they put forth raising us. We are grateful for their efforts and the lessons they imparted, especially their respect for history and their dedication to integrity.

They were part of the generation that grew up after World War I, the war that was supposed to end all wars. A statement that proved to be incorrect. They had to face and defeat an even greater enemy. After which they had to restructure their lives and culture with no clear road map. No wonder they were called "the greatest generation". Despite obstacles, they succeeded. They raised the four of us. They were positive role models, teaching respect for others, honesty and, most of all, perseverance. Traits that we want to pass on.

We can trace some of our earliest ancestors' arrival to the Dutch colony, New Amsterdam, which was founded in 1609, some to the Massachusetts Bay Colony, Plymouth Rock, founded in 1620, others to Pennsylvania and Virginia after 1740. Our ancestry includes British soldiers who arrived during the American Revolution whose capture enabled them to change sides and stay in the new country. One of our family members served as a member of George Washington's bodyguards. His brother fought at the Battle of Kings Mountain. Later, several fought in the Civil War; three gave their lives.

ROBERT ALAN MCDONALD, KATHIE EILEEN MCDONALD COURTNEY, RICHARD EDWIN MCDONALD, MARY JO MCDONALD HELFRICH

Foreword

*It's in the quiet I miss you most.
When my mind has the chance to wander
and my heart has a moment to remember.
By Lola Lawrence*

The Farm as depicted in Biographical Record Stark County Ohio, published by Chapman Bros. Chicago 1892. Mr. John McWhinney's bio can be found in References

Growing up on a farm with the responsibilities that we shared gave us advantages later in life. For these reasons, we put this together for our children and for the generations that follow. We want you to know your heritage, to know something of the way we were raised, and the values we learned.

THE MCDONALDS

Our parents passed on traditional values and ways while having their vision fixed firmly on the future. The farm, buildings, and land provided a bridge from the past and the old traditional ways; self-sufficiency, independence, and self-reliance as preparation for a world which is constantly changing with evolving technology. Our experience was unique even when compared to our contemporaries. We did things, had experiences, and learned skills that even our peer group did not share. This is our attempt to give you a glimpse of how we grew up, to highlight those values and to pass on the understanding that we gained. We attempted to be factual, not glossing over defects. Sometimes, these defects are humorous.

We were raised to be grateful for this wonderful country we inherited, the freedoms we enjoy, and to give thanks to those willing to take up arms to preserve this way of life. We consider ourselves lucky to have known those that served during World War II as it included our father, uncles, neighbors, friends, and a fellow who served in the "red-eye express"— the outfit that moved supplies across Europe who were nearly all Black soldiers.

Our family's history is interwoven with that of the United States. We have found family members from coast to coast. We are grateful to all of them. Had they not done what they did, we would not be citizens of the greatest country the world has ever known.

According to David M. Eagleman in his book *Sum: Forty Tales from the Afterlives*, he states there are three deaths: first when the body ceases to function, second when the body is consigned to the grave, and third when your name is spoken for the last time. A variation of the third is when your story is told for the last time. We are preserving both names and stories.

Looking back on our upbringing, we wouldn't change anything. We think Mom and Dad got it about right. We hope that someday you will say the same about us.

ROBERT ALAN MCDONALD, KATHIE EILEEN MCDONALD COURTNEY, RICHARD EDWIN MCDONALD, MARY JO MCDONALD HELFRICH

Table of Contents

Dedication

Foreword

Chapter	**Title**	**Page**
1	The Farm	7
2	Our Ancestry	23
3	Our Parents	53
4	Getting to Know Marian	71
5	Getting to Know Mack	83
6	The Children	105
7	Friends and Neighbors	117
8	Campers	133
9	Farming Over the Years	137
10	Farm Work and Chores	159
11	The Woods	179
12	Other Goings-on	201
13	Vacation	225
14	Family Time	227
15	Bo's Story	233
16	Bill	251
17	Mary's Jonny	261
18	Ginger	271
19	Animals We Knew	275
20	Butchering	283
21	Weather Events	291
22	A New Beginning	305
23	Family Information	309
24	Family Artistry	337
25	Family Recipes	353

Reference Information

THE MCDONALDS

Chapter One - The Farm

We grew up on what was then a large farm, 152 acres, purchased in 1947 and owned until 2004—57 years. The events recounted primarily occurred between 1945 and 1979, a period of 34 years.

Upon return from military service after World War II, in October 1945, our father, A.C. (Alpha Carl) McDonald and our mother Marian Pauline Jones McDonald, decided on a career in farming. They first rented a farm owned by the Booth family (our maternal grandmother's family) in Harmon for about a year. In early 1947, they purchased The Farm.

The Farm, described in the Abstract of The Title as Part of the Northwest Quarter of Section #23 Township #11, Range #10, (Sugar Creek Township), Stark County, Ohio, was originally part of the land Thomas Rotch obtained by a Government Patent to the Northwest Quarter Section #23 Township #11 Range 10 containing 160 acres May 1, 1823, by James Monroe, President of the United States. (A Patent is the first title transferred from the government to a private party.)

According to our mother's research, Mr. Rotch was the owner of vast tracts of Ohio land which he sold. He was a wealthy man, and the land sales increased his wealth. He was also a ship owner. One of his ships was targeted during the Boston Tea Party.

John R. McWhinney Sr. purchased the farm from the heirs of Thomas Rotch on August 3, 1829. The Farm ownership continued with the McWhinney family from John R. McWhinney Sr. to John R. McWhinney Jr., and then to his heirs until February 1, 1947, when A.C. and Marian McDonald purchased it. This land, excepting certain Rights of Way granted to Railroads, became the McDonald Farm. The McWhinney's were the second owners. Therefore, McDonald's purchase made us the third owners and the last to use the original boundaries.

Mother's recollection and comments are supported by *Massillon History: Thomas Rotch- The Story of Thomas & Charity Rotch;* https://massillonmuseum.org/57. This article describes Thomas

ROBERT ALAN MCDONALD, KATHIE EILEEN MCDONALD COURTNEY, RICHARD EDWIN MCDONALD, MARY JO MCDONALD HELFRICH

Rotch buying Ohio land in two transactions: First, 2500 acres at the Steubenville Land Office and 4000 acres at the Wooster Land Office. Based upon the geography we conclude that the McDonald Farm was included in the second transaction. The Northwest Territory of which Ohio is a part was ceded to the United States by the British in the Treaty of Paris at the conclusion of the Revolutionary War.

The Rotch name is prominent in Massillon. According to Rich's recollection from hearing conversations between our parents and older neighbors, Mr. McWhinney Sr. bought the farm because the trees were larger than were the trees growing on land around Massillon. He reasoned that the land was better.

Rich and Mary recall Grandma Nellie Jones telling them about John R. McWhinney, Jr., a Civil War veteran, riding through Harmon on a large dapple-gray horse. He was ramrod straight with a long white beard. The Harmon kids would hide behind the bushes when he came through. They were in awe of him. *(See Mr. McWhinney Jr.'s biography reproduced in References.)*

THE MCDONALDS

The farmhouse shortly after move-in, viewed from the south. The chimneys accessible in each second-floor room can be seen. The first-floor ground floor room was Mom and Dad's bedroom. The room above theirs was Rob and Rich's. On the east (right side of the photo) was the living room, with Kathie's room on the second floor. The dining room with Mary's room above it was on the north and can't be seen in this photograph. The first-floor room on the left (west) was the TV room with the room above used for storage. The room at the back sticking out on the left (west) side is the kitchen.

The farm was one half mile square, 160 acres with the railroad right-of-way, seven plus acres, taken out. Two different railroads came through, with one crossing the other near Lawndell Road, which bisected the farm. There was also a siding that one of the rail companies used for rail car storage.

ROBERT ALAN MCDONALD, KATHIE EILEEN MCDONALD COURTNEY, RICHARD EDWIN MCDONALD, MARY JO MCDONALD HELFRICH

The Farm Aerial Photograph taken circa 1934

THE MCDONALDS

Lawndell Road was named years after our purchase, and according to Mary's recollection, Dad believed it was originally built as a stagecoach road which ran between Wilmot (then Milton) and Navarre. It is Township Road 303.

Railroads

The railroads when we first moved to the farm were the Wheeling and Lake Erie (W&LE or WLE) and the other was the Baltimore and Ohio (B&O). Over time, the railroad ownership and the names changed. The Wheeling and Lake Erie was leased to the Nickel Plate Road, which later became part of the Norfolk and Southern. The B&O, the oldest railroad in the United States, was acquired by the Chesapeake & Ohio railroad becoming the Chessie System, which became part of the CSX Corp. Our Grandpa Dan Jones would joke, "If the Nickel Plate ran in a circle, would it be an O (B&O)?"

Prior to our ownership, the streetcar line also ran through the farm adjacent to and paralleling the railroads. The streetcar ran from New Philadelphia to Canton passing through Harmon with a stop right in front of our Grandparent's home. The streetcar ceased operations, and the right-of-way land was deeded back to the farm.

Mom told us a story about one of the conductors on the streetcar line, a Welshman. The streetcar was always late getting into Canton despite an on-time start when leaving New Philadelphia. The conductor was blamed for this. To prove that it was the fault of the scheduling and not the operation, this conductor began a run exactly at the scheduled time and took the car without making a single stop for passengers, arriving in Canton right on schedule – pronouncing it using his Welsh accent, "I brought her in right on SHE-GOOL-EE (schedule)," thus proving his point.

The railroad roadbed produced useful things: wild strawberries, elderberries, raspberries, blackberries, and occasionally horse radish grew on the railroad right-of-way, which we harvested. These things are gone now thanks to chemical defoliants.

ROBERT ALAN MCDONALD, KATHIE EILEEN MCDONALD COURTNEY, RICHARD EDWIN MCDONALD, MARY JO MCDONALD HELFRICH

In the days of steam, we would walk the tracks and pick up coal that had fallen out of the engine, tender, or off a gondola car. The railroads used coal to produce steam, and railroads hauled coal to their customers. We added the scavenged coal to our supply and burned it in the winter to heat the house. The coal supplemented the wood that we cut for heat. Occasionally, when we were out on the tracks scavenging, the fireman would often toss us a shovel full or two. This was great coal. The railroads bought and used the best. It really burned hot!

The House

The house we grew up in, viewed from the southeast. The building north of the house (right) is the butcher-house or summer kitchen. Photograph by Marian McDonald after Rich's exterior restoration and remodeling.

The first dwelling was a cabin on a hill overlooking Sugar Creek southwest of the current farm stead. Only traces of the foundation remain.

THE MCDONALDS

The second house, along with the first barn and other buildings, were constructed near the center of the property. In 1872, the third house was constructed. It was the house we grew up in.

The second house was still standing when we took possession. We used it for storage and as a workshop. Later, the old house, as we called it, was torn down to make way for the machine shed built where the garden had been.

The third house was two stories in the shape of a cross. The style was Italian Provincial. There was a cellar under three of the four ground-floor rooms. Each ground floor room had an outside door, access to a chimney, exterior windows, and an exterior door. Each exterior door had a fully functional transom, which allowed ventilation without opening the door. There was a center stairwell with stairs leading to the second floor and another set leading to the cellar. The living room had a bay window which extended to the second floor, so the bedroom over the living room also had a bay. Every room on the first or second floor had a 10 foot ceiling.

The original plan was to build the house in a T shape. But we surmised, they decided it wouldn't be large enough, so they added a wing to the south side resulting in the cross shape. We reckoned that addition was done along with the original construction, but they did not excavate the cellar under it. Instead, there was a crawl space that wasn't accessible for anything except a small animal like a rabbit or a skunk.

After construction, a room was added to the northwest corner which became the kitchen. This room was only a single story built over a crawl space accessible from the cellar. What originally had been the kitchen became the dining room.

There were two pantries off the original kitchen (dining room): one on the east and the other on the west side. Dad, with Grandpa Dan's help, converted the west pantry to a bathroom. The east pantry became a closet, the only one in the house. For years, there was only a single bath. Later, a shower and laundry area were added to the cellar. During the major remodeling, Rich added an upstairs bath, which Mom always wanted. *(See Pictures and Drawings)* Prior to

ROBERT ALAN MCDONALD, KATHIE EILEEN MCDONALD COURTNEY, RICHARD EDWIN MCDONALD, MARY JO MCDONALD HELFRICH

having an upstairs bath, Mom had to carry water upstairs for cleaning and back down for disposal.

The outside door to the east of the dining room led to a covered porch which had a set of covered stairs which provided outside access to the cellar. The exterior door to the north, out of the kitchen, led to a porch with sandstone steps accessing a sidewalk which went to the butcher-house.

The design did not include central heating. Instead, each room had access to a chimney permitting installation of heating stoves. Ohio winters got cold, and a stove heated a single room. The exterior windows and doors allowed cross ventilation during hot weather.

Later, a wood/coal-burning furnace was installed in the cellar. Heat runs radiated from the furnace to the first-floor rooms. One heat run served the kitchen, dining room, and bathroom. It terminated in the dining room wall, so most of the heat went into the dining room. Upstairs they installed floor registers in the east and north upstairs rooms, allowing heat to rise into those rooms. There was also a cold air plenum leading from the east first floor room back to the furnace. All heat movement was based on the principle that warm air rises and cold air falls— convection. The south bedroom that Rich and Rob shared had no access to heat. The stoves were gone before we bought the property, removed after the furnace was installed.

Without any heat source, the second story bedrooms got downright cold in winter. In fact, Rich recalls snow inside the windows in the boy's bedroom.

Linoleum was installed during an attempt to remodel the boy's bedroom. The first winter after installation demonstrated why that was a poor choice. Placing one's feet on a cold floor when getting out of a warm bed is something to be avoided. Mom agreed linoleum wasn't a desirable choice. But it remained until Rich did the big remodeling project.

It was a very well-built house. The main foundation was cut sandstone. As was the custom in those days, the exterior walls were hollow and there was no insulation in the attic. The second-floor rooms were arranged over the first floor. A center stairway and a center hall accessed the second floor east of the stairs.

One of the noteworthy features was a two-story bay window on the east facing side. Likely the ground floor east room had been intended as the dining room and the south facing ground floor room the sitting room or parlor. The purpose of the west first floor room wasn't clear. It could have been a bedroom or a farm office. Because the furnace was immediately below this room it was the warmest room in the winter. We used it as a family room or TV room.

Cooking was done on a coal stove until Dad and Grandpa Jones wired the house for electricity and plumbed it for running water. Looking back, it's incredible to consider that Mom grew up in a home with electricity which supplied power for a refrigerator, stove, lights, and a radio and running water in the kitchen and a full bathroom. Then, after Dad returned from the service, she moved into a house that had none of these features.

Getting electrical power wasn't a straightforward simple task because the power lines were along Justus Avenue but didn't extend down Twp. Road 303 to the farmstead. Since we were the only customer, the electric company wasn't overly anxious to go to the expense of putting up power poles, installing wire, and a transformer so the wiring could be run to the house.

Dad completed an application for power, but the power company was dragging their feet, which irritated Grandpa Dan. Before too many days passed, Grandpa Dan paid a visit to the electric company's office in Massillon. He didn't tell Dad what he was doing; he just went to the office and forcefully explained that Dad was a combat World War II veteran who needed power. Apparently, Grandpa Dan's visit got things moving. Before long, electricity was available. After that, Dad and Grandpa Jones wired the house and extended electrical service to the butcher house, milkhouse, the sheep barn, and the barn.

Once electricity was available, a water well was drilled in the milkhouse, a jet pump was acquired, and water lines were installed to the house and barn. Fortunately, Grandpa Dan had both electrical and plumbing tools. That work lasted 50 years until Rich replaced it.

Having electricity and running water certainly helped Mom!

Surrounding the house were large mature trees. On the west and south facing the road were huge maples, on the north was an enormous weeping birch and to the east there was a pine and a persimmon. Further east were two of the largest sassafras trees in the area. Collectively these trees protected the house from high winds, and in the summer, the trees served as air conditioning.

A half-size door in the west wall of the north bedroom permitted access to the attic space above the kitchen. The window in the adjoining attic was cracked, allowing enough wind to enter to rattle the door. Access to the main attic was through the north bedroom ceiling.

The north room became Mary's bedroom. When younger, Mary was always afraid someone would enter her room through one of these attic doors. This kept her awake. She would come to Kathie's room and get into bed. Kathie thinks Rich could have augmented Mary's fears telling her there was a "boogie man" under her bed. Mary also recalls going downstairs to Mom and Dad's room to sleep if Kathie wouldn't allow her in her bed. Mary would somehow find space in Mom and Dad's double bed. It was a tight squeeze.

Farm Buildings

At various times, three barns had been built. The first two had burned down. The first burning was attributed to a spark from a railroad engine. That barn, the smallest, was closer to the railroad. This barn is depicted in the drawings on the cover and in the Foreword. The second and third barns were constructed on the same foundation: 38 feet by 90 feet on the ground floor and 40 feet by 90 feet on the second floor. The first barn, according to the drawing shown in the *Biographical Record Stark County Ohio, published by Chapman Bros. Chicago 1892,* may have been too small, so they increased the size and in addition to changing the location when building the second. The fire that took the second barn was attributed to spontaneous combustion of damp hay, which can occur when hay is placed in storage before it is thoroughly dry. Its size was considered adequate, so they built the third as a replica of the second. We were always told that the best barn—materials, construction, and finish—was the second, which, of course, we never saw. The framing lumber used to construct the barns was cut from the woods on the farm.

Additional buildings on the farmstead were a sheep barn built at a right angle to the main barn, a combination double corncrib/storage shed, another corncrib located west of the sheep barn, a garage, a summer kitchen or butcher-house, an icehouse which was converted to a milk house, a chicken coop, a brooder house, and a smokehouse.

There were apple, peach, cherry, and pear trees and a grape arbor all producing fruit. There was a garden directly in front of the old house. For a time, Dad had a couple of honeybee hives. Honeybees were a lot of work and had Dad continued keeping them, they would have required investing in equipment. As it was, two neighbors, Ed Miller and Arden Grosklaus, had both the knowledge and equipment. They primarily took care of the bees. Dad didn't feel it was right for them to do the work while we got the benefits, and he wasn't that keen on bee keeping. Eventually he turned the hives over to them and they took them away.

During the period we owned the property, the sheep barn, the old house, the corncrib/storage shed, and the other corncrib were torn down. A large machine shed, a hog farrowing/finishing building, and a much larger corncrib were constructed.

Self Sufficiency

The care that McWhinney's imparted included a large chestnut oak planted east of the house. That tree came from an acorn, Mr. John R. McWhinney, Jr., gathered when he visited Arlington National Cemetery. He was a Civil War Veteran and planted the oak in remembrance of those he served with that lost their lives. That oak produced a bounty of acorns each year. We used to watch a doe bring her fawn to the yard in the fall to feast on the acorns.

The milk house was originally an icehouse built of hollow glazed tile. Ice would be cut in the winter, brought to the icehouse for storage with saw-dust insulation added. The butcher-house or summer kitchen had a wood-burning furnace that could heat two iron or copper kettles simultaneously and a line-shaft for running butchering equipment. We never used the line-shaft as it was unnecessary after electrification.

Taken in total, the farm was self-sustaining. The design was unique in that other neighboring farms did not have a butcher-house or an icehouse. We didn't use all the features as originally intended but did use most of them.

Farming Operations

After the purchase, the next task was to move about two miles from the Booth farm in Harmon. Rob recalls a bit of the move. He was three years old. The primary means of transport was a horse-drawn wagon. Rob recalls crossing the railroad tracks, then turning into the farm driveway. Rob's job was watching kittens in an empty watering trough. He recalls going into the house where the room that became the dining room was piled high with furniture. It wasn't easy for a small boy to get through.

The folks who were renting before the McDonald purchase hadn't yet completely moved out when Marian and Mack moved in so there was a brief time with two families in the house.

Kathie, Richard, and Mary were all born after the move.

The McDonald family included Mack and Marian and four children: Robert, Kathie, Richard, and Mary—in birth order. Everybody on the farm had a job or what we called chores. Mack and Marian didn't work at what we knew as a "public job." They were farmers.

The primary business of the farm was dairy and hogs. We milked about 20 head of Holsteins. Initially, the hog operation was a boar and five or six sows. Dad bought the hog foundation stock from

Arthur Eberly, our Uncle Don Jones' father-in-law. The hogs were purebred Chester Whites.

We sold milk to the local cheese factory in Brewster about 2 miles away. Each day, a truck would come to the farm and pick up about four 10-gallon cans of milk and take them to the cheese factory. Once a month, the dairy sent out a check for the milk they had received. This was operating money. Later, we hauled our own milk to the dairy, and returning with a tank containing about 300 gallons of whey, what's left of the milk after making cheese, which we fed to the hogs.

Dad converted the sheep barn to a hog barn, which was used primarily for finishing, but occasionally for farrowing. Farrowing is the birthing area and finishing is getting them large enough to be sold for meat. We stored straw - usually the barley straw - for bedding in the second story.

The sows would each produce two litters of pigs each year. Later, the hog operation expanded to 16 sows. Finished hogs, weighing 220 to 250 pounds, were sold to a local slaughterhouse. Each litter would wean an average of eight pigs. Initially, the farm produced 80 to 100 hogs per year. Later, more hogs were sold. Thus, the hogs supplied a larger portion of the income. Hogs were known as farm mortgage removers.

Other income came from the sale of wheat, the only grain that Mack sold, and eggs, which was Marian's money often used for school lunches and other things the children needed. Occasionally, Mom would buy something for herself.

Sometimes Dad would need money and, without Mom's knowledge, dip into her funds. Because Mom always knew how much she had, Dad didn't get away scott free. Mom, after finding Dad's stash, would upbraid him for getting into her money often by stating, "Why are you getting into my money when you have all this of your own?" To which Dad would reply, "I'm saving that for something I need." Exactly what his need was he didn't say. However, Dad had money when he wanted to buy a Christmas present for Mom.

ROBERT ALAN MCDONALD, KATHIE EILEEN MCDONALD COURTNEY, RICHARD EDWIN MCDONALD, MARY JO MCDONALD HELFRICH

Typically, the wheat was sold in January and was used to pay the real-estate taxes, the first installment being due in February each year. Later, Mack stopped planting wheat and increased planting barley, which was hog food. All the corn, oats, barley, and hay we grew were fed to the cattle, hogs, chickens, or horses. Besides milk, the dairy cattle produced a calf each year. Most calves were sold as veal after weaning. Some heifers were kept as replacements for older cows that were no longer productive. Old cows would be sold when no longer productive, or they could be slaughtered for meat.

Each of us kids had a dairy cow that was "ours." That meant we got the income from the sale of that cow's calf. That money went into our college fund, a savings account at the Navarre Deposit Bank where our Uncle Don Jones, Mom's brother, worked. From the day we were born, we knew we were going to college.

Each year we butchered at least one head of beef and two or three hogs for our own use.

We had gardens that produced sweet corn, tomatoes, potatoes, squash, pumpkins, onions, cabbage, lettuce, cucumbers, and herbs used in canning and preserving. We also picked wild blackberries, raspberries, and elderberries. Mom canned, preserved, froze, and put-up jams and jelly. Now and then we'd make home-made ice cream using cream and milk that didn't get sent to the cheese factory.

Initially, a team of two horses, Dan and Bird, and a used Farmall F-20 tractor supplied the power. Most of the tillage equipment was horse-drawn or hand operated. Over the years, we added equipment.

In 1951, Dad bought a new Minneapolis Moline Z tractor. With it came a mounted two row corn cultivator and a semi-mounted seven-foot sickle bar mower. The Minnie was a major improvement and led us away from horses. It produced 32 horsepower at the drawbar and could pull two or three 14-inch plowshares. However, Dad always regretted that he did not buy the next larger size, designated U, which had 45 horsepower and could pull three to four 14-inch plowshares.

THE MCDONALDS

1951 Minneapolis Moline Z

We ate very well. We had little cash, but we were healthy. We drank unpasteurized milk. Kathie thinks it made our immune system strong, as we were seldom ill. In fact, the veterinary bill was always more than what we spent on the doctor. And, in those days there was no such thing as medical insurance. When we went to the doctor, dentist, or heaven forbid, the hospital, Mom and Dad wrote a check.

And like all farms, we had other animals. We had dogs, cats, horses, and later sheep. These other animals were primarily pets, but we expected them to earn their keep. Stories of many of these animals is presented later.

ROBERT ALAN MCDONALD, KATHIE EILEEN MCDONALD COURTNEY, RICHARD EDWIN MCDONALD, MARY JO MCDONALD HELFRICH

THE MCDONALDS

Chapter Two – Our Ancestry

We have traced our ancestry and find that we are primarily from the Celtic clans and of Great Britian: McDonald from Ireland, and prior to that from Scotland, and Jones from Wales. However, it is possible to look even further back, and when we do, we find ancestors from The Netherlands, the Walloons – from what is now southern Belgium, and Germany, in addition to England and France.

We have relied on information gleaned from the internet, from a document developed by Clarance L. Booth, from our collective memories of conversations recalled largely by Mary and the rest of us to a lesser extent, to documents found in Mom's Bible in Mary's possession, the Meredith Bible in Richard's, and the McDonald Bible in Robert's.

We are confident that the Joneses came to America in the 1870s as we are the third generation. We believe the McDonalds or McDaniels as they were known at immigration – explained later – arrived in 1740.

But others were already here. Our maternal grandmother's family surname is Booth who immigrated as a British soldier. Our Grandmother Nellie Booth Jones told us that we were related to John Wilkes Booth; yes, THE guy that assassinated Abraham Lincoln. Also the James family of Missouri that produced Frank and Jesse James. According to Grandma, an ancestor of the James family came over on the Mayflower. If correct, that would have been 1620.

Our father's family includes the surname Van Natta which we believe is Dutch. We believe they arrived at approximately 1660 or even as early as 1609, when the Dutch settled New Amsterdam – New York today.

Our earliest paternal ancestor with the surname MacDonnell/McDaniel/McDonald, born in North America is David McDaniel. Two of David's older brothers served in the American Revolutionary Army: James McDaniel Sr. and Henry McDaniel Jr. David's father Henry Sr. was born in County Antrim, Northern

ROBERT ALAN MCDONALD, KATHIE EILEEN MCDONALD COURTNEY, RICHARD EDWIN MCDONALD, MARY JO MCDONALD HELFRICH

Ireland, immigrated in 1740 with his father, and may have served in the French and Indian War.

James Sr., who would be an uncle with six greats preceding uncle, was a bodyguard for George Washinton during the American Revolution. Henry Jr., who served in the same militia as his elder brother, fought and was wounded in the battle of Kings Mountain.

Military service also extends to our maternal ancestors beginning with the American Revolution with the earliest of the Booths coming the colonies as a British soldier, subsequently changing sides and thereby immigrating.

We know that three of our family died during the Civil War. One was a Booth, one was a Melton, and one was a Van Natta. Another Van Natta died in 1865 at 25 years of age, but we cannot determine the cause of death as being the result of the war.

Members of our family have been in North America since colonial times. Our history is part of American history. Part of the reason for this book is to document what we know or think we know in the hope that information will be added over time. We may be in error and encourage correction if better data becomes available.

MCDONALD

Our paternal grandparents were Samuel Sanford McDonald, born March 3, 1881, Mineral Wells, West Virginia, and Julia Naomi Melton McDonald, born October 31, 1889, Bellville, Kansas. They married on December 11, 1907, in Fairvalley Woods County, Oklahoma. Their wedding picture (shown on the next page) was taken in Seaside Oregon. It is highly likely they honeymooned in Seaside near or at the home of Julia Van Natta Rider, Grandma Julia's grandmother, or her sister Hattie E. Rider Hart. Grandpa Sam passed August 28, 1963. Grandma Julia passed February 4, 1980. Samuel and Julia were parents of Jessie Marie, Alpha Carl (our father), Hester Edith, Betty Cora, and Julia Lee.

THE MCDONALDS

Samuel Sanford and Julia Naomi Melton McDonald's Wedding Photograph

Samuel's father was Valentine Washington McDonald, born 1842 in Greenbriar, Virginia – later West Virginia. He died in 1910 at his home seven and one-half miles from Alva, Oklahoma. His mother was Mary Elizabeth Butcher McDonald, born January 23, 1845, and died February 18, 1890. In 1893 Valentine married Hester Kesterson. Samuel was the ninth of twelve children.

All 12 of the children were born to Valentine and Mary and are: Mary Elizabeth b. 11/29/1864, Albert Scott b. 1/10/1866, James Willie b. 11/16/1867, Lilly Dale b. 12/13/1869, John Harrison b. 1/1/1871, Henry Monroe (Mun) b. 2/1/1874, Theodore Madison b. 2/13/1876, Dora Jan b. 11/21/1878, Samuel Sanford (our grandfather) b. 3/3/1881, Arthur (Hun) b. 7/10/1883, Clara Belle 5/16/1885, and Minnie May b. 6/13/1887. The first four children were born in Wood County, West Virginia, as were the last five. The middle three were born in Kansas: John and Henry in Republic County and Theodore in Cabette County. *(This information is from a handwritten document in our mother's hand stored in the McDonald Family Bible in Robert's possession and confirmed in our grandfather Sam's hand in a note in the same location.)*

ROBERT ALAN MCDONALD, KATHIE EILEEN MCDONALD COURTNEY, RICHARD EDWIN MCDONALD, MARY JO MCDONALD HELFRICH

Valentine's father was Nathan McDonald, born February 2, 1810, in Pennsylvania, and who passed in 1883 in West Virginia. Nathan married Harriet Eckelberry McDonald, born 1816 and passed 1894. Nathan McDonald's father was Alexander McDonald.

Alexander McDonald's father was David McDaniel. Alexander was born in 1787 and passed in 1850. Alexander was born in Chadville, Fayette County, Pennsylvania. Alexander married Nancy Springer McDonald, who was born in 1791, and who died in 1880.

David McDaniel was born in 1770 in Fayette County, Pennsylvania. He passed in 1850. David was married to Mary Middlecoff McDaniel, whose date of birth and death are not known.

David's father was Henry McDaniel, Sr. We have two accounts of his birth. One that he was born in Virginia and the other that he was born in 1724 in County Antrim Northern Ireland. Henry lived in Greenbriar (Monroe county), Virginia (now West Virginia) and died in 1819 in Monroe County, Virginia (also now in West Virginia). His mother was Mary Ann Porter McDaniel, born in 1735 and died in 1793.

According to the source that seems to us the most reliable is a Family History of Henry McDaniel Sr. – Monroe County, West Virginia. From "The Ancestry of Grace Carolyn McDaniel" by Kelly Greer. Henry Sr. may have been in the line of the McDonnell or MacDonnell's of County Antrim, Northern Ireland, the first ancestor being Sir Randal MacDonnell, the first Earl of Antrim in 1601, son of Sorley MacDonnell. Please refer to the web site and brief description in the References.

Henry Sr. immigrated with his father John Michael McDaniel in 1740 on the ship *The Bachelor* which arrived in New York. Henry Sr.'s two brothers, Caleb and Sylvester, came later. This information agrees with our father's saying that originally there were three brothers who immigrated. A story handed down through the family.

John Michael McDaniel's father was Sir John McDaniel MacDonnell, and his mother was Rebecca Williams. John Michael was born in Antrim Northern Ireland in approximately 1695. We haven't found the date of Rebecca's birth, nor have we found Sir John's birthdate. His wife was Anises Anne Pasley. They married in 1718. But her birthdate isn't known. It is particularly interesting that Sir John's middle name is McDaniel, and his last name is MacDonnell. Over the years our family has had at least three different surnames.

For the sake of brevity, we have limited the information provided. Included in References is information on the Glenarm Castle and the Dunluce Castle both which we believe to be our ancestral homes albeit at differing times. Please refer to Reference Information and consult the internet for a link to the article "Exploring the History and Mystery of Dunluce Castle" by Colin.

It is speculated that Henry Sr. may have been an officer in the French and Indian War as he was granted land as compensation, but due to the lack of definitive records his service cannot be confirmed.

One of Henry and Mary Ann's sons was James W. McDaniel, Sr. He was an Orderly Sergeant who served with the Bedford County, Virginia Militia during the American Revolution. He was one of General Washington's bodyguards.

Another of Henry and Mary Ann's sons, Henry Jr., was granted a pension due to his service in the Revolutionary War. His recorded statement is that he served as a captain, and was wounded during the Kings Mountain Battle, a turning point in the war. It was fought by the Overmountain Men who traveled 330 miles from Sycamore Shoals, North Carolina – now Elizabethton, Tennessee – to defeat the British Regulars decisively.

It is believed that by being able to trace ancestry to both James and Henry Jr. McDaniel that the women are eligible for membership in the Daughters of the American Revolution, DAR.

Our surname changed over the years. In Northern Ireland, it seems to have been MacDonnell. Upon immigration, it was McDaniel. Henry Sr.'s last name was McDaniel as was David's. David was the first of our grandparents born in America. David's son Alexander's last name is shown as McDonald. However, all of Alexander's siblings' surnames are shown as McDaniel. We have found no information as to why this is so.

ROBERT ALAN MCDONALD, KATHIE EILEEN MCDONALD COURTNEY, RICHARD EDWIN MCDONALD, MARY JO MCDONALD HELFRICH

The following explanation was found during an on-line search: **"When did McDonald become McDaniel and why?"** In Scotland, they say there are no McDaniels. They are supposed to be McDonalds but when they came to America there was not one way to spell words.

The name McDonald, or the variation McDaniel, is claimed to be of Irish or Scottish origin and is composed of the prefix Mac (shortened to Mc), meaning "son of" and the Christian name of Daniel, Donall, or Donell. Both versions – McDonald and McDaniel – are found in the Holden and Talley ancestry. Donell or Donall, a baptismal name was popular in both Ireland and Scotland in ancient times. The Gaelic name Donald or Donnel and the English name Daniel all mean the same thing to Gaelic people. The tradition is that the family is descended from one Muireadach or Colla da Crioch, who was living in Ireland in the latter part of the third century A.D. The direct line of this descent cannot be traced. The McDonald or McDaniel Celtic family descends from Somerled, son of Gillebride, through 74 McDonald or McDaniel Clan Badge "By sea or by land," his son Ranald and his grandson Dhomhnuill (or Donald) of Islay. Somerled is described as "a well-tempered man, in body shapely, of a fair and piercing eye, of middle stature and quick discernment." He traveled "over the sea to Skye," where the Scottish welcomed him as Lord of the Isles. Somerled expelled the Norsemen from the Western Isles in the 12th century and became Regulus of the Isles (king of the isles).

There are still people in Scotland who retain the McDaniel name. Furthermore, there are many people who were Mac-Donald and changed their surnames to Mcdonald or McDonald and visa-versa for their own reasons...in-addition to this, the recording of surnames have been in many cases written as they assumed.

Melton - Grandma Julia's family name was **Melton**. Her father was Albert Kermit Melton Sr., born January 16, 1862, and died June 6, 1957. Albert was first married to Adella Alice "Della" VanNatta Melton, who died in 1884, the same year as her marriage, and then

THE MCDONALDS

to Cora Mae Rider Melton, born September 22, 1866, and died December 6, 1955. Albert Sr. and Cora were married for 70 years.

Albert's father was Isaac Thomas Melton (1837 – 1904), and his mother was Naomi Rebecca Mason Melton (1833 – 1921). Cora's father was Samuel T. Rider (1827 – 1924), and her mother was Julia Maria Van Natta Rider (1842 – 1934), who is buried in Seaside, Oregon.

It is interesting that Albert K. Melton's first wife was Della Van Natta, and his second wife, and mother of all his children, was Cora May Rider. Her father was Samuel T. Rider, born in 1837, died 1924. Her mother was Julia Van Natta Rider, born 1842, and died 1934. We do not know if the two women were related, but it seems likely that they were.

Samuel T. Rider's father was Joshua Rider, born in 1811 and died 1896. Joshua is buried in Schoharie County, New York. We haven't located Joshua's spouse, but he is shown to have had five children. Two of Joshua's children, both males, lost their lives during the American Civil War. The eldest, Asa B. was 22 or 23 and David S. was 24 or 25. We have been able to confirm Asa's service in the Civil War but were unable to confirm David's although he passed in 1865, or our Great Great Grandfather Samuel's although he was of military service age at the time. We were able to find two Samuel Riders listed as serving in two New York infantry Regiments but neither lists a middle initial. Confirmation wasn't possible. Tracing the Rider history before Joshua wasn't successful.

However, tracing Julia's ancestry a bit further was possible. Her parents were Henry Van Natta, who was born in 1794 and died in 1874, and her mother was Hannah Montanye Van Natta, who was born in 1797 in New Jersey and who died in 1874. Unfortunately, we couldn't find Henry's parents' names, but we did find that Hannah's parents were William Montanye, born 1772 and died in 1855, and Elizabeth Wintersteen Montanye, born in 1734 and died in 1800. Both were born in New Jersey. That was as far as we could trace the Montanye lineage, but Elizabeth's parents were Jacobus Christian Wintersteen - 1708 to 1780 - and Anna Engel Wintersteen - 1711 to 1758. Both Jacobus and Anna were born in Germany and

ROBERT ALAN MCDONALD, KATHIE EILEEN MCDONALD COURTNEY, RICHARD EDWIN MCDONALD, MARY JO MCDONALD HELFRICH

were married there in 1728. They must have immigrated after their marriage. They are the parents of 13 children.

Memorial for Joshua, Catharine Ann, Asa B., and David S. Rider in Esperance, Schoharie County, New York

THE MCDONALDS

The name Rider is derived from the Middle English Ridere for horseman. Thus, emigration from Britain, England, or Scotland can be surmised.

Both Samuel T. Rider and Julia M. Van Natta Rider were born in New York as was their daughter Cora May, our Great Grandmother. The surname Van Natta and the New York residence give rise the possibility of Dutch heritage. In fact, the surname can be traced to Dutch records as early as the 1630s, giving rise to the possibility that some of our ancestors could have been among the earliest settlers which was in 1609.

According to family lore, the Riders moved to Oregon via the Oregon Trail. According to Julia M.'s obituary, she was a Republic County, Kansas, pioneer in the 1870s until moving to Oregon in 1894. Our Great Great Grandmother Julia Van Natta Rider was born in Burtonsville, Montgomery County, New York. She died in Woodburn, Marion County, Oregon in 1934 and is buried in Canby, Clackamas County, Oregon. Her daughter, Cora M. Rider Melton, was also born in New York. Thus, our Great Great Grandparents Rider journeyed from the east to the west coast in their lifetimes and so did their daughter, our Great Grandmother Melton.

ROBERT ALAN MCDONALD, KATHIE EILEEN MCDONALD COURTNEY, RICHARD EDWIN MCDONALD, MARY JO MCDONALD HELFRICH

Melton family: *Top Row: Hattie Elmina b. 9/28/1891, Roy Everett 8/21/1886, Julia Naomi (Grandma Julia)10/31/1889, Dora Mae b. 1/2/1888, Second Row: Henry Isaac b. 8/19/1898, Albert Kermit Jr. b. 3/31/1903, Mervin Samuel b. 9/1/1901, Albert K. Sr. b.1/161862, Ernest Chester b. 7/7/1906, Cora M. Rider b. 9/22/1866, Carrie Elizabeth b. 2/11,1896. Ethel Louise (not pictured) died at about age 8.*

Grandpa Sam moved frequently. Why he moved frequently isn't entirely clear, but he always found work. We know that Grandpa Sam apprenticed as a plasterer, but we have no record of him practicing the trade. He favored farming.

Our father was just the opposite. Once he settled on the farm, he didn't move again. In later years, he travelled, especially after productive oil and gas wells were drilled enabling him to buy a motor home.

THE MCDONALDS

We aren't sure where Grandpa Sam and Grandma Julia met. It is possible that they met in Oklahoma as our research indicates that both families were in Woods County at the same time, and both families were in Kansas not far from each other and at similar times. Grandpa Sam's father, Valentine, lived in Woods County prior to his death in 1910, and one of Julia's brothers, Henry, lived in that same county, although later.

Prior to meeting Julia and prior to their marriage in 1907, Sam left West Virginia. He lived for an unknown amount of time in Kansas as did one of his brothers who was married at the time. We do not know which of Sam's brothers this was. We know that Sam and his brother, who, with his family, moved from Kansas to Oklahoma. We know that Julia was born in Bellview, Kansas and the Melton's moved to Oklahoma and later to Colorado as they lived in Lamar and Greeley. We do not know the details of Sam and Julia meeting, but their families were in close proximity both in Kansas and later in Oklahoma.

There is speculation that Julia's parents were not fond of Sam, which could be because Julia became pregnant with their first child, Jessie Marie—born June 17, 1908, prior to their marriage. Sam and Julia homesteaded near Fairvalley, Woods County near Alva, Oklahoma. Jessie, Alpha, and Hester were born in Oklahoma. The family moved to Colorado by covered wagon. They settled in Lamar, Colorado – in the southeast part of the state on the Arkansas River.

Mary recalls Dad telling her that in the summer he would stay with his grandparents, Albert and Cora. It was his job to help Cora with her garden. Lamar is in an area Dad referred to as the "dry land." Rattlesnakes were plentiful and inhabited Cora's garden. Her instructions to Dad were, "If you see a snake, stand still and I'll know there is a snake. I'll come with my hoe and chop its head off."

ROBERT ALAN MCDONALD, KATHIE EILEEN MCDONALD COURTNEY, RICHARD EDWIN MCDONALD, MARY JO MCDONALD HELFRICH

Dad said he saw snakes; stood still as instructed, and Grandma Cora chopped their heads off, then threw the snake carcass out of the garden. Dad described Grandma Cora as a small woman barely 100 pounds soaking wet. Water wasn't plentiful in that area, so they caught rainwater in a barrel. Dad recalled taking his bath in the rain barrel.

Homestead Living in Oklahoma

According to both Dad and Grandpa Sam, Grandma Julia and her mother, Great Grandma Cora had similar personalities. We have a letter from Grandpa Sam written late in his life in which he states he liked Pa Melton but didn't care for Ma as much. Dad's description of the two women was similar: no nonsense, straight forward to a fault, a bit standoffish, and unloving as they weren't prone to displays of affection.

From Colorado, Sam and Julia moved their family to Akron, Ohio, where Betty and Julia were born. Then, in the depression 1929, Grandpa Sam bought a farm and moved the family to Bolivar, Ohio. Later, the farm was purchased under eminent domain by the government as part of the Bolivar Dam watershed. Grandpa Sam then bought a farm on Poorman Road in Navarre, Ohio.

Grandpa Sam had a leg crushed by his tractor which required amputation. He lived with our Aunt Betty Wisselgren while recovering. After that he and Julia separated—no record of divorce has been located—and Grandpa Sam, after selling the farm, moved to Monet, Missouri. After living alone for years, until his money ran low, he lived with his niece Mable McDonald Fox.

It was strange with Grandpa Sam living with Aunt Betty and Grandma Julia living with us that they didn't visit each other being less than two miles apart, but they didn't. This separation prevented Kathie and Rich from getting to know or even having a memory of their grandfather. Rich relates that his only memory of Grandpa Sam was him in his casket. Mary, being younger, wasn't born before Grandpa Sam went to Missouri.

After the farm sale Grandma Julia initially moved in with our Aunt Dudy, where she provided nanny services for pay. Later, she moved to the farm with us. Her room was the north bedroom on the second floor. She lived with us for several years. She made an extended trip to Colorado, staying with her siblings for about two years. Upon returning to Ohio, she lived in Massillon.

We never had an opportunity to get to know our Aunt Jessie. She contracted tuberculosis and passed away at the age of 23, after spending considerable time in a sanitarium. She had married Jack Walker. They had no children. Mr. Walker was reported to be a gambler and Aunt Jessie was flamboyant or flashy.

Mary recalls a conversation with Mom about the way Grandpa Sam treated both Grandma Julia and his daughter Jessie during Jessie's illness. Mom related that Dad, who had passed before this conversation, held hard feelings toward his father as Grandpa Sam wouldn't give Grandma Julia money for train fare to visit Jessie who was hospitalized for over a year in a sanitarium in Cleveland, Ohio. The sanitarium later became part of Cleveland Clinic. According to Mom, Jessie endured treatment that included deflation of her lungs one at a time, insertion of medication, removal of the medication and reinflation, all over a period of days or weeks. The procedure successfully restored the lung function, but the disease had invaded her spine. She spent time in a full body cast near the end of her life. According to Mom, Dad harbored resentment toward his father as Grandpa Sam was extremely strict with Jessie, not allowing her

ROBERT ALAN MCDONALD, KATHIE EILEEN MCDONALD COURTNEY, RICHARD EDWIN MCDONALD, MARY JO MCDONALD HELFRICH

much of a social life. When once she got out from under Sam's control, she went a bit wild, which Dad felt contributed to Jessie's medical problems. And, for not giving Grandma Julia money to visit Jessie more often. Dad blamed his father for both conditions.

Rich recalls family lore that Grandpa Sam and Grandma Julia were not the first in the family to homestead in Oklahoma. According to that information, a husband and wife were part of the April 22, 1889, opening of the Cherokee Strip. The husband was an official, perhaps a marshal, charged with the responsibility of keeping early settlers' (Sooners) out until noon. This required the wife to drive the covered wagon. Which family this was isn't known, but it would be either the Riders' or Melton's.

Grandma Julia wasn't the easiest person to live with. Not that Grandpa Sam was any better. They did things to annoy each other. While living with us, she did things that got under Mom's skin. How Mom held her tongue is something that, looking back, none of us understand, but she did. One of the things she did was count everything. She would count the teaspoons, the dishes, and the clothes that went into the wash. If the count was off, she would report it to Mom. If Mom and Dad were going away for even a few hours during the day, she would arrange to go to Aunt Betty's or Aunt Duty's, so she didn't have to watch us and fix us anything to eat. When Rob got old enough to drive and go out at night, he learned Grandma couldn't stay up past 2 AM, so he made sure he came home after that time so she couldn't give an accurate report on the time he got home.

Richard was Grandma Julia's favorite. She showed her favoritism in many ways. At mealtime, Grandma would pick out the best cut of meat, put it on Rich's plate, cut it up for him, and would say to one or the other of the girls, "Here Kathie or Mary is a piece of meat, you can cut the fat off." Rich was certainly capable of cutting his own meat at the time.

As a treat, Grandma Julia baked homemade cinnamon rolls, but being very frugal (i.e., cheap even though she wasn't paying for it), she scrimped on the sugar. The rolls weren't too good, but they were a treat. Both Dad and Rob complimented her extensively on the rolls, but Rich, when asked, said they could use more sugar. That was the end of the cinnamon rolls. If Rich didn't like them, then no more would be made — and they weren't.

A brief word about Mable Fox, Grandpa Sam's niece, and our cousin; she and her husband owned a grain harvesting business. They bought combines in the spring, and all summer followed the harvest, custom combining wheat, and other small grains from Oklahoma to the Canadian border. Mable drove the school bus they had converted to a kitchen. She fed the crew all summer. At the end of the season, they returned to Missouri in the bus. They sold the combines when they were finished with them and bought new ones the next year.

Grandma Julia attended the Baptist Church in Massillon. Based on his comments, Dad was baptized in the Baptist Church.

JONES

Our maternal grandparents were Daniel Jones, born April 1, 1889, in Justus, Ohio, and Nellie Frances Booth Jones, born May 1, 1894, in Goshen, Ohio. They were married on October 11, 1914, in a double ceremony with Grandma's sister Eva and Ford Welty. Grandpa passed December 29, 1965, and Grandma passed August 21, 1984. Daniel and Nellie were parents of Donald Franklin, Marian Pauline (our mother), and Eleanor May. All the children were born in Harmon.

ROBERT ALAN MCDONALD, KATHIE EILEEN MCDONALD COURTNEY, RICHARD EDWIN MCDONALD, MARY JO MCDONALD HELFRICH

Wedding Photograph Daniel Jones and Nellie Francis Booth Jones

Grandpa Daniel Jones was a first generation American. His parents had emigrated from Wales. His father was David M. Jones, and his mother was Eleanor Jones Jones, both having the same surname but were unrelated coming from different parts of Wales. He was the second youngest of six children, who in birth order were: Taliesin, Morgan, Elizabeth, John, Daniel, and Aeron (who died at five months).

THE MCDONALDS

Jones family: Bottom Row – Elizabeth (Lizzy), David—Photograph, Eleanor; Top Row – Daniel (our Grandfather), Morgan, Taliesin and John (Jack)

Our great grandfather, David M. Jones, died as the result of a mining accident. Rich and Mary have the clearest recall of conversations describing the event.

According to the Brewster, Sugar Creek Township Historical Society, coal was discovered in Stark County in 1806. Approximately 100 mines were operated in the county. There were three mines around Justus: Fisher Mine, Elm Run Coal Company, and the tracks. Coal was the most important fuel in the early 1800s, and its importance continues.

Many men worked in coal mines. A number of these men were Welsh, having been miners in Wales or had grown up in mining families. Our great-grandfather filled both descriptions.

ROBERT ALAN MCDONALD, KATHIE EILEEN MCDONALD COURTNEY, RICHARD EDWIN MCDONALD, MARY JO MCDONALD HELFRICH

The mines in our area of Ohio were referred to as "deep" mines, meaning a shaft was often dug down into the ground to locate coal seams. Steam powered elevators were installed and used to lower men and equipment into and out of the mines, and to bring the coal to the surface. Our grandfather obtained a stationary engineer's license while working in coal mines.

During the workday, coal was loaded into carts which were moved to the surface where the coal was off-loaded and stored prior to being sold. Coal mining involved hand labor with picks and shovels. To increase productivity, blasting was used to loosen the coal in the underground seams. Near the end of the workday, charges would be prepared and set off. The resulting blast created a huge amount of dust, which took hours to settle. Blasting at the end of the day allowed settling to occur overnight when no work was occurring. This was safer for the men.

On the day of David Jones' accident, charges were set and the fuse lit. But the blast did not occur as expected. They waited, as sometimes the explosion did not occur as planned, and they didn't want anybody to be caught unexpectedly. Eventually, the decision was made to check and reset the charge. David went into the mine, and it exploded.

Other men were able to get him out, but his injuries to his chest and back were extensive. He likely had broken ribs, with resulting lung punctures, and may have had a broken back. To transport him home, about a mile, he was placed on a board, then put into a wagon. Medical care was summoned. His condition was grave, and it got worse.

Over the next three days, fluid built up in his lungs. Medical care available at the time had no way of draining the fluid or managing the resulting infection. This was before antibiotics, and diagnostic equipment such as X-rays weren't available. Before he passed, his children were able to see their father— Dah as they called him. He told them he wasn't going to make it. Reportedly he said, "I'm no good." They got to say goodbye, but our grandfather's memory of that experience was with him the rest of his life. This occurred in 1896. David was 42 years old. Our Grandfather Daniel Jones would have been seven years old at the time.

David is buried at the Welty Cemetery where Lawndell Road meets Route 93 and US Route 62. According to our Aunt Eleanor, our Great Grandmother Eleanor Jones regularly walked to the Cemetery, over two miles each way, to shed tears over David's grave for many years. She now rests beside him.

She had five children to raise, and she did so. Although she had a house in Justus, she had few other assets. One skill she possessed was the ability to launder woolens, especially blankets, so that they did not shrink or suffer damage during the washing process. That skill turned into a money making venture. To support her family and raise her children, Great Grandmother Eleanor took in laundry, cleaned for people, raised a garden, and received help from the community.

The boys quit school and went to work in the mines. None finished school. They brought their pay home to their mother. We aren't sure what Lizzy did. It is likely that she helped her mother. Our grandfather was the youngest. His family encouraged him to finish school, but he too quit school after completing the eighth grade and went to work in the mines.

Jones is one of the most common Welsh surnames. Its origin is from the name John. Thus, a person named John Jones is actually John John, a double name. Double names are common in Wales; a practice that continued after immigration to the United States.

While living in Great Britain, Robert inquired about the practice of double names and the lack of middle names, as our grandfather and his siblings had but a given and a surname. Here's the story Robert got: Wales was conquered in 1282 by Edward I. At that time, the Welsh gave their children a name but didn't use surnames at all. Thus, a person named John was simply John without any additional identification. The King, when introduced to one of his Welsh subjects, inquired as to his name and the person responded "John." To which the King replied, "John what?" The person responded "John." Similar inquiries of other Welsh subjects resulted in names

ROBERT ALAN MCDONALD, KATHIE EILEEN MCDONALD COURTNEY, RICHARD EDWIN MCDONALD, MARY JO MCDONALD HELFRICH

such as David, Evan, William, Thomas and so on with no surname. The King didn't like that and decreed the use of surnames. Therefore, surnames were created. John became John Jones, David became David Davies, Edward became Edward Edwards, Reese (or Ryse) became Reese Reese, Evan became Evan Evans, and so on. Since the King didn't decree the use of a middle name, use was optional. The practice of double names continues to this day. Many of our grandparents' friends of Welsh lineage had double names. The practice included girls, so we knew people named Jenny Jones and Thomas Thomas as well as the others noted above.

Mary recites family lore as being told to her by either Aunt Eleanor and/or Mom regarding Eleanor Jones and David Jones' meeting and marriage. Great Grandmother Eleanor Jones was betrothed to another man, arranged by her father. Eleanor wasn't in favor of marrying this man although he was said to have means, a man of property. She and her sister Meg (Margaret) went on holiday (vacation) to Brighton in the south of England. While in the marketplace, they saw a redheaded man and Eleanor commented to Meg, "That's the one for me!" She introduced herself and they fell in love and married. Eleanor's father wasn't happy about her breaking the betrothal.

Before immigrating, she purchased a collection of Lusterware, fancy pottery which is finished with a second metallic glaze, which they brought with them. While waiting to leave the ship, they watched the unloading. Great Grandmother Eleanor saw her box containing the Lusterware dropped breaking nearly all the contents. She prized the remaining few pieces.

Grandpa Dan told us the preacher often came to their house for Sunday dinner, even though they were poor. Apparently, Great Grandma Eleanor was a good cook and hostess. To illustrate how closely Great Grandmother Eleanor watched her funds, Grandpa Dan told us they had to show the bread to their mother before she would allow them either butter or jelly. They weren't to have both.

He said that they could sometimes get both by buttering one side and having it turned down before getting jelly.

Aunt Eleanor told us she would invite Great Grandma Eleanor to come for Sunday dinner as they were having chicken, her favorite, regardless of the actual menu. After church, Great Grandmother Eleanor would ride the trolley from Justus to Harmon. They hurried out to greet her at the trolley stop which was in front of their house. They were delighted when they saw her hat on backwards playing a game with Mom and Aunt Eleanor, pretending she didn't realize her hat was backwards. She must have been a delightful Grandmother

Because of Grandpa Dan's father's early death, the boys all went to work when they were young, quitting school around the fourth grade. The work they found was primarily coal mining. They brought their earnings home to their mother. Grandpa Dan, being the youngest, got the best education because he stayed in school through the eighth grade. Then he quit even though his family wanted him to finish high school. Grandpa Dan said he wanted to do his part, not wanting to take advantage of being younger.

Grandpa and some of his brothers were partners in the Jones-Price Coal Company. Rich has a ledger, part of the financial records of the Company for the years 1921 and 1922 in Grandpa Dan's handwriting.

Rich also recalls Mom telling of Grandpa Dan's bill collecting technique. Coal sales were to people in the community for home heating. Sales were cash, and some were credit.

Mom related Grandpa Dan's business practices may have reflected his early years. He often gave coal to needy people, especially widows often around the winter holidays. Mom thought that seeing his own mother struggle influenced Grandpa. When Grandpa would see someone who had the means to pay, but whose bill was past-due, he would walk right up to them and tell them they needed to pay their bill. According to Mom, it didn't matter where they were at the time. Grandpa didn't hesitate to demand his money.

Later, Grandpa got a job at the Wheeling and Lake Erie Railroad as a stationary engineer in the powerhouse, a job that he performed for over 30 years, and from which he retired when he was over 70.

ROBERT ALAN MCDONALD, KATHIE EILEEN MCDONALD COURTNEY, RICHARD EDWIN MCDONALD, MARY JO MCDONALD HELFRICH

He initially obtained a stationary engineer's license while running coal mines.

Grandpa Dan was a record keeper. Rich has a ledger he kept when working at the back shop at the railroad. He recorded engines and rail cars worked on, and the purpose and extent of the work.

We were told by old-timers who knew him that Grandpa Dan was an outstanding baseball player. They said he would have been a professional if his mother had allowed him to play Sunday ball.

He maintained physical fitness all his life and could perform feats of balance and strength. He could walk on his hands all around the yard, he could stand on one leg, extend the other straight out in front of him, then lower himself to the ground on his other leg, then stand up without the use of his hands or arms while the leg remained extended. Rob recalls seeing him do that when he was over 50. Rich recalls working with him and while cleaning up he picked up a broom, held it in both hands, then jumped through it without letting go and jumping back through. He asked Rich, "Can you do that?" He was over 70. Grandpa never drank or smoked. None of us ever recall him saying a swear word.

Grandpa Dan was as fine an example of a grandfather as can be imagined. He could be counted on to take his grandchildren where and whenever needed. He also enjoyed sweets. His favorite ice-cream was butter-brickle. And he liked black liquorice. He used to buy liquorice buttons at a store in Navarre, Muskoff Drug, and carry them in his pocket. Rich remembers crawling all over Grandpa like a monkey to get the liquorice out of the white bag in his pocket.

There were things Grandpa Dan wouldn't eat. One of them was chocolate, another was Jell-O. Someone told him they made Jell-O from horse's hooves, and he did not drink while eating. He would eat his meal and then drink his glass of milk after he'd finished eating.

Because Grandpa Dan's birthday was April 1, April Fool's Day, we would always try to prank him on his birthday. Our favorite was to tell him that one of the women—it could be Grandma or Mom or

THE MCDONALDS

Aunt Eleanor was making him a cake, and it sure looked good. He'd ask what kind, and we'd tell him it was chocolate—which he wouldn't eat. He'd get a pained look but would be visibly relieved when we'd say, "No, it's a white cake."

Rich recalls seeing a bunny out in the yard and Grandpa telling him that if he put salt on its tail, he could catch the rabbit. Rich says when he saw a bunny, he'd get the saltshaker and sneak up on it. He got close a couple times, but never quite close enough to get that salt on its tail. Rich says this is one prank Grandpa pulled on him. He didn't figure it out until he got older.

Physical dexterity ran in the family. Mom told us that her Uncle Jack could walk up and down stairs on his hands. And Grandpa told us Uncle Jack could walk through a marble match while barefoot and pick up the marbles with his feet.

Grandpa Dan worked hard and was both frugal and creative. He would get extra use out of his Gillette Blue Blades by stropping them to restore the edge. He turned used hacksaw blades into paring knives by shaping wooden handles which he riveted using copper rivets to the blades he had hand formed. Mom had quite a few of his knives. He also made larger knives, butcher knife size. What he used for the blade we can't recall. He made tweezers that worked very well for removing splinters. And he made at least one meat fork.

For the grandchildren, he created horse swings. The first one he designed and built was placed in the basement of his house in Harmon where the grandchildren could use it in all kinds of weather. The horse head was modeled from the head of a stick horse one of the grandchildren had. He built the body from pine one-inch boards. It was suspended from the basement ceiling with ropes he placed through holes he drilled on either end. He used dowels for hand and footrests and designed an adjustable seat. Since the first one worked well and each of the grandchildren liked it, he built one for each of his children's families. We enjoyed riding the horse swing immensely.

He had a workshop in the basement where he created the knives, toys, and did other work. He didn't have a lot of tools, but he was

ROBERT ALAN MCDONALD, KATHIE EILEEN MCDONALD COURTNEY, RICHARD EDWIN MCDONALD, MARY JO MCDONALD HELFRICH

skillful with what he did have. His basement was always neat and tidy.

The house he and Grandma Nellie owned had space for a garden which Grandpa Dan spaded by hand every spring. He would come home from work and go out to the garden where he would spade for a time. In a few days, he would have the garden ready for planting. The garden was very productive.

The house had a cistern which captured water when it rained. Grandma Nellie used the rainwater for laundry because it was "soft" water, requiring less soap, as did the "hard" water they got from the well which was used for drinking. Grandpa Dan installed plumbing he designed which brought the water from the cistern into the house by way of an electric pump. This meant less work from Grandma; she didn't have to use a hand pump.

Grandpa Dan acquired plumbing tools when installing the plumbing in his house. Those tools were used on The Farm when installing running water as were Grandpa's talents. He also provided his expertise and tools when he and Dad electrified the Farmhouse.

Our Grandma, Nellie Frances Booth Jones, was raised on a farm in Harmon. She was born in Goshen, near New Philadelphia, Ohio, the eldest of seven children: six girls – Nellie, Eva, Annie, Dorothy, Bea, and Norma, and one boy -- John. The building lot on which she and Dan built their house, located at the corner of Day Avenue and Navarre Road (Federal Route 62) in Harmon, was originally part of the Booth farm.

Our mother related that her mother and father would entertain themselves by reciting stories and especially poems they memorized when growing up. They made it a competition to see who could be the most elaborate and accurate. Mom told us that Grandpa Dan repeated the fourth grade. Not because he didn't complete the work, but because he really liked the fourth grade. The way children moved from one grade to another was to ask them if they felt they mastered the work and wanted to move on. Grandpa Dan enjoyed the year so much he told the officials he wanted to stay in the fourth grade, so he repeated it. The result was an extremely easy year for him, and he memorized the fourth year McGuffie Reader. No doubt those poems he recited to Grandma in later years were in that reader.

They also celebrated April 1, April Fool's Day, but not necessarily because of Grandpa's birthday. Each year Grandma Nellie would say, "I'm going to get him this year!" and each year Grandpa would best her. It was a standing joke between them. But since they were both competitive, it became a complex undertaking as the years went by.

Clarence Leroy Booth compiled the Booth ancestry of which we have a copy. According to that document, the Booths can be traced to Edwin Booth, born in England in 1744, who, along with his brother and 11 other British soldiers, came to America during the Revolutionary War. They hadn't been in the Colonies long when both were captured. They were given the option of remaining prisoners or changing sides. They changed sides which enabled them to remain in the United States after cessation of hostilities. Edwin served until the conclusion of the war, 1883. The brothers were separated and never saw each other again.

Edwin married Rachel Reynolds around the year 1781. Rachel was from a prominent family in Cecil County, Maryland. In 1812, Edwin and Rachel moved to Ohio with their nine children.

Grandma's father, J. Franklin (Frank) Booth, was married to Flora Augusta Meredith Booth, whose father was Roland Jones Meredith. Roland was born February 2, 1839, and died May 26, 1902. Roland's wife was Mary Ann James Meredith. His mother was Martha Jones. We presume Martha immigrated from Wales. We do not know Roland's father's name.

ROBERT ALAN MCDONALD, KATHIE EILEEN MCDONALD COURTNEY, RICHARD EDWIN MCDONALD, MARY JO MCDONALD HELFRICH

Four Generation Photograph
Grandma Meredith, Nellie Jones,
Donald Jones (baby), Grandma Booth

From the internet, Mary obtained information that the Meredith's immigrated to Ohio in 1830. (See *All the Way Back to Wales with the Meredith's | Whispering Across the Campfire* (wordpress.com) From the Meredith Bible in Richard's possession, we are able to confirm accuracy.

Grandma Nellie's parents were politically active. She was interested in politics her entire life. She finished high school in Justus, completing all 11 years. Having a high school diploma meant the person was qualified to teach school. Grandma Nellie didn't work away from home after marrying Grandpa Dan, as was the custom then.

THE MCDONALDS

Grandma Nellie served on the School Board during construction of one of the Navarre school buildings and our Uncle Don Jones was the Treasurer. *(See Navarre School Dedication in Photographs and Drawings.)* She was highly intelligent, finishing first in her high school graduation class. She was a natural teacher. She taught piano to her grandchildren, and she tutored our cousin, Sue Foster, in math all through high school and may have helped when Sue was in college. Sue became a high school math teacher. Grandma had words of wisdom that she passed along. One of her sayings was, "If you expect to rate high in society, you must not expectorate on the street."

Frank Booth was a Stark County commissioner for 12 years. Grandma Nellie was a staunch Republican. Her interest in politics seemed to have passed to Mom, as she also was involved. In fact, after Mom's passing, we received a letter of condolence from President George W. Bush.

J. Franklin Booth, this photo believed taken for his political campaign

ROBERT ALAN MCDONALD, KATHIE EILEEN MCDONALD COURTNEY, RICHARD EDWIN MCDONALD, MARY JO MCDONALD HELFRICH

Rich recalls being told Frank Booth was a 32nd Degree Mason. This affiliation may have helped with his political career.

Mary recalls that in family lore Frank Booth had a disagreement with his father when he was in the second grade resulting in Frank quitting school, leaving home, and growing up with another family. He had no formal education beyond the second grade.

Robert recalls Mom telling us that Frank Booth was an early riser and insisted on getting a good night's rest. Should there be visitors when Frank's bedtime came, which was quite early in the evening, he would stand up and announce, "You can stay as long as you like. I'm going to bed." And did so, leaving Flora to continue entertaining the guests.

Another of Frank Booth's traits was an absolute insistence on honesty while in office. Grandma Nellie would tell us he wouldn't take part in any dealings that had the slightest appearance of a political favor and wouldn't have any personal business dealings with the county or state while in office. We could tell that she was enormously proud of her father and his honesty. Grandma Nellie had no patience with a dishonest politician or any other dishonesty, for that matter.

Flora Augusta Meridith Booth
Mother of Nellie F. Booth Jones

Both the Booths and Merediths lived in Harmon, Ohio, one on either side of Day Avenue.

Grandma and Grandpa Jones were devoted to their churches. Grandpa Dan attended the United Brethren Church (now United Methodist Church) in Justus and Grandma Jones attended St. Paul's Evangelical & Reformed (now United Church of Christ) in Navarre.

Mom told Mary that originally Grandma attended the Justus church but because of a squabble in the congregation, she switched her membership to Navarre, where she remained. There was no noticeable friction between them. Grandma once told Robert that she should have gone with Dan.

Aunt Eleanor told Mary that while attending Sunday school in Justus, the Sunday School teacher threatened to lock an unruly boy in a closet, as he wouldn't behave. This frightened Aunt Eleanor because she thought this punishment might happen to her. So, she went into the sanctuary and sat between Grandpa Dan and her Uncle Tal, the two men she trusted the most in the world, where she knew she would be safe. Men and women sat on different sides of the aisle

ROBERT ALAN MCDONALD, KATHIE EILEEN MCDONALD COURTNEY, RICHARD EDWIN MCDONALD, MARY JO MCDONALD HELFRICH

in church. Thus, it was quite remarkable that a young girl would sit with the men.

Mom was a member of St. Paul's in Navarre and we children went with her.

The lesson gained from knowing a bit about our ancestors is that they were strong, independent people. That certainly includes the women.

Our Grandpa Dan, when commenting on someone he admired, would often say, "They come from good stock."

Chapter Three – Our Parents

*Marian Pauline Jones McDonald & Alpha Carl McDonald
wedding photograph December 29, 1942*

Dad was born June 27, 1912, on a homestead near Alva, Oklahoma to Samuel Sanford McDonald and Julia Naomi Melton McDonald. Mom was born April 27, 1919, to Daniel Jones and Nellie Frances Booth Jones, who lived in Harmon, Ohio. Dad passed away January 27, 1985. Mom passed away April 23, 2004.

ROBERT ALAN MCDONALD, KATHIE EILEEN MCDONALD COURTNEY, RICHARD EDWIN MCDONALD, MARY JO MCDONALD HELFRICH

Mack's Early Years

Dad's parents lived in a soddy—a house made from sod cut from the ground—when Dad was born. Part of the house had been a corncrib. They used tumbleweeds for a Christmas tree. Later, Grandpa Sam sold the homestead and moved the family by covered wagon to Colorado where he ran an alfalfa milling plant. Dad said his playmates were the children of Mexicans who worked at the alfalfa plant. He described the Spanish he learned as swear words. Among the phrases he taught us was 'loco in cabeza,' crazy in the head.

Before long, the family moved again, this time to Akron, Ohio, where granddad worked for the Firestone Tire and Rubber Company. The family lived in Firestone Park near the plant. Dad said that life in Akron was the easiest Grandma Julia ever had. She was not in favor of leaving Akron.

Dad went to school in Colorado and Ohio. When they came to Ohio, officials at the school where Dad was enrolled, decided his education was lacking, so they put him and his younger sister, Hester, (Tiny as we called her) back one year. Dad said that was the easiest year of school he ever had; it was all review. Holding them back wasn't necessary.

THE MCDONALDS

A.C. or "Bud" McDonald on right.
The caption on back of the photograph is Feb. 7, 1925.
Dad would have been 12 years old.

Dad became the Akron city marble champion. Marbles were a big sport when Dad was growing up. He remained quite a good marble shooter but couldn't pass the talent to his sons. He was also good at spinning tops, a game scored similarly to marbles. You get to keep the marble or top knocked out of a ring, but if the knockout fails, you may lose your shooter or top. He had success teaching Rich tops.

Because of being held back a year, Dad entered Akron Garfield High School older, bigger, and stronger. He went out for the football team and was a starter his freshman year. *(See copy of the certificate and varsity letter in Chapter 23.)* The coach, who Dad really admired, told him, "Play football for me through high school and I'll see to it you go to college."

ROBERT ALAN MCDONALD, KATHIE EILEEN MCDONALD COURTNEY, RICHARD EDWIN MCDONALD, MARY JO MCDONALD HELFRICH

Living in Akron, Dad got an education that wasn't all in books. He met a professional boxer, Meyer (K.O. for knock out) Christner pictured to the right. Dad learned boxing and sparred with this man. Christner was a heavyweight contender whose fights included Primo Carnera and Jack Sharkey, both highly rated heavyweight contenders. Rob can testify to Dad's punching prowess, recalling that he got knocked into the milk cans after saying something that Dad didn't like. Rob says he's glad that Dad walked away after he got back on his feet.

Dad told Rich about a fight he got into shortly after moving to Bolivar. According to Dad, a guy was mouthing off, so Dad knocked him over a woodpile. Rich didn't know whether the story was accurate, he had his doubts but said nothing to Dad. Sometime much later, unexpectedly, a fellow drove up to the farm, stopped, and asked Dad if he was Bud McDonald. Dad said that he was. The fellow said, "You don't remember me, do you?" Dad agreed he didn't. The guy said, "I used to think I was pretty tough until you knocked me over a woodpile." Rich got his question answered.

Dad provided advice about fighting. "If there's going to be a fight, and it can't be avoided, hit the other fellow as quick and as hard as you can. That may end it right there. The man that lands the first hard punch usually wins." But we can't recall Dad ever getting into a fight. His presence and obvious willingness to fight always ended it.

In 1929, between Dad's freshman and sophomore years, Grandpa Sam purchased and moved the family to a farm near Bolivar, Ohio. Keep in mind this was during the Depression. To help pay for the farm, Dad had to quit school and go to work cutting and installing mine posts with Grandpa Sam. Because of the move and quitting school, Dad lost the opportunity to go to college.

THE MCDONALDS

For his work on the mine posts, Dad was paid, but Grandpa Sam kept Dad's wages. Dad said Granddad paid for the farm during this time, so Dad's wages helped. Dad said that his father gave him a quarter — once.

While working in the mine, there was an accident and Dad injured his back. He never went to a doctor and never had a thorough examination until he was over 70. When examined, the doctor told him he had a broken back. He lived with it the rest of his life, including military service.

For a time, Dad worked for and lived with the Sickafoose family whose business included house moving in the East Sparta, Magnolia, Ohio, area. Dad remained close to this family his entire life. One of the sons, Donald, who was a bit younger than Dad, owned a private airfield and a drag racing track. In later years, Dad arranged for Donald's flying service to take him and Mom to North Dakota to visit Mary.

Dad had a large clear-glass beer stein, pictured below with a quart jar for size comparison. It was displayed with other collectibles in one of two step-back cupboards Mom had. He told us that he had gotten it when he was part of the crew that dismantled and tore down the Falls House Tavern, which was done about 1934 - 1936. The exact date isn't documented or the tear-down but it took two years.

ROBERT ALAN MCDONALD, KATHIE EILEEN MCDONALD COURTNEY, RICHARD EDWIN MCDONALD, MARY JO MCDONALD HELFRICH

The Falls House Tavern was located near the falls on Sugar Creek which were destroyed when the Beach City Dam was constructed. Dad would have been 22 years old in 1934. It is possible that Dad was working for "Pop" Sickafoose at the time. The stein is now in Stuart Courtney's possession. For additional information on the Falls House Tavern, please refer to References.

Military Service - Dad entered military service June 25, 1941. After serving nearly three months, he was transferred to the Enlisted Reserve Corps (ERC) September 21, 1941. He returned home and returned to making glazed structural tile in East Canton, Ohio. After the Japanese attack on Pearl Harbor, December 7, 1941, the United States entered World War II declaring war upon the Axis Powers.

On April 3, 1942, Dad was recalled to active duty and served until October 20, 1945. He was assigned to the 692nd Tank Destroyer Battalion. From recall through September 11, 1944, Dad trained stateside in Camp Gordon, Georgia, Camp Hood, Texas, Camp Phillips, Kansas, and had winter maneuvers in Tennessee.

Dad didn't describe the training he received, but he often said, when performing an unusual task, "I learned how to do that in the Army." A brief description of the training is found in the book "THE TANK KILLERS" by Harry Yeide, published by Casemate. That description is reproduced here:

Training the Men

The Tank Destroyer Force gained full control over its own training, a situation that differed considerably from the haphazard arrangements that characterized the Army's separate tank battalions. A Unit Training Center became the heart of Camp Hood and was subsequently augmented by an Individual Training Center and a Replacement Training Center.[56] Battalion records during the war suggest that while units did not always get as many replacements as they needed, the ones they did get were generally properly trained to fight in TDs. Separate tank battalions, in contrast, often had to hastily train replacements who had never seen a tank before.

Tank killers were trained not only to fight with their guns but also to conduct "dismounted tank hunting." Crews of disabled TDs were expected to ambush enemy tanks and raid his tank parks using small arms, grenades, mines, and improvised weapons. Bruce sent Maj Gordon Kimbrell to visit the British Commando School and patterned tank-hunting training on the Commando model. The course employed live grazing fire and exploding practice grenades for the first time in the Army during simulated battlefield conditions.[57] The men underwent a grueling schedule that included conducting night reconnaissance, crossing deep streams, climbing slippery barbed-wire-covered banks, scaling steep walls, detecting booby traps, street fighting, and mastering demolitions.[58] The training in urban warfare would prove particularly important in Europe, where crews in separate tank battalions would face a steep learning curve because they had received no such instruction.

After surviving this unusually rigorous training regimen, the TD men tended to think of themselves as an elite force.

After reading this, one can better understand Dad's knowledge of explosives, shooting, and improvisation. Also, each man's obvious pride in themselves and the battalion.

ROBERT ALAN MCDONALD, KATHIE EILEEN MCDONALD COURTNEY, RICHARD EDWIN MCDONALD, MARY JO MCDONALD HELFRICH

Military Training– Dad in the center front has an X on his helmet

Captain John B. West commanded "B" Company of the 692nd Tank Destroyer Battalion during Dad's entire tour of duty both before and after deployment to Europe. Captain West was highly respected. The orders he gave were carried out.

But even the most respected officer has a hiccup now and then. While stateside, the men were getting a little bored with constant training so discipline slipped. Pranks began and this type behavior increased in frequency and foolishness. In fact, some downright dangerous actions were taking place. Captain West tried soft warnings that were simply ignored. That made him angry! He put the entire company in formation at attention and expressed his displeasure beginning, "Henceforth, forthwith, and as of now, this shittery will cease!" He went on from there chewing them out collectively. Dad couldn't remember the rest of it. According to Dad's account, the foolishness stopped at once. Fortunately, before serious injuries resulted.

When on the rifle range, Captain West was firing from the prone position and he wanted to experience violent earth movement so that he could train to recover his firing position. He fired a round and

THE MCDONALDS

ordered Dad, who was a sergeant at the time, to shake him simulating earth movement. Dad said he shook the Captain, but not too violently. Captain West wasn't satisfied and responded, "Goddamn it, Sergeant, I said shake me!" To which Dad responded, "Yes Sir!" When the captain fired again Dad bent over the captain, grabbed him by the epaulets, raised him completely off the ground and shook the captain till his eyes rattled, then dropped him. To which Captain West responded, "That will do Sergeant! That will do!"

Dad told of a young officer who was introducing some realistic training. He had read that equipment such as the jeeps were designed to withstand abuse such as jumping over ruts and over streams, so he began ordering the men to put the equipment to the test. It didn't take too many days before those orders were countermanded. Senior officers became unhappy with the amount of damage being inflicted.

The 692nd Tank Destroyer Battalion shipped to Europe on September 12, 1944. It landed in Cherbourg, France, September 26, 1944. They served through the end of the war, May 8, 1945, as part of the occupation forces until July 1945. Along with his unit, Dad returned to the United States. He was discharged October 20, 1945. His total service was four years, three months, twenty-six days.

Tank Destroyer Battalions were conceived to defeat heavy armor using high velocity artillery. They were tank killers. The thinking at the time was that the U.S. tanks then in service, primarily the M4 Sherman with its 75- or 76- millimeter gun, would not be successful against the larger more powerful German tanks, specifically the larger Tiger with its 88 millimeter gun and heavier armor. This concern resulted in formation of Tank Destroyer Battalions. One of the ways tank destroyers were used was attaching them to infantry divisions. This is how the 692nd was used.

Initially, the unit consisted of half-tracks (heavy-duty trucks which had tracks instead of tires in the rear) which towed a three-inch gun, high velocity artillery gun that could be fired both as direct or indirect fire. Each gun required a crew of 13. While in that configuration, Dad's unit was attached to the 104th (Timberwolves) Infantry Division. Later, they received M36 tank destroyers, which

ROBERT ALAN MCDONALD, KATHIE EILEEN MCDONALD COURTNEY, RICHARD EDWIN MCDONALD, MARY JO MCDONALD HELFRICH

were the lower portion–running gears of the Sherman medium tank–M4 coupled with an open turret mounting a 90 millimeter cannon. A crew of five was required to operate an M36. Later, the 692nd was separated from the 104th, and was then attached to the 42nd (Rainbow) Infantry Division. The 692nd served in continuous combat for 195 days.

M36 crosses the Rhine on an engineer bridge March 24, 1945. In addition to Dad, our Uncle Pink (Varner) Foster, combat engineer, served in this battle

The 692nd received 3 battle stars affixed to their European Africa Middle East (EAME) ribbon worn on their dress uniform. The battles were: <u>Freeing of Antwerp</u>– Oct. 23, 1944 to Nov. 8, 1944, <u>Breach of the Siegfried Line</u>– Nov. 8, 1944 to Mar. 7, 1945, and <u>Rhein Crossing</u>– Mar. 8, 1945 to May 9, 1945. While attached to the 104th, they were in two battles. They breached the Siegfried line twice; the only unit to do so. The last battle was while attached to the 42nd.

Company B, the company Dad was in, received the Presidential Unit Citation.

Personal decorations that Dad received included the Bronze Star Medal for action in penetrating the Siegfried Line, World War II

Victory Medal, Good Conduct Medal, and National Defense Medal. He was a staff sergeant in command of an M36 Tank Destroyer in a platoon of Company B of the 692nd Tank Destroyer Battalion.

After the war, Mack, as most people called him, was tired of taking orders and decided that upon discharge, he would farm and take orders from no one again. He stuck to that declaration.

Mack's Character - Dad was a physically large man. He always said he was six feet one and one-half inches tall and weighed 190 lbs. The height was correct, but after his time in the service, his weight increased and so did his muscle mass. Dad had to be well over 250 lbs. Dad was strong. When he grabbed something, it moved. Later in life, he lost weight, primarily because of high blood pressure. and to help ease the burden on his knees. His two very noteworthy features, besides his size and strength, were his eyes and his hands. Rich always describes Dad's eyes as steely blue, and Mary adds they changed to cobalt blue when he got angry. We all knew that when those eyes flashed, we needed to get right immediately.

Dad's hands were like no one else's hands. They were thick with fingers that looked like sausages. Dad gave Rob the ring that Mom had given him. While he was in the service, Dad wore that ring. Dad liked the ring but couldn't wear it anymore because it couldn't be made large enough to fit either his ring or pinky finger. Rob took the ring to Duncan Jewelers in Massillon, Ohio, to be sized to fit his finger. Before starting work, the jeweler decided to see how large it was. He put it on a measuring stick and the ring went right over the entire stick. Rob thinks the last measurement was a 16. Our best guess is Dad's fingers had to be well over size 20.

Another interesting thing about Dad's hands was they never got cold. He would be working outside carrying whey to the hogs in 5-gallon buckets in the dead of winter with no gloves on and his hands would be warm even with cold whey running over them. We could never understand why he didn't get cold, but he didn't seem to. Mary remembers constantly being cold in the winter. Her feet never got warm. She thinks it could be an early symptom of an autoimmune disease she suffers from after getting older. Rob also remembers being cold in the winters. Part of the reason was not having a good heavy coat. We always had hooded, lined sweatshirts which were supposed to keep us warm. They really didn't do the job. After getting felt lined boots, Rob's feet stayed warm throughout the winter no matter what he was doing.

When Dad spoke, we listened. His word was law. Whatever he told us to do, we had to do it – no excuses. Disobedience, misbehavior, and just failing to live up to his or Mom's expectations resulted in unpleasant consequences, and those consequences were as certain as the sun rising in the east. In short, we feared and respected Dad.

He wasn't just a scary person to us. He had the same effect on other people. One guy in his tank destroyer crew, Bob Kuehner, told Mom that the only thing that scared him during the war, including all 195 days of combat, was "your husband!" One of Rich's friends, who stood about six foot six inches and dressed out about 275 lbs. told Rich the only man he ever met that scared him was "your dad." At the time, Dad was over 60.

We never saw anybody willing to take him on and he confronted armed people while unarmed himself and they backed off quickly.

Careless Hunters - One such incident occurred during squirrel hunting season. A fellow from Massillon, who frequently visited the farm and always asked permission to hunt or fish, was down in the woods with permission to be there. Dad wasn't aware of anyone else hunting and told him to go ahead. Dad didn't want anyone to get shot, so he wouldn't give permission if someone else was there first. A couple of guys were also in the woods, but they hadn't gotten permission and Dad, of course, didn't know they were there.

The man who had permission came back to the house after only being in the woods a brief time and told Dad someone had shot and hit the tree right over his head. Rich was there so Dad and the person with permission immediately walked down the road and into the north pasture where these guys were supposed to be. They were coming out of the woods and were armed. Dad wasn't, but it made no difference.

Rich recalls Dad verbally tying into them, telling them he had a mind to take those guns away from them and wrap them around their necks. They must have believed Dad because they didn't argue and left with orders not to come back. Rich says he couldn't believe what Dad did with them being armed and all. All the while that Dad was chewing them out, all they said was "yes sir," "no sir."

To Dad, the man from Massillon had permission, and the others didn't, and that made all the difference. The fact that the Massillon guy was Black and the others weren't had no bearing. What Dad instilled in us was right was right, and wrong was wrong. Disrespecting others' property was always wrong. A person's color didn't mean a damn thing. What counted was how that person treated you and your property.

Mary says she always had a feeling of perfect safety when Dad was around. Nothing or nobody would get through him. Mary surmises that Mom had that same feeling as she wanted Dad with her when she had to testify during a legal proceeding at the school. Dad sat right outside with his arms crossed. Mom said everyone who entered was intimidated. Dad never said one word to anybody.

Dad had a hard life, and he didn't get to finish his education either in high school or college. He really was counting on going to college, and Dad was certainly smart enough to have done so.

Marian's Early Years

Mom's education began in a one room school 300 yards down the road from her home in Harmon, Ohio. She always insisted that the education received was as good as or perhaps better than what she would have received in a school with a single age group in one room. They could hear all the other classes reciting, which served as either review or precursor for what was to come.

ROBERT ALAN MCDONALD, KATHIE EILEEN MCDONALD COURTNEY, RICHARD EDWIN MCDONALD, MARY JO MCDONALD HELFRICH

Marian and Donald Franklin Jones about 1920

One opportunity she received was unintentional. Because the school was so small, girls had to be included on the baseball team. At the time, there weren't many opportunities for girls in sports. When she told the story, you could tell that Mom was proud of being part of the team and that she liked competition. Mom recalled their team beating another school easily. Later, the two teams were going to play again, and Mom's teacher encouraged their team to throw the game so the other team wouldn't feel bad. Mom said she reported this to her Dad, Grandpa Dan, who was totally incensed. According to Grandpa, you always do your best. It's up to the other team to stop you. That was a life lesson Mom passed on.

Mom went to high school in Navarre, Ohio, graduating in 1937. She was valedictorian of her class, and her class included a cousin who became a chemist and international consultant and another classmate who was a successful attorney who took and passed both the CPA and Bar the first sitting in the same year. Pretty stiff competition.

Marian's high school graduation announcement and photograph

Mom wanted to go to college, but in 1937, times were bad. For a while, she was the only one in her family with a job. Neither her older brother, Don, nor her dad were working. At that time, it was considered more important that boys got an education as they were the primary breadwinners, so Mom went to Canton Actual Business College where she learned bookkeeping, typing, and shorthand. These skills were important as she got a position in the Muskingum Conservancy District and later in the home office of the Wheeling and Lake Erie Railroad in Brewster, Ohio. Later, Mom worked in the Treasurer's office at the local school system. But while we were younger, Mom didn't work away from the farm.

ROBERT ALAN MCDONALD, KATHIE EILEEN MCDONALD COURTNEY, RICHARD EDWIN MCDONALD, MARY JO MCDONALD HELFRICH

Marian Pauline Jones- High School Graduation, 1937.

Mom was living with her parents when she and Dad, who was in the Army, married. She continued living there until Dad got out of service.

Marian's Character - Mom stood about five foot four with a slim build. Mom was never heavy. In fact, she had trouble gaining weight. Her mother and her sister, our grandmother Nellie and our aunt Eleanor were both about five feet six inches tall. At approximately nine months of age, Mom contracted whooping cough and nearly died. She was so ill that they had to take her outside so she could breathe cold, denser air. Mom was so weak she couldn't walk until she was 18 months. When she began talking, it was complete sentences. The whooping cough may have kept her from reaching her full height.

Mom was strong, both physically and mentally, and vigorous her entire life. She had to be strong to deal with Dad. She was the only person who could stand up to Dad and win. Mom didn't do so willy-nilly, but when she felt she needed to she did and came out on top. She kept the books for the farm and managed the money– what little there was of it. But the bills were paid, and we were clean, well fed, and healthy. Mom saw to that.

THE MCDONALDS

Shared Characteristics

One thing that Mom and Dad had in common was they both wanted to go to college, and neither were able to do so. When we kids came along, we were going to college! And we all did. Rich recalls Mom telling her minister just before passing that the one thing she was the proudest of was that all her children were professionals.

Both Mom and Dad were attuned to the flora and fauna on the farm. Mom could name every plant, cultivated or weed. Dad could walk through the woods in winter when all the leaves were gone and name every tree. Both were particularly good at math. Dad could calculate the dimensions of the things we were building or repairing in his head. He hardly ever used a pencil and paper.

Marian at retirement

They weren't just book smart. They understood people. We learned quickly how hard they were to fool. Rich laments that he couldn't get away with anything. They knew what he was going to do before he did. Since Rich was number 3 in birth order, they learned a great deal from Robert and Kathie; likely more so from Robert, as Kathie was well-behaved.

Both Mom and Dad liked feeding people. Anyone who was at the farm at mealtime got a seat at Mom's table. Not only did they feed people great meals, but they supplied garden produce to their brothers and sisters and their families. There is no way of knowing how much fresh produce they gave away.

Getting something on Dad was difficult, but he'd get things on himself. From time to time, something would remind us of something funny Dad had done. We'd remind him of it and go about making a joke about it. Dad would let that go on for a bit, but when he's heard enough, he'd say, "That's enough." And it was. We'd

ROBERT ALAN MCDONALD, KATHIE EILEEN MCDONALD COURTNEY, RICHARD EDWIN MCDONALD, MARY JO MCDONALD HELFRICH

either shut up or talk about something else. As Rich says, "He'd fix you with those steely blue eyes and you knew you were in serious trouble."

Although Dad hated making a mistake, he would comment, "If you never do anything, you can't make a mistake."

Chapter Four – Getting To Know Marian

Drive and Ambition

Marian was 110 lbs. of ambition, with an incredible capacity to get things accomplished. Her Dad, Grandpa Dan, knew how hard she worked physically with her slight frame. He tried, after he retired, to help her as much as he could. Nowhere was her hard work more evident than in the care of her garden and canning.

Mom didn't manage the heat well. She tried helping make hay. But, after working briefly, she turned bright red as her body temperature increased. Her skin would be dry. She stopped sweating; thus, her body didn't cool itself.

Mary was little when Mom suffered heat stroke working in the garden. She had passed out. When Mom came to, she told Mary to get Dad. Mary was scared; afraid Mom was dying and wouldn't leave Mom. Finally, Mom recovered enough to make it to the house while leaning on Mary, who was terrified. Mary says when Mom felt better, she was scolded, but good!

When canning, Mom frequently stayed up well past 2 in the morning, chained to the cycles of the pressure cooker. First it had to steam for 10 minutes. Then by setting the petcock to restrict the escaping steam, she forced up the pressure till it reached 10 lbs. for most items. There were varying times it had to be kept at 10 lbs. For example, quarts of green beans required 25 minutes. Mom was vigilant about the pressure and was constantly adjusting the heat on the stove. Then it had to cool so the pressure would go down. Finally, remove the petcock before opening.

Kathie and Mary remember the volume and variety of the items that were stored on the basement shelves for winter eating.

- 80 qt. green beans
- 220 pt. of corn – later the corn was frozen.
- 120 qt. of tomato juice – there were also canned tomatoes and catsup.
- red beets; regular and pickled.

ROBERT ALAN MCDONALD, KATHIE EILEEN MCDONALD COURTNEY, RICHARD EDWIN MCDONALD, MARY JO MCDONALD HELFRICH

- sauerkraut (Dad helped shred this and he carried the crock in which it was fermented up and down the steps.)
- lima beans
- apple sauce
- sour cherries for pie
- grape juice and jelly (from Grandma's grape arbor)
- pears
- peaches (bought)
- apricots (bought)
- apple butter (sometimes made in the butcher-house as a community effort)
- red crabapple jelly (from Johnny Wilson's trees)
- black raspberry jelly
- blackberry jelly
- elderberry jelly
- strawberries & strawberry jam (the strawberries were bought and picked at a local grower's farm)
- several varieties of sweet pickles (one of which took an entire week of soaking and washing off brine daily for one batch)
- bread and butter pickles
- quarts upon quarts of dill pickles

Mary remembers all of us helping with picking from the garden or trees. Kathie and Mary both got to help with canning preparation, but Mom ran the canner–pressure cooker. She was afraid of it all her life. Mom used the pressure cooker for green beans, plain beets, and corn. The rest of the canning was done using a cold packer.

Mom would cook crab apples, blackberries, and grapes. For jelly, Dad would carry the huge pot containing juice and fruit to the basement. There it was strained in a flour sack tied shut with string and suspended from the ceiling to drip into a clean 5-gallon bucket.

When it finished dripping, Dad would twist it round and round to squeeze out all the juice until only pulp would remain. He was the only one strong enough to accomplish this feat with ease. He would carry it upstairs where we added sugar and Sure Gel. The mixture boiled, skimmed, and boiled some more. Then Mom ladled it in jars sealed with melted paraffin.

It would frequently be close to 100°F in the kitchen when canning. Mom sometimes opened the ceiling vent, which was still present from the cook stove. This allowed the heat to rise into the attic. She would be on her feet from 6 AM till 2 AM and the next day more of the same. In between, she cooked 3 meals, did the dishes (no dishwasher), fed chickens, ironed, washed clothes which were dried on the line, and tended the garden. Our sheets were changed every week and pillowcases and sometimes sheets were ironed along with our clothes.

Feeding Everyone

Nearly every Sunday, Mom fixed and served a large five course meal: salad, potatoes, vegetables, meat, and complete with dessert, after church to us and whoever visited. We had homemade noodles, pies, cakes, and cooked puddings. Our favorite pudding was cornstarch pudding, which was like custard served hot. Mom's angel food cakes and pies were famous. Emily (Aunt El's youngest) recalled that Mom always made angel food cake for her birthday because it was her favorite.

Rob's favorite after-school snack was Mom's red crab apple jelly spread on Roman Meal bread with chunky peanut butter. It was an afternoon snack beyond compare. Two or more of these sandwiches after school carried us through the evening chores until supper.

Another great combination was Mom's catsup poured on browned hamburger to make sloppy Joes. What a wonderful sandwich.

Mom showed her love by her countless devotion in feeding and clothing us. She never missed ball games or concerts. She was

ROBERT ALAN MCDONALD, KATHIE EILEEN MCDONALD COURTNEY, RICHARD EDWIN MCDONALD, MARY JO MCDONALD HELFRICH

always by our side, and we were never told, but we knew how proud she was of each of us for our different talents.

In the earlier years, bums who traveled the rail lines would stop at the farm for handouts. Mom would always feed them. It might be just a cheese sandwich, but they always ate and got something to drink. Kathie recalls bums stopping by at Thanksgiving. They really ate well that day.

Now and again, a bum would ask to sleep in the barn. The barn was Dad's department. He would give them permission with the proviso that they didn't smoke in the barn. Dad would explain he didn't want the barn burned down. He took them at their word, and they didn't break it.

Mom was a member of the United Church of Christ in Navarre, Ohio. She attended faithfully and made sure we children attended as well. We gained knowledge of the Lord from an early age through Sunday School, Bible School in the summer, and catechism when we were old enough.

Rarely in Error

Finding a mistake or getting anything over on Mom was rare, but not entirely impossible. Mom didn't like it when she made a booboo and sure didn't like being reminded of it. About all you got was a pained expression and little to no comment.

Rob recalls getting something over on Mom - once. In the winter, we worked outside and used cloth gloves. Those things got wet and a wet glove in the cold wasn't worth anything, so we'd bring the gloves into the house and put them on the register to dry. There were always several pairs of gloves on the register, and they all looked the same. Rob came to the house to trade gloves as his were wet. He didn't want to take the time to take off his dirty boots and then put them right back on again, so he asked Mom to throw him a pair of gloves. Mom wasn't in the best mood because she was doing something else and really didn't want to be bothered. Without really looking at them, she threw Rob the gloves. When Rob got the gloves he said, "Hey, you threw me a right and left!" to which Mom replied, "I can't help that." And threw another glove. She then thought about what had been said and done, then cracked a small smile, realizing she'd been had.

Rob recalls one other instance when he was two. It was winter with just a little snow on the ground. Mom dressed Rob in a snowsuit, boots, a cap with flaps that she tied under his chin, and mittens.

Rob in his snowsuit with Mom at the Booth farm

At the time, they were living on the Booth farm near Harmon. To get from the highway, Federal Route 62, to the farmhouse, one had to go down a lane which crossed a small creek via a bridge. The bridge was basic and had no guard rails or anything else to keep something or someone from going over the side.

Somehow, Rob was left on his own for a brief time. He began walking up the lane toward the highway, which meant he first came to the creek bridge. Rob recalls bending down to look at the water flowing below. He must have bent too far because he fell in, flipping over, and landing on his back in the shallow water. The drop was only about three feet, but when you're only two, that's a long way. Then the trouble began. Rob didn't know how to get out. He recalls standing at the side of the creek, grabbing plants (dead grass) along the bank, and trying to use them to climb back out. Every time he'd grab one, the plant would break, and he'd fall back down. Finally,

ROBERT ALAN MCDONALD, KATHIE EILEEN MCDONALD COURTNEY, RICHARD EDWIN MCDONALD, MARY JO MCDONALD HELFRICH

he found one that didn't break and got back on the lane. As he started back toward the house, Mom met him. He remembers being scolded, but also Mom putting him in a warm bath to warm him up. Rob says he doesn't remember being cold or the feel of the water, but it was winter, and it must have been cold.

Rob says he used to remind Mom of this episode by telling her, "You sure didn't watch me very well." To which Mom would reply, "You had no business going to that creek."

One day we were making ice cream. As Rich remembers it, we were in the basement cranking the ice cream machine. Mom had prepared the mix, put it in the metal freezing container and sent the whole works down to the basement. We had the ice down in the basement chopped into pieces that would fit into the machine. Mom also sent salt down for us to use.

We cranked and cranked. All the while adding ice and spreading salt on it. But the ice cream wouldn't freeze. So, we kept cranking; changing off as one of us would get tired. This was very unusual as normally it was a one-person job to crank until the ice cream froze, but not this day. Finally, Rich tasted the salt. When he did, he found the salt was sugar. Mom sent the wrong stuff down. She cared little for being reminded of that one.

Mom usually gathered the eggs as the chickens were hers. Plus, her big strong boys were afraid of the chickens, as both Rob and Rich always got pecked when gathering eggs. Rich recalls using a stick to push the hen off the eggs so he could gather them. But the hens would ignore the stick and peck Rich anyway. At that point, Rich would hit the hen to get her to move. This resulted in a non-laying hen for a few days. For this, Rich got in trouble with Mom.

Lye soap or whitewash was used to clean the chicken coop. This had the advantage of being a disinfectant.

Mom always wore her engagement ring. As she would say, the stone wasn't large, but it was decent quality. One day after coming back from gathering the eggs, Mom looked at her ring and the stone was gone! One chicken had seen it and pecked it right out of the mount. The stone had become loose. Had Mom known which chicken got the stone, we would have had a chicken dinner, but she couldn't tell one from another.

Mom had to quit wearing her engagement ring. There wasn't any money to replace the stone. Years later when circumstances improved, Mom bought a new stone, with Charlotte's assistance, and had it installed. She went back to wearing her engagement ring.

We could tell when Mom got upset with one or more of us, she would call us yaps and if really upset dumb yaps. One of the girls, thinking that Mom may have made up the word yap, looked it up. To her shock, a yap is a person of low intelligence – a ne'er-do-well. So, being called a yap was bad, but a dumb one was worse.

Keeping the Family Well-Cared For

Mom was terrific in the kitchen. Every day, she prepared two large meals: dinner (lunch) and supper (dinner). She also prepared breakfast, but it wasn't as substantial. As Rich and Rob recall very often cocoa and toast, or cinnamon bread was what we ate. Occasionally, we would get eggs or pancakes.

We worked hard and could really put away the groceries. Rich says he never really remembers getting full. He'd just eat till the food was gone. Both Rob and Kathie remember putting a slice or two of bread on their plates after the potatoes were gone and eating the remaining gravy that way. Nearly every meal would include dessert, usually a couple of pies or cake. The dessert, like the rest of the food, would be gone at the end of the meal, but somehow there would be leftovers.

Mom would put the leftovers in containers and refrigerate them. When the leftovers built up, Mom would take them out and make slum-gullion. It was never the same twice, but somehow it was always good. It was a casserole with lots of veggies and scraps of meat.

To support all the pickles Mom made, we raised cucumbers. The best pickle patch was across the railroad near the bottom of the hill.

ROBERT ALAN MCDONALD, KATHIE EILEEN MCDONALD COURTNEY, RICHARD EDWIN MCDONALD, MARY JO MCDONALD HELFRICH

We also harvested garlic on the railroad and dill both off the railroad and in a small patch near the house.

Mom didn't just prepare superb meals, but she also fixed treats. Her home-made ice cream was top shelf. Occasionally, she would make deep fried donuts. She also made root beer and bottled it. With all she had to do, taking time to make these special treats for us was wonderful.

Mary doesn't remember getting many cooking lessons from Mom. But she was taught how to can and bake. Mary says when she was about 12, Mom made a big pot of vegetable soup. Mary was to warm the soup for Dad's lunch. Mom was working at the school and wouldn't be home. Mary turned the stove on high and scorched the soup. She says Dad ate a couple of bowls but told her to throw the rest to the dogs. Mary recalls getting in trouble with Mom for wasting so much food. But, at 12, she didn't know how to warm food. Mary says she learned to cook from observation. Grandma Julia taught her how to make gravy.

Kathie cooked side by side with Mom. Kathie thought it was cool that the flour was kept in the flour bin in the lower cupboard on the south wall. Sometimes Kathie made the entire meal with Mom assisting with the meat. Kathie recalled that her brothers always said the food she cooked wasn't any good, but they ate it and if they didn't know she cooked, then they would say it was good.

One thing Mom did for the boys was to make sure they could cook enough so they wouldn't starve. Rich recalls learning to make gravy and mashed potatoes. He really liked doing those things and enjoys cooking and helping even today.

Rob recalls his cooking lessons going well until he went into the kitchen to learn how to make pie crust. Mom was downright famous for her pie crust. Mom got the ingredients out – lard, flour, water, and salt – along with the rolling pin and board. Rob was trying to take notes. Mom just tossed ingredients onto the middle of the board and started mixing stuff together. Of course, Rob asked the pertinent questions: How much of this and how much of that and how does it go together? Mom didn't really have a recipe; she went by feel. When Rob persisted, he was told, "Get out of my kitchen!" Rob still isn't good with pie crust.

Rich always liked the rolls Mom made of the leftover pie crust. It was simple. Roll out the leftover pie crust, sprinkle on sugar and cinnamon, roll them up, and bake. Mary recalls Dad liking these rolls as well.

Rob is grateful that Mom taught the boys a little cooking. It gave them an appreciation for what some might think of a girl's work, and it really came in handy when Rob had to do the cooking later in his life.

When she and Dad first started farming, the only way of preserving food was canning. They bought a National pressure cooker. It had a pressure gauge which was controlled by a petcock. When using the pressure cooker, the proper pressure had to be maintained for the required time and the pressure had to be relieved before opening.

Mom was canning. The canner was at pressure when Dad came in the door. He saw the canner and decided he wanted to see what's for supper, so he opened the lid. It blew the contents straight up, damaging the ceiling. Mom was really upset. She always said he could have blown us all up. She never trusted that pressure cooker after that and really watched Dad around the stove. Mom always said she never could understand how he could open it when it was under pressure.

Laundry was a major chore for Mom. She had a washing machine: a single tub with an agitator and a wringer on top. It was better than doing laundry by hand, but it sure wasn't automatic. It had to be attended constantly. Mom made lye soap with the lard we made when butchering. She used it to wash the heavily soiled farm clothes.

Mom had a long handled wooden spoon, which she used when doing laundry. Over time the spoon got considerable wear causing the spoon part to break off. But that didn't deter Mom, she kept using the handle. When asked about the stick or spoon, Rich and Kathie would say it was a stick, and Rob would tell you it's a spoon. In any case, Mom found it handy when reaching into the very hot water she used when doing laundry.

Kathie and Rich found a gray/green toy alligator. To prank Mom, they would put the alligator in the washer. Mom would poke around with the stick and up would come the alligator. The first time it happened, it startled her. She got used to it, but she never knew when it was going to happen.

Monday was laundry day. After getting washed, baskets of clothes were taken outside and hung on clotheslines. There were two lines in the front yard and four lines behind the butcher-house. In the winter, the clothes were taken downstairs to the basement where they were air dried. After drying, the clothes were carried into the house. Tuesday was ironing day. As we got older, we helped with the clothes, but Mom did the bulk of the work.

Mom always worked in the gardens. She had one hoe that she used. Mary recalls it being a woman's hoe. The handle seemed to fit her better, as it was thinner than the other hoes and just a little shorter. Dad would sharpen it. Between sharpening and Mom's constant use, the blade was worn thin, and the corners were rounded off. Rich recalls using that hoe and found that it was very sharp, making easy work of cutting weeds and due to the rounded corners, it could get close to the plant without damage. This meant less weed pulling. That hoe was so worn that it developed a crack. Mom tried without success to find another hoe of this type and never could. Mom used it till the end of her gardening days in her flower garden.

Mary recalls getting in trouble with Dad for playing the radio in the Oldsmobile we had. When she and Mom went somewhere in the car, they would play the radio. Sometimes they would forget to turn the radio off before shutting off the car and when next started, the radio would come on. When Dad heard the radio, he would say, "Who's been playing the radio? It will run down the battery." It wasn't that Dad didn't like music or the radio, but he thought having the radio on would discharge the battery, making it impossible to start the car. The battery always seemed questionable at best anyway. He refused to believe the automobile companies no longer wired the radio directly to the battery as they previously had done. When Mary and Mom went somewhere, after getting out of earshot, Mom would say, "Turn on the radio." Finally, after hearing Dad's complaints, Mom asked, "Why do you suppose they put radios in cars if you're not supposed to play them?" Dad could not come up with a response.

Near the end of her life, Mom experienced visions of things that had happened and of things that we could not see. She said to Mary, "Put down that pig!" Mom was remembering the days when we used to bring the newborn pigs into the house to warm up. Mary used to like carrying the cute little pigs around. Mary says, "Even though they were white and clean, they still smelled like pigs." One of her visions was of a person who she didn't know and instinctively didn't like. She told Mary about the person and that she didn't like them. Mary said, "Tell him to go away." Later Mom said she did that, and the person left.

ROBERT ALAN MCDONALD, KATHIE EILEEN MCDONALD COURTNEY, RICHARD EDWIN MCDONALD, MARY JO MCDONALD HELFRICH

THE MCDONALDS

Chapter Five – Getting To Know Mack

Dad learned a great deal in the military. He also worked with a house mover and as a kiln fireman. He had skill with explosives, machinery, building trades, and he managed a gun and tank destroyer crew. His military training began in 1941 and ended after D-Day in 1944 when they landed in France. The entire outfit was well trained. As Mom used to say, "They were a crack outfit!" They were. They had a low casualty rate and saw more combat than some other outfits.

Spending Money

Dad was not a big spender. An example of Dad's inability to spend money was his work belt. His old belt wore out. But Dad wasn't without resources. He had kept the harnesses when he stopped farming with horses and no longer owned any horses. So, he went to where the harnesses were lying on the floor of the old house, picked out a good strap, made it into a belt, and used it for over 20 years. If he could find something to put to a different, productive use, he'd do it. He felt that he had time, but he didn't have money.

Dad would spend money on us kids, just not large sums of it. Dad carried his money in a soft rubber squeeze purse that he'd gotten from the bank as a free give-away. Mostly his money was coins, but rarely he would fold up a bill or two and put them in there. Dad didn't carry a wallet; he was worried about losing it.

Concern about losing a wallet may have come from Grandpa Sam plowing his wallet under when doing spring planting. Fortunately for him and his family, the next year when plowing the same field, the wallet re-appeared. There was over $600 in it, a substantial sum in the '40s. Grandpa Sam liked having money on him, unlike Dad.

ROBERT ALAN MCDONALD, KATHIE EILEEN MCDONALD COURTNEY, RICHARD EDWIN MCDONALD, MARY JO MCDONALD HELFRICH

Shortly after moving from Bolivar to the farm on Poorman Road, Grandpa Sam when into Navarre to one of the two feed mills. He walked up to the counter, said to the person at the counter, who happened to be the owner, "I need to open an account. I just bought a farm on Poorman Road, and from time to time I may need credit." The owner replied, "I'm sorry, I don't know you. For now, until I get to know you, I'll have to ask you to pay cash." To Grandpa Sam, this was an insult. So, Sam waited until he sold something and had hundreds of dollars in his wallet, walked up to the owner, threw his bulging wallet on the counter, and asked, "Think I can get credit now?" He was granted credit.

We would go with him to the dairy in Brewster. In the dairy retail store, which had a lunch counter, they also sold ice cream, popsicles, cheese, butter by the pound, and milkshakes. A single dip ice-cream cone or a popsicle was a nickel. Milkshakes cost more, perhaps a quarter. Rich remembers going with Dad one morning with Mary along. At the time, Mary was in her 'not talking much or at all' stage. But Mary wanted a treat, so she looked at Dad and said, "Do you have any money?" A complete sentence. Rich says it tickled Dad so much he belly-laughed. Rich thinks they got milkshakes that day.

Mary recalls Dad and his change purse in this fashion: it was green and extremely firm plastic, so firm that Mary could not squeeze the ends to get it open. Dad would give Mary the change purse when taking milk to the dairy in the morning after milking. If she could get the money out by the time they got to the dairy, she could have a treat. He typically gave her the change purse around the area of the bridge, which meant Mary only had 2 miles to work that money out. To get the money out, she had to slip her pinky finger in the holes at the end and try to slide a coin out of the middle. Mary recalls that when she reached the second bridge, the one on 93 that went over Sugar Creek, she frequently didn't have the money out. This was when the panic would ensue. Now there were only about 4 blocks left till the dairy. Next came the Brewster City Limit sign and 35 MPH speed sign. Three blocks left and still no money. Somehow, through sheer desperation, Mary always extracted the coin, usually as they were turning into the dairy. Mary believes Dad did this to keep her quiet and busy. "She is positive," he chuckled, watching.

One day, upon getting out of the green truck to get her treat, Mary spotted a dollar bill lying on the ground right beside the truck. She showed Dad. He said, "What should we do with that found money?" Mary replied, "Milkshakes for everyone." Dad must have added extra money because Mary bought 6 milkshakes that day.

Dad was not only reluctant to spend money, but he wouldn't consider price increases. Rich says Dad was always about 10 years behind on prices. He would go to buy something, and he'd get mad because the price was higher than it had been 10 years ago. Rich says he would just shake his head.

Rob recalls Dad not accepting price increases, but he had the same problem with getting paid. Dad would tell Rob when he went into the Army, he was paid $21 a month. Rob would counter that he was only getting $70 a month. Dad would say, "See you're making a lot more than I did." Rob would counter, "But you were in the service in 1941, this is 1967. Things have gone up. I'm not really making more that you did." Dad response was always, "$70 is more than $21."

One of Mom and Dad's rules was you never eat or drink anything in front of anyone unless offering to share with them. If you don't have enough to share, you don't eat or drink yourself. If there was a guest at mealtime, they were expected to eat with us – no exceptions.

At the dairy, Amish would come with their children. At one of those times, the Amish man went into the dairy store and came out with an ice cream cone for himself. He had children in the buggy but got nothing for the children. That really upset Dad. His remark was something to the effect, "Look at that dumb s.o.b.; he got something for himself and nothing for the children." It was one of those things that really makes an impression on how a person should treat others, especially members of one's family.

ROBERT ALAN MCDONALD, KATHIE EILEEN MCDONALD COURTNEY, RICHARD EDWIN MCDONALD, MARY JO MCDONALD HELFRICH

Mack Buys a Truck

Farm equipment has a nasty habit of wearing out or no longer being suitable for the work that needed doing. The farm reached a point where a decent truck was necessary. The ideal size would be a 1-Ton pickup, something like a Ford F-350. It would be used daily to transport milk to the cheese factory with a return load of whey, in addition to other hauling jobs.

Mack looked around the area and hadn't located a suitable truck. He knew a guy who was a salesman for the Ford dealer in Bolivar, Ohio. He asked the salesman to keep his eye out for such a truck. Mack had others looking, but the Bolivar guy found one first and brought it to the farm.

The deal was that Dad would use the truck. Drive it around, haul things, and see if it was a good fit. So that's what he did. It was a green F-350 Ford with a 300-cu. inch six-cylinder engine, four-speed manual transmission with a granny gear and a stake body. It was used but seemed in decent shape, just what we needed.

While evaluating it, Mack took the truck into the woods. There was no reason to take the truck into the woods. To get there, we had to go west on Lawndell Road, cross the bridge on Sugar Creek, and go into the north pasture. Into the pasture we went, across the shallow drainage ditch into the woods. The truck was rear wheel drive, not four-wheel drive.

Rob recalls the rest of the story this way: he was in the truck bed, looking over the cab in the same direction Dad was driving. Rob remembers thinking, *Why are we going into the woods? This truck isn't four-wheel drive, but the ground was dry, and it was a nice day, so it should be okay, right?*

Rob knew Dad was going to do what he was going to do and asking why we were doing it would be seen as questioning Dad's judgement. That wouldn't be smart, so Rob kept his mouth shut.

Along we went, deeper into the woods bouncing over the rough spots. Presently, we came to a spot that had two medium-sized hickory trees growing on either side of the clear track Dad was on. Rob, having the same view Dad had, knew that the truck would not fit between the trees, but rather than risk Dad's ire, continued to keep his mouth shut.

In between the trees Dad went, keeping a steady pace – using the theory the quicker through the more likely to make it. Rob recalls thinking the best that will happen is we'll knock the mirrors off. In the gap we went, and sure enough, Dad wedged the truck between the trees. It stopped short of denting both front fenders identically. Rob nearly went over the hood when it suddenly stopped. Dad reversed and somehow the truck extricated itself from the predicament. The good news was that the mirrors were intact.

Rob recalls Dad driving back to the house, where Dad went in to explain it to Mom. Dad started the conversation saying, "Marian, we're going to have to buy that truck." Naturally, Mom asked, "Why?" Dad explained that he'd dented both front fenders and would have to either pay for the repairs or buy it. Of course, Mom asked how it happened. Dad replied in all seriousness, "I thought it would fit."

So, Mack bought the truck. We used it for years on the farm, and when he finally got rid of it, the fenders were still bent.

Special Mail Service

Mary recalls Mr. Hammond, the mailman, taking the mail to Dad one winter day. Rich recalls that Dad had a unique way of getting people to do stuff for him. Probably because Dad would do things for other people. Dad had prevailed on Mr. Hammond to get the Wednesday Massillon Evening Independent newspaper to him promptly, as Dad needed to see the grain and livestock reports.

Being a good guy, Mr. Hammond hand carried the mail to Dad on Wednesdays. This day, Mr. Hammond figured out where Dad was following the sound of the machinery used to clean the hog pens.

The expanded hog operation included a farrowing house (how it was insulated is another story) and six finishing pens. A gutter

ROBERT ALAN MCDONALD, KATHIE EILEEN MCDONALD COURTNEY, RICHARD EDWIN MCDONALD, MARY JO MCDONALD HELFRICH

surrounded the hog pens, equipped with a gutter cleaner, which moved the hog waste to the deepest part— a shallow pit. From there, it took the waste up a short ramp into a manure spreader. Nothing wasted.

It was winter and, although the sun was out, it was still cold enough that there was ice around the gutter and light snow on the ground. Mr. Hammond stepped up on the concrete surrounding the shallow pit to hand Dad the newspaper. He slipped on the ice and fell into the pit. Mr. Hammond went to his knees. The man was a mess.

Thinking quickly, Dad gathered Mr. Hammond up and took him to the milk house, about 100 yards away. In the milk house, Dad used a hose connected to the well to wash Mr. Hammond off. Well water is always cold and would seem doubly so in winter. That must have been a tough shower.

Mr. Hammond, being a loyal, hard-working person, decided he needed to finish his mail route. So, he cranked the heater in his car up as high as it would go to keep warm and to dry off. He set off to finish the route. The further he went, the warmer it got, and that activated the odor in the hog waste. Finally, the smell got the best of him, and he had to turn down the heat. At last, he finished and got to go home.

After cleaning himself, he went to work cleaning the car, but alas that hog waste proved more than a match for cleaning. After a couple of months during which the car was subject to repeated cleanings, Mr. Hammond gave up. He finally had to sell the car. He also burned all the clothing, including the shoes he wore that day.

After that, Dad got no more special delivery. When Dad told Mom about this, she asked, "Why did you take him to the milk house? It was cold." Dad responded, "Where else would I take him?"

THE MCDONALDS

Nap Time

Rich recalls Dad enjoying an afternoon nap occasionally. On rainy days when work wasn't too pressing, Dad would slip off to the straw mow in the barn and catch 40-winks. The rain beating on the slate roof put him right to sleep. Rich says he tried it and found it worked very well.

Getting Assistance

Dad certainly had a way of getting what he wanted or needed from others. It wasn't just folks like Mr. Hammond.

A few miles away in the little village of Trail was a slaughterhouse that made Trail Bologna: all-beef bologna, made from the meat of older animals that weren't suitable for the table. At the time, the company was family owned. The owner lived in Trail, walking distance from the business. Dad got to know the owner. How they met we aren't sure, but it could have been as simple as Dad walking into the business and striking up a conversation. The owner was Amish or Mennonite. Dad got on very well with those folks.

Dad found that they would custom process animals for a fee. From time to time, we would have an old cow that was no longer productive for milking or producing beef calves but was a suitable candidate for Trail Bologna. Dad would load the cow into the stock trailer and haul her to Trail, about 10 miles away. The time of day that this happened could be during normal working hours or not.

Rich recalls helping Dad load a cow and hauling her to Trail. It was late in the evening, and the slaughterhouse was closed for the day. That didn't deter Dad. He stopped at the owner's house, knocked on the door, talked for a bit, and told the owner he had a cow he needed processed. The owner said, "Well, I better open up so you can unload her." And he did. We don't know if the owner was as accommodating to other people, but he sure was for Dad.

We always had Trail Bologna and Dad sold a fair amount of it to others.

ROBERT ALAN MCDONALD, KATHIE EILEEN MCDONALD COURTNEY, RICHARD EDWIN MCDONALD, MARY JO MCDONALD HELFRICH

Insulating the Farrowing House

Labor wasn't a problem on the farm. That's precisely why there were four of us – free labor. We used to say there are three ways of doing anything: the hard way, the easy way, and Dad's way, which was much more difficult than the hard way. Insulating the farrowing house was a case in point.

The hog operation comprised of two buildings connected by a common back wall. The first building was the farrowing house and two growing pens and the second building enclosed six finishing pens. The farrowing house was fully enclosed, so it could be heated. The growing pens were partially enclosed, being open to the east. The farrowing house was divided in half with the growing pens separated from the farrowing pens by a block wall and internal door.

We decided it would be easier to heat the farrowing house if we insulated the ceiling. Above the farrowing house was a second story with a solid wood floor sitting on two by eight floor joists. So, we used quarter inch plywood to seal the bottom of the floor joists, leaving an eight-inch space we were going to fill with fiberglass insulation.

Where to get fiberglass insulation cheaply? Dad had an idea. A neighbor who lived east on Lawndell Road had a junkyard in which were junk appliances which contained fiberglass. All we had to do was cut open the appliances: stoves, refrigerators, freezers, and water heaters and remove the fiberglass. So that's what we did. We took axes, hatchets, and other small tools and spent days tearing apart appliances. The water heaters had the best yield, but there weren't enough of them to do everything we needed, so we cut up a lot of stuff.

After liberating the fiberglass, we then took it to the farrowing house and pushed it into the void. The first time we did this, we did it bare armed. The itching was terrible, so we got long-sleeved gloves and finished the job using them.

THE MCDONALDS

How much did we save? Given the time we spent tearing apart those appliances and the cost of fiberglass insulation, which was cheap, we lost money. Our time could have been better used doing something—anything—else. Most people can't believe we really did this. Rest assured; we did. As Rich says, "Dad never got over the Depression."

Rob's Driving Lessons

Rob recalls a time when he drove the old truck that Dad originally owned. The truck may have been a Dodge and as near as we can remember, it was a rusty red or orange and black. It was large, over one ton and Mom hated driving it because she wasn't strong enough to steer it – no power steering. Rob was about 4 or 5. Dad was doing a repair and needed the truck moved while he was outside. He put Rob in the cab and said, "Put it in gear and move it." Rob had no idea how to drive or even how to put the thing in gear – floor shifting manual transmission. Rob protested that he didn't know what he was doing. Dad was adamant, "Move the truck!" So, Rob got it started, pushed the clutch in with his foot, and jammed the gear shift into a gear. When he let out the clutch, the truck stalled, but it moved a little bit. Dad said, "Good, just what I wanted." Rich recalls a big scratch on the dash that Dad put there lighting those old Blue Tip matches he used to light his cigarettes.

Dad purchased a new Studebaker Commander automobile before WWII. When he got out of the service, the car wasn't in good shape. It had been parked at Granddad McDonald's farm. Grandpa Sam used it for storage. Mice and other vermin got into it. But the car would still run and since we had nothing else, it was used.

One day we used it to go to the Brewster Dairy. Exactly the reason for this trip has been lost in time. Rob recalls the trip this way: Dad parked the car at the back of the building at the top of a hill that led downward and across Ohio Route 93 and into an open field. Since Dad wasn't going far, just inside the dairy, and would be right back, he turned off the ignition, put the car in first gear and left Rob – then about 3 years old – standing in the front seat of the car. The car had a manual transmission, as almost every car had, so it was customary practice to place the car in first gear when parked. The car also had an emergency brake that could have been set as a further safeguard, but Dad didn't use it that day.

Rob recalls Dad getting out and leaving after cautioning him to stay in the car. He may have also said, "Don't touch anything." But Rob isn't sure about that. Dad was gone and Rob was all alone. Rob recalls seeing Dad shift, so he took hold of the gearshift on the steering column and pushed it up. The upward push put the car in neutral, and it began rolling down the hill toward Route 93, picking up speed as it went. Rob recalls trying to pull the gearshift lever back down, but that didn't work. The car rolled down the hill across 93, going about halfway across the field where the land rose, acting as a brake, causing the car to stop.

Rob recalls the ride, hoping they hit nothing, because he didn't know how to steer or stop it. When the car came to a stop on its own, Rob's wish had been granted. The car hit nothing except grass and Rob was still standing upright in the front seat. Rob recalls thinking, *I'm in trouble now*. But Dad came running to the car with someone from the dairy. Dad opened the door and checked to see if Rob was hurt, and found he wasn't. Rob says Dad never said a thing to him, so there never was a reason to tell Dad how the car got into neutral.

Coon Hunting

Dad had a pair of AKC registered Black and Tan Coonhounds, Drum–male and Lady–female. Dad acquired both as pups by boarding a full-blooded bitch who was about to whelp, for a friend. After weaning, Dad got his choice and selected a male and female. Dad and another friend, Ray Geis, trained the dogs. Drum was a silent tracker. Only when the 'coon was up a tree – treed – would Drum bark. When Drum barked, you knew you had a 'coon and it was treed. Lady was a bit harder to train and in her early years would get distracted by a rabbit or another animal. But she became much better as she got older.

Lady was the better killer. Once the 'coon was on the ground Lady would grab the 'coon behind its head and poor old Drum would grab its gut and they'd stretch the 'coon until it died. In this position, Drum usually got bit or clawed. If Lady got it by herself, she would grab it behind its head, shake it and snap its neck.

'Coon hunting could be an adventure, especially since it was done at night. We would go out hunting after finishing the milking, about 8:30 PM. Of course, we hunted our own woods, but often someone would beat us there. They would start hunting about 5:00 PM just as it was getting dark. We would still have to eat supper and milk. It used to irritate Dad, but the hunters would be gone before he could do anything about it.

One place we hunted was the woods around the strip mines east of the farm. It was rough country, and we had little hunting competition there. Arch Croy (Barney) owned the strip-mined land, so we always had permission to hunt. Rob always worried about walking over a "high wall" in the dark. The high wall was what the sheer bank left when the strip mining removed the "overburden" – the material above the coal seam. Dad knew where the high walls were, and we didn't have an accident.

Dad wasn't particular about cleaning his guns. He'd use the gun and place it in the corner until the next time. Guns didn't get cleaned or oiled with any regularity.

One evening we were up on high ground just above the Muscoff farm. The dogs treed four 'coons in one tree. We loaded the gun and Dad tried a shot. The gun wouldn't fire. The firing pin was rusted and wouldn't move. Dad told Rob to go down to Muscoff's and ask them for coal oil (kerosene) to free the firing pin. Rob did as he was told and came back with it. The remedy worked, and we got all four 'coons.

Another brief word about the gun we took 'coon hunting. It was an old rolling block single shot 22 caliber rifle. The spring holding the rolling block tight to seal the combustion chamber was old and worn and didn't create a good seal. When it was fired, smoke hit you right in the eye. Not a fun experience. It caused flinching or shutting your eye at the critical time. Later, Rob got a bolt action 22, and we used it instead.

We, along with Ray Geis, were hunting near Navarre. Drum wasn't acting right. He kept hanging around us instead of ranging ahead like he should. Finally, Ray went up to Drum and gave him a kick in the butt. Drum moved out and within a couple minutes began to bark.

Knowing that Drum only barked when he had a 'coon treed, we were sure it was a 'coon, but his bark didn't sound right, like the way he normally barked treed. When we got to him, we found out why. Drum had the 'coon on the ground. Apparently being silent on the trail allowed Drum to come right up near the 'coon before the 'coon knew he was there. There was a tree right behind the 'coon, but if he tried for the tree, the dog would get him, and the dog didn't want to get bit or clawed so he didn't attack with the 'coon facing him. They had a standoff.

Lady wasn't with Drum when he cornered the 'coon, but Lady heard Drum's bark and knew he had a coon. Lady broke the standoff as she came charging into that 'coon. There was a good fight as the 'coon was in good health. At one point, the 'coon shook loose and started up the tree, but Drum leaped up and picked the 'coon off the tree like a good basketball center. Back on the ground, the fight resumed. Finally, the two dogs seemed to have the 'coon done in. We got the dogs off the 'coon and Dad picked it up by the hind legs and smacked its head against a tree trunk to be sure it was dead. Dad put the 'coon in the game pocket of his hunting coat. It was a large 'coon.

We headed back to the vehicle as we were finished hunting for the evening. All at once, Dad started taking off his coat. Ray asked Dad, "Mack, what's the matter?" Dad replied, while getting out of the coat, "It came back to life!" Dad got the 'coon out of the coat and smacked his head on a rock this time. That was one tough 'coon.

Another night we went to a spot known as the 40-acre swamp. The overgrowth was thick, and the underbrush was worse. There were places we couldn't walk. We were down on our hands and knees trying to get through. We nearly got lost because we couldn't see the sky to determine what direction we needed to go. Fortunately, we got out of there, but we didn't get any 'coons.

But likely the worst experience was one late December evening when we went hunting. We didn't have a good hunt, got nothing. When we got back, Mom informed Dad that this was their wedding anniversary. Dad seemed truly embarrassed about forgetting their anniversary. He didn't try to make an excuse, but the look on his face told it all. Mom had fun reminding him of that one for quite a while.

Mary recalls Lady being placed in the granary for breeding. Another Black and Tan coonhound was supposed to father her pups, as Lady and Drum were litter mates, so Dad put those two in the granary. Mom said he patted his pocket and said, "I have the key right here." The next morning, three dogs came out of the granary. Drum joined the party. The slots in the granary were on the top about 12 feet off the barn floor and only 6 to 8 inches wide. So much for locking her in. The sad part of this story is that Lady died having that litter of pure-bred Black and Tans, so Dad never got a litter.

Coon hunting was primarily sport, although the 'coons were skinned, and the hides sold at the end of the season. At the time, hides weren't particularly valuable, so the income wasn't close to paying for the dog food.

The Last of the Romantics

Dad liked to get Mom presents for Christmas and other occasions, but nothing too frivolous. He would occasionally bring Mom irises from the night pasture. Also, he enjoyed showing Mom dog-tooth violets growing in the woods. But he wouldn't pick them as they weren't plentiful, and he was afraid they would be gone.

One Christmas, Dad gave Mom open stock dishes Mom was collecting. Another time, he got her nice pots and pans. Seeing those gifts, Grandma Nellie, Mom's mother, dubbed Dad the last of the great romantics.

Dad also liked to play jokes or pull pranks. One Christmas, he made a double-barreled slingshot for Aunt El. It was a large bra that he got from his sister, our Aunt Betty. Dad attached it to a tree fork, wrapped it carefully in burlap, and tied it with binder twine. He gave it to Aunt El, who never said or did anything remotely out-of-line. When she unwrapped the present, she turned beet red, much to Dad's delight.

The common theme with Dad wasn't so much that he didn't like spending money, but the fact that he never had much of it. So, he found other ways of getting things done that didn't involve money.

Honeydew Melons

What makes this remarkable is Dad planted something he knew nothing about.

Dad used a few feet of the field immediately west of the house for a garden. In those couple of rows, Dad planted potatoes and melons, both watermelons and muskmelons. The crop did exceptionally well that year. We had all the potatoes we needed for the entire year. The melon crop was terrific. The watermelons were big and sweet, but some muskmelons were strange—at least Dad thought they were. Because melons grow on vines, it's hard to tell where one plant ends and the other starts. The fruit gets mixed up.

Dad liked muskmelon, which has an interior salmon color. So, he'd go out and pick a melon, cut it open and if it were nice and pink/salmon colored, he'd take it in and eat it. But some were green. Dad would open one of the green ones and shake his head, saying, "I thought it was ripe; it looked ripe." He'd take the green ones to the sow and boar lot and feed it to the hogs. The hogs really liked these melons. But Dad was really puzzled. He couldn't understand why all the melons weren't ripe when they looked like they should be.

THE MCDONALDS

That fall, Mom and Dad were having a cookout in the butcherhouse and had invited neighbors, relatives, and friends. Dad was planning to serve corn (roasted in the husk done in the furnace), hamburgers, hotdogs, potato salad, and melon- both watermelon and muskmelon. But he was concerned that the green melons would be served, and he didn't want to serve something that wasn't ripe. He mentioned the predicament to one neighbor who stopped by. The neighbor took one look at the green melon and asked Dad, "Have you ever tried eating the green melon?" Of course Dad replied, "No, he wasn't interested in eating anything that wasn't ripe." That's when the neighbor told Dad about honeydew melons, and Dad took a bite. At that point, honeydew melons became Dad's favorite, and the hogs lost out. Even Dad had a chuckle.

Fish Tales

We hadn't lived on the farm long when we had a spring flood. Fortunately, it was early enough that it didn't stop or seriously interfere with the spring planting. But what it did was strand a bunch of carp in a low place south of what we called berry hill. During floods, carp leave the creek bed and go where they can find food as they are bottom feeders. Other fish species don't seem to do this.

Slowly, the water receded, and the carp became increasingly visible. Dad, and one neighbor, probably Nick Schonlen, decided they would gather the fish in wash tubs, take them to the poorer area in Massillon, and sell them. That's what they did. The venture was successful as they came back with money. They said they could hear people scraping the scales off those fish before they left town.

Carp getting stranded was a common occurrence. It didn't happen every year, but it wasn't unusual. One of the places was a low area in the night pasture west of the barn. This area held quite a bit of water and some years it held water the entire year. Often, we could ice skate there in the winter.

One year, a bunch of carp were stranded, and they became increasingly visible as the water receded. A Black family from Massillon were frequent visitors. The older gentlemen frequently

ROBERT ALAN MCDONALD, KATHIE EILEEN MCDONALD COURTNEY, RICHARD EDWIN MCDONALD, MARY JO MCDONALD HELFRICH

came to fish and sometimes to hunt. He and his family were very respectful, always asking before coming onto the property. Dad liked them and enjoyed talking to the older man. He had served in the Army during World War II in the Red Eye Express, so he and Dad had a shared history.

This family stopped by one summer day as they wanted to fish. The family group included the older gentleman, his daughter, and her son, the older man's grandson. Dad told them to fish wherever they wanted to, but before they did, would they be interested in catching carp that were trapped? At first the older man said he wasn't interested in carp. He wanted to catch catfish. But Dad took them to the top of the hill where you could see the pond and see the fish fins breaking the water as the fish swam around.

This sold the grandson. He told his grandfather that he wanted to catch these fish. It looked so easy with fish fins breaking out of the water all over the pond. So, grandpa gave in, and Dad gave them a couple pitchforks, and we walked down to the pond bank with them.

The grandson took off his shoes, carefully rolled up his trouser legs above his knees and, armed with the pitchfork, waded in. He would see a fish's fin, move to stab it with the pitchfork, but would miss. He was careful at first to keep his pants dry. Pretty soon, he forgot about staying dry and began chasing the fish all over the pond. All the while stabbing with that pitchfork and missing. Now and then, he'd step on a fish. It would move and he'd jump. He was having fun but not being successful. He'd say, "I stabs where he is, but he ain't there!"

Grandpa couldn't stand it any longer. He, too, took off his shoes, carefully rolled up his trousers, grabbed a pitchfork and waded in. Pretty soon, he, too, forgot about staying dry. Water was flying in all directions, and those two guys were stabbing all over the pond, often right next to each other. How they missed each other's feet was a miracle, but they did. They weren't successful in getting carp. We, along with the daughter, stayed out of the pond, but we were all laughing so hard we could hardly stand. Even the two fishermen were laughing.

By the time they finished, they were a muddy mess. We took them up to the milk house and hosed them off. Both the grandfather and the grandson were tired, so they decided they had enough fishing for that day. They may have gotten a fish or two, but certainly no more than that.

Affinity to Wintergreen Lozenges

Dad had a particular affinity to pink, wintergreen flavored lozenges. The kind that tastes like Pepto-Bismol. Mom also bought him Reed's cellophane wrapped candies. Dad would get a supply of either of them and secret them in a pocket. He'd slip one in his mouth when working. But Kathie had a great nose and ear and could sniff them or hear the cellophane rattle from clear across the barn. Dad would slip one in his mouth and almost immediately Kathie would exclaim, "I smell candy!" Dad knew the jig was up and he'd have to share.

Dad frequently got a stomach upset after eating. This happened during the evening milking after the evening meal. We always knew it was going to happen when Dad began spitting, then coughing. The cats knew, too. They'd gather around Dad in a semi-circle waiting. Up it would come. Never a great deal but the cats liked it. When asked, Dad's response was, "This is a sign of a strong stomach." His stomach would get rid of anything that caused the least upset. At least that was his story, and he stuck to it.

Dad also suffered from occasional blood sugar lows. Rob recalls once having to get him some pink lozenges one afternoon when we were cleaning out the horse stable. After a few lozenges, Dad perked right up. He said when he felt weakness coming on, he would get something to eat. It could be candy or a sandwich.

ROBERT ALAN MCDONALD, KATHIE EILEEN MCDONALD COURTNEY, RICHARD EDWIN MCDONALD, MARY JO MCDONALD HELFRICH

Military Tales

Dad's army buddies would visit. The two families that visited most often were Bob Kuehner, his wife Ann, and their son Bobbie as well as Gene Jacobs, his wife Dorothy (Dot), their son David, and daughter Debbie. During the evening milking, Dad and his buddies would reminisce about their service time. Often the stories were humorous but not all of them. Listening to these stories gave us a great appreciation for what these men went through.

While training stateside, Dad had most of his pay sent home as support for Mom and Rob. Once he was down to six cents. So, Dad thought, *What the heck, this is not much better than being totally broke, so why not take a chance.* So, he got into a penny-ante poker game. Dad said he won about $12 and made it through the rest of that month.

They spoke of the dangerous actions such as taking a town without using ammunition, not once but twice, on successive nights. Their orders prohibited ammunition because the Allied forces took extreme care to preserve historical buildings, especially cathedrals. They said the Germans knew this and used the information to their advantage. For example, they'd position snipers in cathedral bell towers knowing the Allied forces wouldn't fire on them.

They added protection to their tank destroyers, sandbags to augment the armor, as a tank destroyer's armor was lighter than a tank and a German 88-millimeter gun would go right through if they were hit. They added a 30-caliber machine gun to augment firepower and allow multidirectional fire from both the 30- and the 50-caliber machine guns while engaging the enemy with the 90-millimeter main cannon. Tank destroyers had an open turret, which meant a hand grenade or guns in the hands of snipers posted in raised positions could attack from above, so they added a closable steel cover.

They told of raiding a winery. They looted so much wine, champagne, and cognac that after loading it on the tank destroyer, the turret would hardly turn. But they did an excellent job of putting the contents to beneficial use. In fact, during a transit, one guy fell off. They stopped to find him and here he came, weaving up the road holding the bottle. When he got close, he exclaimed, "I never spilled a drop!"

Blake Brenner, who was part of the family that rented The Farm after Dad retired, related a story Dad had told him that occurred during action in Cologne, Germany. When fighting in urban environments, they would try to take out snipers who hid in the church bell towers. Then they would find an alley, dead end ones were the best, back the tank destroyer in with the cannon pointing forward so they could shoot anything that came in front of them. They were about to use this tactic. Dad ordered the driver to back into an alley. The driver refused and said, "The lieutenant and his jeep are behind us!" To which Dad responded, "Run over the son-of-a-bitch!" Blake told this story to Stuart Courtney.

The battle of Rhein Crossing lasted three months and involved crossing the Rhein once, the Main five times, and the Danube once. Seven river crossings all while under fire or threat of fire. During this battle, one guy in the battalion set up a still and was making booze on the front lines. It seems quite amazing that the mash had time to ferment, seeing how the unit was moving constantly. This guy was talented.

Dad later told Mary about liberating the concentration camp at Dachau. How those prisoners that lived through the horror were walking skeletons. There were body stacks. When looking over the bodies, one of them moved. They discovered a living person. They took immediate action, and that person lived. In fact, he attended one of their reunions.

Dad said that their commanding officer made sure that each one of them knew they had permission to go in and see for themselves what when on, but by seeing what was outside, Dad said he had no desire to see any more.

Dad commented to Rich that during combat, the ideal situation was to have just enough alcohol in you so you didn't care, but not enough to be drunk. In that condition, you were one mean son-of-a-bitch and could get through anything.

After the war officially ended, while acting as occupation troops, Dad's unit captured a young German youth. The Nazis thoroughly indoctrinated these young people. Being so young, he wasn't searched properly and concealed a pistol with which he tried to shoot Dad in the back. Fortunately, Dad or someone else stopped him. Dad told Rich that he really chewed out the guys that did such a poor job. Dad said that had the young man succeeded, Rich and his sisters wouldn't have been here.

Those stories taught us that our parents were tough, resourceful, and enormously proud of their country. They were part of the generation that refused to allow world domination by a dictator.

Stepping Out

Dad managed the boy's social lives without resorting to a lot of rules. He used the same technique on both Rob and Rich. When the boys got old enough to become interested in girls, we were permitted to go wherever and with whom we wanted. But the milking had to be done first. We could use the car, and it always had plenty of gas because we filled it from the farm tank.

Dad wasn't a particularly early riser, usually around 6 o'clock, which meant that the morning milking started between 6:30 and 7:00 AM. Milking is scheduled twice daily, 12 hours apart. Milking took at least an hour, more like an hour and a half, especially in the winter when the cows had to be fed silage while milked.

The boys could leave after the milking was done and they had to be back in time to milk the next morning. That rule was iron clad. The later they stayed out, the less sleep they got. The boys remember falling asleep when trying to milk on more than one occasion. Rich recalls a couple of Rob's friends coming to pick him up. They would be all dressed up and would wait for the milking to be finished so Rob could get cleaned up and ready to go. It seemed that the more anxious the boys were to go, the slower Dad moved. It was always 9 o'clock or later before Rob left. Rob recalls wondering what went on before 9 PM? When it was Rich's turn, he was in the same predicament.

Dad's rules were rigid for the boys, but there were exceptions for Dad and the rest of the family. Each year the town of Magnolia, Ohio, held a homecoming festival and Dad made it a point to go. That evening, milking was over by 6 PM and by 7, we were in the car heading for Magnolia, all cleaned up and smelling good. Dad always had a fine time at the homecoming. He knew a lot of people who attended.

Magnolia is located close to Bolivar where Grandpa Sam owned a farm after leaving Akron. Dad worked for and lived with the Sickafoose family who lived in Magnolia, so Dad considered it his hometown. Dad lived and worked there during his late teens or early 20s, but we don't know why he lived with the Sickafoose family.

Similarly, on special occasions the milking got done earlier. Our cousin, John Wisselgren, was getting married in the evening in Sugar Creek, Ohio, about 15 miles away down Route 93, a very crooked road. Dad left the boys to finish milking which included putting the cows out in the night pasture and taking the milk to the milkhouse and cleaning up the milking equipment. By the time the boys got to the house, the rest of the family was getting into the car. At this time, Rob had a 1954 Ford V-8. The boys got cleaned up, dressed and were on the road in record time. Knowing they we already late, Rob pushed it. They were sliding through the turns trying not to slow down too much. Rob was hanging onto the steering wheel and Rich the seat. There were no seatbelts. Fortunately, they didn't hit anything and didn't get hit. Coming into town, they spotted a car with a PT license plate. PT was Brewster's identification. They thought the car must be going to the wedding the same as they were, and they were right. They walked into the church right behind the rest of the family, they heard Dad say, "They probably won't make it. They don't know where they're going."

ROBERT ALAN MCDONALD, KATHIE EILEEN MCDONALD COURTNEY, RICHARD EDWIN MCDONALD, MARY JO MCDONALD HELFRICH

THE MCDONALDS

Chapter Six - The Children

As in all families, each sibling is different, unique in their own ways. Knowing those characteristics may help visualize our daily life.

Robert, the eldest, was born during World War II while Dad was serving. Mom told us she nearly finished giving birth before the doctor got there. Dad couldn't get leave and didn't get to see the baby for over a month. Grandpa Dan Jones had this comment when he first saw Robert, "Well, I guess he'll be alright." Rob looked a little rough.

Mom and Rob lived with Grandma and Grandpa Jones until the end of the war. Rob was always close to that set of grandparents. He was their oldest grandchild. Rob thought this may have resulted in a little distance from Dad, as they didn't bond until after Dad came home. Also, Rob was headstrong and outspoken, a trait that got him in trouble with Dad from time to time.

Being the eldest, he was the first to get chores assigned. He had regular barn chores to be done each day by the time he entered the first grade at age five. Rich remarked he thought he'd escaped getting barn chores, but upon entering the first grade at age six, he got them too.

Rob always got the job of naming the milk cows, and if something needed to be climbed, he got that job as well. Rob always wondered if Dad thought he was a good climber or expendable.

Rob recalls his first farm job. He was three. They put hay up loose. After cutting and drying, they raked it into windrows, and loaded onto a wagon using a hay-loader hooked to the back of the wagon. Horses or the tractor could pull the wagon. We used horses. On the wagon, a person spread the hay using a fork. Once loaded, the wagon went to the barn to be unloaded and put into the haymow.

ROBERT ALAN MCDONALD, KATHIE EILEEN MCDONALD COURTNEY, RICHARD EDWIN MCDONALD, MARY JO MCDONALD HELFRICH

The first year on the farm, the haying crew was Mom driving the team, Dad loading, unloading, and mowing, with Robert riding along. This "crew" matched neighbor Walt Lantzer's four-man crew load for load.

Bird and Dan pulling the hay ladder

Unloading was done using hay forks that were operated on a track at the peak of the barn roof. The forks would be lowered, set into the hay then raised using a rope attached to the forks which ran through a series of pulleys mounted at the roof peak from there down to the floor where it made a 90-degree turn, then hitched to Bird the horse that pulled it down the barn bank thus raising the load and pulling it to one of two mows at either end of the barn.

Dad put Rob on Bird's back. Being only three, he really added little to the task. The horse knew what to do and pulled the load. When she felt the load trip, she would come back up the hill to do it all over again. Dad said he put Rob up there just so Bird would think somebody was guiding her. Sure! That makes sense, right?

Rob became a business consultant.

Robert- High School Graduation 1961

THE MCDONALDS

Kathie came into the world early one cold December morning. Mom and Dad didn't have a running car and even if they did, it wouldn't have been any use. The road through the farm was snow and ice covered. Getting up the hill to Justus Avenue wasn't possible by car. The township didn't plow or clear ice and snow. In fact, sled riding down the hill from Justus Avenue to the railroad crossing was great because it was solid ice. For the first few years, this was the condition every year. Eventually, the township began plowing and salting, which, of course, ruined sled riding.

The plan to get Mom to the hospital was to have Grandma and or Grandpa Jones drive to the farm and take Mom to Massillon to the hospital. This morning, they couldn't get to the farm because of the road condition, so Dad took Mom up the icy road to Justus Avenue where she got into Grandpa Jones' car. From there, they took her to Massillon where the hospital was. Dad couldn't go to the hospital until later because he had to milk. But the birth was successful and in time, a healthy Kathie came home.

Kathie was always obedient and a hard worker. Both Rob and Rich felt she got more work assigned as Dad expected her to help outside and Mom expected her to help in the house. She did both and didn't complain, at least not too loudly or too often. Strange things happened to Kathie that she really didn't cause or have control over. One day she was in the bed of the truck while Dad was filling 55-gallon barrels with whey at the dairy. Dad shoved a barrel back toward the cab and it hit Kathie, knocking her off the truck onto the hardtop driveway. She got scraped and needed first aid. While it wasn't life threatening and didn't do permanent damage, she got hurt and shouldn't have. Dad said, "I knew when I let go of the barrel it was going to hit her, but I couldn't stop it."

Kathie helped Mom in the house, in the gardens, and with the chickens. On Saturdays, the entire house was cleaned. Kathie helped Mom with cooking, dishes, laundry, ironing, and canning. She also helped with the barn chores after Rob left for college.

When Mary was two or three, she would change clothes frequently ... making extra laundry for Mom, and extra ironing for

ROBERT ALAN MCDONALD, KATHIE EILEEN MCDONALD COURTNEY, RICHARD EDWIN MCDONALD, MARY JO MCDONALD HELFRICH

Kathie. Mom let Kathie iron pillowcases, hankies, and Mary's play dresses. A sprinkling bottle dampened the clothes. Then the clothes were rolled and allowed to sit while moisture spread over the entire cloth. The ironing was done promptly, so clothes didn't mildew.

Kathie loved riding horses and continues to own and ride them. Although she learned to ride Bill, she wanted her own horse. Mom and Dad had a friend, Fred Thompson, who had a mare he wanted to sell. Her name was Ginger. Kathie tried the horse out, found her to be a good fit, and bought her. Ginger was a fine riding horse but wasn't much for working cows. So that job remained Bill's.

A short way down Justus Avenue, Kathie and her husband, Dick Courtney, purchased a farm, which they've added to over the years.

Kathie became a registered nurse.

Kathie- High School Graduation 1966

Richard, like his two older siblings, entered the world during a cold month- February. This February didn't disappoint. It was cold and snowy, with difficult driving conditions. But this time, there was a better plan. Dad was going to the hospital with Mom. This meant that Rob was going to go to the barn while someone else milked— Uncle Pink (Varner) Foster or Uncle Bud (Roy) Wisselgren. Grandma Jones was staying with Kathie, who had a bealed ear. (A bealed ear is a viral infection which is very painful and cannot be treated with antibiotics because it's viral. The only treatment is time and a dry warm compress.) Rob was seven and Kathie was two.

On the way to the hospital, Dad said to Mom, "What's wrong with this car? It seems sluggish." That's when they discovered Dad forgot to shift into third gear. Like his siblings, Richard entered the world successfully. At the proper time, he came home.

Rich was always athletic. He learned to walk by nine months, and his theory seemed to be that there's no need to walk when you can run or jump. Even when he was little, he'd leave the house by charging out of the dining room through the screen door. He'd hit that screen at full stride and never touched the two sandstone steps leading to the ground. He'd be out across the porch and driveway by the time the screen door banged shut. Dad would just shake his head with a half-smile on his face. Mom would yell, "Shut that screen door! Don't let the flies in!"

Rich was good at pounding nails. Dad bought a half keg of nails and Rich used them to build a doghouse. He had nails so close together that it was almost made of metal. Kathie recalls Rich taking the handles off the kitchen cupboards when he was little. Mom would tell him to put them back on, and he would.

Rich also remembers going upstairs alone and taking the mortised locks off the bedroom doors, taking the locks apart, then putting them all back together again. He says the first time he took one lock apart, he almost panicked when he had difficulty remembering how it all worked. But he figured it out and then it was easy.

Rich was a talented baseball player, a pitcher, even playing a bit at the NCAA Division 1 college level. Rich became a carpenter with his own contracting business.

ROBERT ALAN MCDONALD, KATHIE EILEEN MCDONALD COURTNEY, RICHARD EDWIN MCDONALD, MARY JO MCDONALD HELFRICH

Richard- High School Graduation 1969

Mary, unlike the others, entered the world in a hot month- August. There was no drama getting to the hospital. The roads were dry; the weather was fine, but hot. Dad took the three siblings to the hospital with him when it was time to bring Mom and Mary home. Children could only enter the hospital at certain times, so we had to stay outside. Dad left us in the car with strict instructions to stay in the car and to keep it warm for the baby. That meant keeping the windows rolled up.

There we sat on a sultry August afternoon in a dark-colored car, in the middle of a large black topped parking lot, with the windows rolled up because Dad said to keep it warm. In fact, he specifically told Rob he was responsible if anything went wrong. Rob was twelve, Kathie was seven, and Rich was five. It got hot in the car! Kathie finally had enough. She got out and stood outside. Rob and Rich stayed in the car trying to follow Dad's directive. Eventually, Mom, Mary, and Dad came out and got in the car. The first thing Mom said was, "Roll the windows down. It's too hot in here!" Rob and Rich just looked at each other, but Kathie had a big smile.

Mary, being the youngest, benefited by being able to get away with more than any of the rest did. Mary had a mind of her own and seemed to know what she wanted and how to get it, and that included praying. The three older siblings were glad to have a little sister and catered to her. Mary was the slowest to learn to talk, mainly because she didn't need to talk. If she wanted something, she'd just point and grunt and one of the others would get it for her. Mom would say, "Is this child ever going to talk?" She did and when she did, it was in full sentences—no baby talk.

Rich recalls complaining to Dad that Mary was spoiled. She was good at getting her way. To Rich's surprise Dad didn't disagree. Instead, he remarked, "You all helped spoil her." To which Rich had to agree.

Mary was also athletic and loved riding horses. She started like we all did with Bill, then her own horse, Jonny. Mary recalls getting into Bill's stall, standing in the oats box, climbing on his neck, and then sliding down to sit on his back. She would sit there while Rob and Rich did barn chores. Today she loves nothing better than riding. She owns a retired thoroughbred.

Mary recalls Dad trying to get the best of her. Mary, being five years younger than Rich, was a surprise baby. When Mary was nearly grown, Dad said to her, "Mary, you know you were a mistake?" Mary immediately responded, "The best one you ever made." Dad had no response. Mary had the last word that time.

Mary and Dad frequently traded cows. Dad came to the house with the news that one cow had twins. This meant that there would be two calves to sell, so Dad was pleased. Mary asked which cow had twins. When Dad told her, she said, "That's good. Those are my calves. Don't you remember, we traded?"

When she was little, Mary didn't like to wear shoes. She would take them off wherever she was and leave them. We would ask her where they were, but she couldn't remember, then we hunted them.

Because of the age gaps between the siblings–twelve years between Rob and Mary, five years between Rob and Kathie, two years between Kathie and Rich, and five years between Mary and Rich. Mary was the last to finish high school and leave the farm. This meant she got stuck doing both outside and inside work.

Once during haying, Dad hired two boys to help. Dad was baling and Mary was running the crew. These two were more interested in Mary than they were doing any work. Mary was working and they were getting paid. Mary fired them. She recalls Dad asking where they were and she replied, "I fired them!" She figured she was in trouble, so she lit into Dad before he had a chance to get on her. Dad accepted what she told him but hired no more help. If any of the rest of us had fired people, it wouldn't have gone as well as it did for Mary.

Mary became a speech and hearing teacher.

Mary- High School Graduation 1974

School Days

The Farm's physical location was in the Beach City School District, but the mailing address was Navarre, and the telephone number was Brewster. It didn't seem unusual to us. It's just the way things were. But it did confuse some folks.

The Sugar Creek Township school districts were Beach City which included Wilmot and Brewster which included Justus. The surrounding land which wasn't in the villages was included in the school districts. School buildings were in all four villages, all of which were incorporated except Justus. Later, the two school

THE MCDONALDS

districts were consolidated with Navarre, which is in Bethlehem Township, and became the Fairless School District.

Beach City and Brewster had high schools, Wilmot and Justus did not. All the Wilmot kids went to Beach City for high school, but the Justus kids had a choice. They could go to Brewster or Navarre. This was true even before consolidation. For example, our mother who lived in Harmon, had a choice when she was ready for high school. Her family chose Navarre. Her cousin, Bob Evans, also chose Navarre even though he lived in Justus.

We went to school on the big yellow limousine, the school bus. It came right down 303, stopped in front of the house, and picked us up. In the afternoon, just the reverse. When Rob first went to school, it was important that he was ready and could not miss the bus because we didn't have a car. If Rob missed the bus, Dad would have to take him or get him using the old truck. On his first day of school, he got on the bus with Mom waving bye. This wasn't unusual, everybody rode the bus. Mom or Dad had spoken to Flossie Lantzer, a neighbor girl, who was in high school and asked that she keep an eye on Rob, which she did. Kids didn't get taken to school or picked up unless they had something important, like a doctor's appointment.

The Beach City campus covered an entire city block. It was south and west of the center of town. There were three buildings. All built at various times. The oldest was a two-story structure with four rooms, two on each floor and with a center staircase. There were five or six grades in the building, so some classes had to be split up. The first grade (there was no kindergarten, in fact none of us went to kindergarten) was all in one room. The second grade was split, part in the first-grade room and part with the third graders. The first through third were on the first floor and the fourth through the fifth or six were on the second floor. The bathrooms were in the basement. Girls on one side and boys on the other. The heating system was also in the basement along with the plumbing.

After getting through the fifth or sixth grades, you moved to the middle building. Then after the eighth grade, you went to the high school building. At first there was no cafeteria so most carried their

ROBERT ALAN MCDONALD, KATHIE EILEEN MCDONALD COURTNEY, RICHARD EDWIN MCDONALD, MARY JO MCDONALD HELFRICH

lunch. We certainly did. But kids that lived in town could go home for lunch. It was a big deal when they put a cafeteria in the high school.

School was a straightforward progression until a couple years after consolidation. The School Board decided that revising the bus routes would improve efficiency. And subsequently, other changes were made. We were caught in the changes. Mom and Dad were told that the Beach City bus would no longer go past the house on 303, but if they wanted Rob, Kathie, and Rich to continue at Beach City, they could; but they had to walk up the hill and catch the bus where 303 intersected with Justus Avenue, about a quarter mile away. The alternative was to catch the Brewster bus, which was routed right past the house, but it would take us to Brewster. Mom and Dad reasoned that the biggest impact would be on Rob since he was in high school. Kathie and Rich were still in grade school. We discussed it and decided we would go to Brewster. Rob liked the idea because Brewster had a better football team, or at least he thought they did, and they played 11-man football.

Brewster's school buildings were split between the north side and south side. The north side was a small building and was only early grades. All the rest was in the south side located two blocks off Wabash Avenue, Route 93. Wilmot and Justus each had one building. Navarre's buildings were consolidated right on US Route 21 next to Nichols Bakery.

It took years before the voters approved a bond issue to build a new high school building. Before Rob's senior year, the School Board decided to consolidate the high schools even though they didn't have a building for it. They put the entire high school in the Navarre building. Eventually voters approved a bond issue, and a new school was built in Justus.

Changes continued and affected each of us. Rob went to Beach City for grades one through nine, then Brewster for grades ten and eleven, and finally Navarre for the twelfth grade. Kathie went to Beach City for the first through fourth grade. Then she went to

THE MCDONALDS

Brewster for the fifth and sixth grades, then to Justus for the seventh, then to Brewster for the eighth and ninth, and finally to Navarre for the tenth through twelfth. Rich also had multiple changes. His first grade was in Beach City, then Brewster for the second through sixth grade, then Justus for the seventh, then back to Brewster for grades eight and nine, and finally into the new high school building in Justus for his last three years. Mary had the most straight forward schedule. She went to Brewster for the first through eight and then to the new high school in Justus for nine through twelve. Here's a chart that may help:

Grades	Rob	Kathie	Rich	Mary
1	**Beach City**	**Beach City**	**Beach City**	**Brewster**
2	**Beach City**	**Beach City**	**Brewster**	**Brewster**
3	**Beach City**	**Beach City**	**Brewster**	**Brewster**
4	**Beach City**	**Beach City**	**Brewster**	**Brewster**
5	**Beach City**	**Brewster**	**Brewster**	**Brewster**
6	**Beach City**	**Brewster**	**Brewster**	**Brewster**
7	**Beach City**	Justus	Justus	**Brewster**
8	**Beach City**	**Brewster**	**Brewster**	**Brewster**
9	**Beach City**	**Brewster**	**Brewster**	Justus
10	**Brewster**	**Navarre**	Justus	Justus
11	**Brewster**	**Navarre**	Justus	Justus
12	**Navarre**	**Navarre**	Justus	Justus

During our school years and after, land was purchased, and new buildings were constructed. This began with the high school in Justus. Thus, the older school buildings and land were no longer needed. At first, property no longer in use was sold, but now old buildings are torn down. Only the Wilmot and North Side Brewster buildings remain, having been sold before the law requiring tear down was changed. All the rest, Beach City, Brewster south side, and the Navarre are all gone.

Paying for College

Although each of us had a savings account, it wasn't adequate to defray college costs. To compensate, we went to work off the farm. Three of us went to Ohio University in Athens, Ohio. Rob had gone there as a delegate to Buckeye Boy's State, sponsored by the American Legion. Rob picked the school due to familiarity and the fact it was cheaper being a state school than a private school. Rich and Mary had other reasons for going there but it became an almost unanimous choice.

Robert worked at the Brewster Dairy for nine months and then two summers. After that, he got a job during summers at Union Drawn Division of Republic Steel thanks to the efforts of Uncle Ed Bartko, Aunt Dudy's husband. Being a steel worker paid better than being a cheese maker.

Richard worked at Superior Meats in Massillon. He could make enough working in the summer and at Christmas time to pay for a full year of school with a little left over.

Kathie went to nursing school. It was a three-year program with no summers off. She was able to "work for pay" on weekends which helped defray the costs.

Mary got a job at the Navarre Deposit Bank, working summers. Our Uncle, Don Jones, worked there. When he retired, Uncle Don was President of the Bank.

THE MCDONALDS

Chapter Seven – Friends and Neighbors

Living on a farm, you don't have neighbors and friends 50 to 100 feet away. Mostly they are hundreds of yards or even miles away. But that doesn't make them less important, often just the opposite – more important. Farmers are always helping each other. An important lesson that we learned was that while you may not always agree with your neighbor, you always helped them when they needed help. They would do the same for you.

Our nearer neighbors were Charlie and Anna Grossklaus, Arden and Lois Grossklaus, Johnny and Dorothy Wilson, Ed Miller - who inherited his farm from his sister Carrie, who was Sterling McWhinney's widow – Walt and Minnie Lantzer, Harry and Helen Pepper, Howard and Mardel Harold, the Paul Latzenhiezer Family and Arch Croy. Sterling McWhinney was John McWhinney Jr.'s son and had sold The Farm to Mom and Dad after inheriting it from his father. Mary recalls that Dad always referred to people using both their given and family names, never by just a single name. With Dad, you always knew exactly who he was speaking about.

Ed Miller would help with a lot of things, including putting up hay. Since he didn't have a TV, he would come into the house most evenings and watch westerns with us after we got done milking.

Ed was around so much, he was part of the family. Kathie recalls pretending to be asleep so Ed would carry her to the house. If he knew better, he didn't let on.

Ed pulled the "salt on the bunny's tail" trick on Kathie. The same trick Grandpa Dan pulled on Rich. Kathie says she got the salt on the bunny's tail, but when she reached for it, it hopped away.

We found out that Ed was terrified of and wouldn't touch a toad. He thought toads gave you warts. Armed with this information, Kathie and Richard would find a toad and chase Ed with it. For an older person, he could move quickly when confronted with a toad.

Ed was raised and lived all his life – except for the time he served in the Army during WW I – on a farm across Justus Avenue. He had worked on The Farm for the previous owners. That work included

ROBERT ALAN MCDONALD, KATHIE EILEEN MCDONALD COURTNEY, RICHARD EDWIN MCDONALD, MARY JO MCDONALD HELFRICH

tiling the fields. Ed's memory was the only map of the tiling system Dad had. If we had a drainage problem, Ed was consulted.

Ed had other knowledge as well and he and Dad had an informal work sharing system. He often helped with haying, butchering, and with bee keeping. He wasn't paid for the work he did, but Dad, and sometimes one of us kids, would do work for Ed. Some of the butchering tools were probably Ed's, but he left them in the butcher house. When he passed, the tools stayed with us.

His knowledge of beekeeping was impressive. Arden Grossklaus, Ed's nephew, was also a beekeeper. He would also help or supply equipment such as a smoker. If Dad had questions about the bees, Ed was consulted. He also helped during honey harvest and with cleaning the hives.

Rob recalls Ed petting the bees. One or more bees would land on Ed's arm or hand where his skin was exposed. Ed would calmly reach with the other hand, using one finger, gently stroke the bee that had landed. The bees seemed to like being petted and never stung him.

The farm Ed owned was south of ours with part of it bordering Justus Avenue across from our southeastern field which also bordered Justus Avenue. In addition to his sister Carrie, Ed had two brothers, Mart and Happy. Mart was short for Martin, but we're not sure what Happy's given name was. Neither Ed nor any of his siblings had children. Because Ed lived the longest, he inherited all their possessions which included the farm he lived on of 80 acres, and investments which were rumored to include a fair amount of AT&T stock. His brother Mart's gun collection, we believe, went to Arden. Happy's possessions and Sterling and Carrie's also went to Ed.

When Ed got too old to live alone and manage the farm, it was sold. Chuck Gonner bought it. By this time, Ed's nephew, Arden Grossklaus, had died leaving his widow, Lois, alone. Ed moved in with her where he remained until his passing. That house was directly across Justus Avenue from our northeast most field. Years later, when Lois got too old to live alone, Rich bought it.

Walt and Minnie Lantzer lived on the farm directly across Justus Avenue. They didn't own it. They were sharecroppers. George Grossklaus' heirs owned the farm. The Lantzers lived and worked the farm for part of the profits. They were good tenants, treating the property as their own.

The farmhouse was quite large, three stories. It was said that the top floor was a ballroom where dances had been held in times past. Whether that was true or not we didn't know for sure. Rob recalls eating in Minnie's kitchen and being on the first floor but doesn't recall ever being on the upper floors.

Dad and Walt helped each other sometimes by sharing equipment. Walt had an Allis Chalmers round baler that we used to bail our hay and straw. The Allis Chalmers round baler produced a bale about the same size as the square balers of that time. Hay bales weighed about 40 pounds, similar to the square bales. Round bales were more difficult to work with when mowing as they were round and thus uneven making them hard to stack and walk on and were harder to put in the mangers when feeding. However, round bales worked very well when bedding. In turn, Dad combined for Walt. No money changed hands. It worked out well for both.

Walt and Minnie were older than our parents. Most of their children were grown, left the farm, and had lives of their own. One of the married children had a son, Lee, who was close to Rob's age. Occasionally, Rob and Lee played together. The Lantzer's son, Bud, also lived at home. He wasn't married. For a time, he ran an auto repair business out of the garage at the S curve about a half mile south on Justus Avenue. Later, he bought an over the road tractor trailer and began a career as an independent trucker.

When Walt and Minnie decided to retire, they needed additional income. They bought a few acres of land that bordered our farm southeast on Justus Avenue and built a house large enough for them and Bud.

They also built a chicken coop and raised laying hens. The hens produced a bounty of eggs which they sold or which Minnie, after separating the egg yolks from the whites, turned into egg noodles, which she also sold. This left Minnie with a large quantity of egg whites that she had no use for. Minnie put these egg whites in quart jars which she regularly gave to Mom. Mom turned these egg whites into angel food cakes. She made so many angel food cakes we got tired of them. If there was a special occasion that required a dessert, Mom was sure to provide at least one angel food cake.

We liked to top the angel food cake with strawberries, either frozen or fresh. Rich, to vex Mom, would smash his cake flat before spooning on the strawberries. Mom was justifiably proud of her cakes, especially getting them to rise properly. Rich says he didn't especially like flat cake, but it annoyed Mom, so he kept doing it.

After the Lantzers retired, the farm was sold and Paul Latzenhiezer bought it.

Barney

Arch Croy lived east on Lawndell Road about a half mile away. Arch worked for the Goodrich Mining Company that operated coal strip mines on the farm that Arch owned and in other places not far away. The strip mine on Arch's farm ceased operation and they had reforested it with locust trees. The spoils hadn't been returned to the previous land contours resulting in pits, so the 'high walls' remained. We used to coon hunt on Arch's property. Rob recalls being afraid of going over one of the 'high walls' in the dark. Fortunately, that never happened.

Arch was older than Dad, had no teeth, and was nearly deaf. His job involved heavy equipment, which robbed him of his hearing. For a time, Dad used the barn on Arch's farm. Arch wasn't using it, and he didn't charge Dad rent. A good deal. Dad kept sows in Arch's barn. Frequently these sows had to be moved back and forth from our place to Arch's. Arch had a Chevy pickup that we used to move the sows. The pickup had a bed that fit between the wheel wells and a stake body suitable for hauling farm animals.

THE MCDONALDS

Dad, Rob, and Rich went over to Arch's and loaded a sow into Arch's pickup. Arch drove and Dad got in the cab with Arch. Rich—being small—got into the cab between Arch and Dad. That left Rob with no place to sit, so he got into the truck bed with the sow. Arch cranked up the truck. Since he couldn't hear the engine, he always revved it high enough to be sure it got moving without stalling when he popped the clutch. He did exactly that this time as well.

Off we went, gaining speed quickly. Arch's driveway was rough with bumps and hollows. Arch hit one of those hard, and it launched both Rob and the sow into the air. Rob says it felt like we were up about three feet. Rob remembers grabbing the stock racks to keep from flying completely out of the truck. The sow couldn't do that since she didn't have hands. Rob recalls thinking, *What if the hog breaks a leg when she comes down?*

What goes up must come down; Rob and the sow did. It was a hard landing. The sow decided she'd had enough of that, so she backed up into a corner of the stock rack and sat down, with her front feet jamming her posterior into the corner. She rode that way all the rest of the trip. She required no urging when it was time to get out. When we got to the farm, Rob looked at Arch and said, "Who are you, Barney Oldfield?" (Barney Oldfield was an old-time auto racer that Rob had only heard about.) From then on, Arch was known as Barney. Arch got a big cackle out of it, grinning that toothless grin of his.

The topic of baseball often came up because of our interest in the sport. Barney let us know that he, too, played baseball. He told Dad and Rich about the time he tried to steal home. He got a good jump on the pitcher, and had it stolen, but the batter didn't know about it, swung at the pitch, and missed, but hit Barney right square on his nose. Barney said that being hit that way stopped him in his tracks, about four inches short of home plate. He never did touch the plate and ended up with his nose flattened the way we see it. Rich recalls Dad getting a hearty laugh out of that story.

Barney used to chain smoke Camel cigarettes—humps, as we called them—but he didn't inhale. It remains a mystery why he bothered to light them; the smoke only got into his mouth.

ROBERT ALAN MCDONALD, KATHIE EILEEN MCDONALD COURTNEY, RICHARD EDWIN MCDONALD, MARY JO MCDONALD HELFRICH

Maple Syrup

Not long after moving to The Farm, Dad and Mom met and became friends with Mr. and Mrs. Jeffers who owned property on the west side of Federal Route 62 and State Route 93 where the two roads combined across from the end of Lawndell Road. The Jeffers owned a farm which included a swampy area right across the roads, the woods beyond, and several tillable acres along the roads with space for the house and barn.

Mr. Jeffers always had a pair of glasses sitting well down on his nose. Most likely he only needed them to read, but he wore them faithfully. Rob can't recall Mr. and Mrs. Jeffers' given names, but Dad always called him Jeff or Jeff Jeffers when referring to him. Rob believes this was in deference to his last name rather than being his first.

Mr. and Mrs. Jeffers were older than Mom and Dad. They had one son who was an airline pilot. Quite an impressive job in those days. Highly likely he learned to fly in the Air Force as most pilots in those days started that way. In any case, the son did not live nearby. Rob really liked going to visit the Jeffers because Mrs. Jeffers always had cookies for him.

Mr. Jeffers had an off-the-farm job. He could have been an engineer for one of the companies in Massillon or Canton as he was a well-educated person and knew his way around machinery and construction.

The Jeffers' woods were full of maple trees. Not just any type of maples, of which there are hundreds, but the variety that produces sap used for maple syrup in the spring. Dad and Jeff decided that they would tap the maple trees and make maple syrup. Jeff would supply the sap. He and Dad would tap the trees. And the syrup boiling would take place in the Butcher house since we had a furnace and copper kettle in there.

Tapping maple trees requires equipment. Taps (short lengths of small diameter pipe which are placed in the tree after drilling an appropriate hole), small buckets with bails that can be placed on the taps to catch the sap, and metal cans with lids to transport the sap from the woods to the butcher house. The metal cans were acquired from Nickels Bakery in Navarre. These cans were supplied to the bakery as containers for shortening and were discarded when empty. The trees were tapped with a brace and bit. Maple syrup is made in the early spring when there are warm days and cold nights. The warm days cause the trees to begin pulling moisture up the trees into the branches. With the moisture, the tree sends sugar from the roots.

Rob remembers going through the woods with Dad to gather sap. The hay wagon drawn by Dan and Bird was used. We would move through the woods emptying the sap into the cans as we went. After gathering, we would go back home and store the cans in the butcher house. This process went on for days until enough sap had been gathered to begin boiling.

The sap was emptied into the copper kettle which was heated over the furnace boiling the sap. Rob remembers looking in the butcher house while the syrup was boiling and not being able to see across the room because of the steam coming off the kettle. It takes about 10 gallons of sap to make 1 gallon of syrup. Boiling syrup gave off a very pleasant aroma.

Things were going well until one day while the sap was being boiled. Dad put Junior Kepler in charge of the fire. To augment the wood, Dad had old tires that he decided to use to increase the heat output. Dad told Junior to use the tires but may not have given specific instructions. Or Junior may not have understood the instructions. Junior wasn't the brightest bulb on the string. By having a good wood fire and then adding tires, Junior got the fire so hot that the 1/2-inch steel plate on the top of the furnace was cherry red in places. He nearly burned the butcher house down. Fortunately, Dad came back, saw what was happening and had to pour water on the fire. Junior knew he had a problem but justified it by repeating over and over, "He told me to do it! He told me to do it!" Junior never fired again.

The intense heat permanently damaged the front of the furnace. It loosened the bricks surrounding the door. The only way to repair it would have been to tear down the furnace either completely or partially and rebuild it using new mortar. That was never done.

Junior Kepler was from Harmon. He and his mom and dad lived next door to our Aunt Eleanor and Uncle Pink. As noted before, Junior was a bit slow. He did have jobs, one being on the section gang with the Wheeling and Lake Erie Railroad. Section gangs are railroad employees who repair or sometimes build the railroad tracks. Each gang has a foreman and several workmen. The story goes that one day the gang was working near a farm with an electric fence. The gang members got Junior to urinate on the fence which resulted in a shock to his manhood. Junior said when describing the incident, "It damn near knocked the thing off!"

Building the Swimming Hole

Jeff and Dad did another project together. Jeff decided to build a sand bottom swimming pool where the swamp was. He got equipment and cleaned out the swamp, drilled a well to supply clean water and began building a bath house on the hill overlooking the pool. Jeff made Dad a deal: if Dad would help build the bathhouse, our family could have use of the facilities at no charge. Dad agreed and helped build the bathhouse. Jeff got the facility up and running, but decided to sell it, which he did to Jack Baylor. The facility is now Baylor's Beach with a sand bottom pool and camping where the woods used to be.

Jeff's selling out ended not only our free swimming but ended maple syrup making, too. Mr. and Mrs. Jeffers moved to Strasburg, and we didn't see them a whole lot after they moved. In all fairness, they were older and were reaching retirement age. Selling the beach helped a great deal.

THE MCDONALDS

Bob Kuehner

Robert Kuehner Sr. was one of Dad's Army buddies. He and Dad remained close after the war. As mentioned elsewhere, Bob and his family were frequent visitors, often on weekends. Bob contributed to many farm projects so having him visit and feeding him, his wife Ann, and son Bobby - Robert Jr. - was an even trade. Plus, Rob, Bobby, and Rich found plenty of things to do when they were together.

Bob was a skilled sheet metal fabricator. He worked in a shop in Canton and seemed to be well respected in the trade and had the run of the shop with full use of the company tools. One of the projects Bob worked on was for one of the meat packing companies, either Superior Meats in Massillon or Sugardale in Canton. The project was to design and manufacture a device that would capture animal blood on the killing floor without air encountering it when the animals were killed and bled out. The project wasn't successful, but Bob was the tradesman selected to run the project. Considering that engineering firms could have been used or that other craftsmen could have been chosen, Bob seemed to have a stellar reputation for sheet metal design and layout.

Around The Farm, he designed and built the gravity bed for the grain hauler installed on the '41 Mercury, the hopper installed in the floor of the east haymow used to store chop, designed and built the hopper for the end of the elevator so it could be used to get the small grain into the wheat and oat granaries, and he designed and built the outdoor bar-b-que we used for many years. Everything he designed and built worked well. Gravity beds are used on wagons so that grain and corn can be unloaded by opening a tailgate allowing the grain to run downhill by force of gravity; essentially, a floor with a slanted bottom.

When laying out the gravity bed, Rob recalls going with Dad to Bob's workplace and watching Bob cut the sheet metal to the specified size and then use the power brake to install stiffening bends in the metal. The parts were brought to the Farm where the finished product was assembled and installed. Bob was a skilled

ROBERT ALAN MCDONALD, KATHIE EILEEN MCDONALD COURTNEY, RICHARD EDWIN MCDONALD, MARY JO MCDONALD HELFRICH

welder. The fit and finish of that gravity bed was as good as any built anywhere.

Bob liked hunting, and he ate what he harvested. He hunted rabbits and pheasants in the fall and winter. One year, pheasant was particularly plentiful. Bob and his wife hosted a dinner party for us and his family at his home in Canton. Bob's home was one of the most frequently visited by our family. This was something of a treat for Mom as she didn't have to do the cooking, although she did help.

Bob liked turtle soup, which is made of the meat from snapping turtles. In the spring, snapping turtles leave the streams and ponds to lay eggs in the soil. Dad would often find a turtle on the road or in a hay field when they were making their journey. Dad would catch them by the tail and carry them to the house where he would put them in an open top barrel for safekeeping before turning them into meat. Carrying a large—and these turtles were large weighing more than 15 pounds—turtle by the tail held far enough away from one's body that it couldn't bite, wasn't easy. Sometimes even Dad had to rest it on the ground before getting it to the barrel.

To butcher the turtle, its head needed to be removed. Dad or Bob would entice the turtle with a broom stick so that it would snap. When it did, the turtle's neck was exposed, and it would be severed with a hatchet. After that, it was a matter of cracking the shell open and removing the meat. Mom usually cooked the meat and made the soup. Turtle soup is like beef vegetable soup.

Bob's eating wild game began when he was a youngster. He would tell us that when growing up he would be out of the house doing things around Canton. He would take a potato from home and some matches, snare a bird (a robin was preferred because it had a large breast), build a fire, cook the potato, and bird meat for his meal. Mom commented he must have been extremely poor because there couldn't be much meat on a robin.

One day we were talking about nicknames. Bob made the mistake of telling us that when growing up he was called Buzz. From then on, we called him Buzz. Finally, the joke got old, and we had to quit.

Charley Barkheimer was a friend of Bob's and Charley became a friend of Dad's. Charley was also in the sheet metal trade and may have worked at the same place that Bob did. Bob and Charley looked a little bit like Mutt and Jeff. Bob was about five-feet seven-inches tall, and Charley was six-feet three or four. Charley was always ribbing Bob about being short, especially when height was needed to perform a task that was above Bob's reach.

Our furnace needed to be replaced. Dad bought a Boomer furnace made in Massillon. Bob and Charley were installing it. They had the plenum elevated and were hooking up the heat runs before putting the burner under it. Bob walked right under the plenum and began installation. Charley was having a heck of a time because his height required him to nearly bend double. Bob looked at Charley and told him, "See, there are advantages to being short!"

Drummers

In the 1940's and '50's, salespeople who knocked on doors were commonplace. Even in the country, where houses were further apart, it wasn't unusual. In addition to the salespeople, there were in-home delivery services such as the Nickles Bread man with baked goods, the milkman who had milk, butter, eggs, and juice, and others such as Fuller Brush and McNess Products. For a while, Mom got bread from the Bread man, but since we had cows and chickens, the milkman gave up quickly.

And of course, there were the salespeople who sold products that didn't require frequent replacement. Things like vacuum cleaners, lightning rods, books, and even fire extinguishers. Those we didn't buy from stopped coming by after being turned down a few times. But Mom and Dad did buy a fire extinguisher that was mounted on the cupboard near the sink. It was an interesting contraption with a glass container filled with a fire suppression chemical, equipped with a spring-loaded hammer device that was supposed to break the glass if the temperature got too high. We never had a fire, so we

ROBERT ALAN MCDONALD, KATHIE EILEEN MCDONALD COURTNEY, RICHARD EDWIN MCDONALD, MARY JO MCDONALD HELFRICH

really don't know if it worked. It was eventually dismounted and thrown away, but it was a feature in the kitchen for years.

Initially the driveway only went in one direction. After turning off the road, the driveway went straight north to the barn. To go to the house, after about 30 yards, it made a left turn to the west. To leave meant turning around or backing up. Later, Dad finally agreed to allow the driveway to make a left turn past the house to go back to the road, but it took years for Dad to make that concession. The reason Dad wouldn't agree was that right in front of the bay window was a spot that got soft when it rained. Rob remembers walking through it after the rain, getting stuck, and having to walk out of his boots to get out of there. He was young, less than five, and he went into the house with muddy feet, which Mom didn't like, and he had to have Mom or Dad retrieve his boots for him.

There was no gravel in that area, but that didn't stop people from cutting past the house to get to the road. Even Grandma and Grandpa Jones did it, and Dad compounded the problem by driving the tractor through there, and we did it, too. Monkey see monkey do. So, even though it wasn't graveled, there were tracks.

It was a constant battle for Dad to keep people from using it as a turnaround. We don't know if Dad didn't like the idea or look of a driveway right in front of the house or if he didn't want to spend money on limestone to make a roadbed.

One day, the Fuller Brush man stopped by to peddle his wares and drove right into the soft spot, pulled through (making a mess as he did so), and stopped. Instead of fixing the mess or just leaving, he went right on and knocked on the door. Mom may not have seen the damage and let him in to see his wares. As Rich recalls, he was something of a pretty boy which didn't endear him to Dad. And Dad happened by and saw the mess he made of the yard. Dad marched into the house and confronted the Fuller Brush man. After a few choice words from Dad, he packed up his goods and left. He wasn't seen around our place again.

THE MCDONALDS

The McNess man, whose name was John McCann, was a completely different story. Dad liked him and looked forward to his visits. Dad would always ask, "Have you got any samples?" To John's credit, he came up with something. He began keeping Chiclets gum in 2-piece packets and giving them to us kids which put him in Dad's good graces. Rich thought Dad appreciated the gesture.

Mom and Dad knew Mr. McCann's story. While they never told us all of it, over time we pieced together what we could. We think Mr. McCann lived in Massillon and at one time may have been an abuser of alcohol, but he got himself straightened out. He went to work for the McNess company, built up a nice route, and made his living off it.

The McNess man had a station wagon, which he kept well stocked. Usually, he could go to his car and fill Mom's order on the spot. Mom's favorite McNess products were spices especially pepper, soft drink flavorings of Nectar, lemon pie filling (used to make Mom's lemon meringue pie), and salve which we used on the cows' udders. The salve was also good on our hands. Dad used it and we think Mom did as well. Nectar came in multiple flavors: orange, grape, lemon-lime, root beer, and others. Our favorite was orange. At mealtime, Mom would mix up a half-gallon pitcher of orange drink using her own sugar. It would be gone before the meal was over.

Having the McNess man come by was a benefit to Mom. She didn't have to go to town to buy the products she got from him, and his prices were reasonable. We wouldn't have had sweet drinks at mealtime if we weren't on his route.

Local Stores

Eight miles from the farm was the town of Strasburg which boasted Garver Brothers Department Store and Shafer Bakery, two of our favorites. It seemed that visits to these stores were special or only happened before special occasions like going back to school or

ROBERT ALAN MCDONALD, KATHIE EILEEN MCDONALD COURTNEY, RICHARD EDWIN MCDONALD, MARY JO MCDONALD HELFRICH

before Christmas. Mom seemed to like going to Navarre or Massillon to shop, but Dad liked Garver Bros. and so did us kids.

Garver's was three floors with a large center stairway. Various goods were at each level. Groceries were on the first floor. The upper floors had clothing (men's, women's, and children's), housewares, and furniture. Prices were reasonable and the quality was good. At Garver's is where Dad bought the good dishes Mom wanted and got for Christmas.

Shafer's Bakery was a small shop right on Route 21 that ran through the center of town. We all clamored to stop, and we usually got our way. Dad certainly didn't object. Mom would always buy maple frosted rolls. We couldn't wait to get into them. No matter how many dozen Mom bought, getting any home required stern warning that we'd eaten enough. Sometimes we would wait while the rolls came out of the oven. Those were the best.

The farm was located less than a mile from Justus and about two miles from Harmon, both unincorporated villages. Neither was more than a wide spot in the road. But both claimed stores. Justus had Dye's Store on Anglemont, stuck between the railroad tracks, and Baughman's Store on Justus Avenue. Harmon had Mrs. Kepler's right on Route 62 in the center of the village. Of the two villages, our Grandmother Nellie commented, "Justus was the ugliest town in the state!" It did not concern Grandmother that Grandpa Dan had grown up there, a mile from their home.

Of the three stores, only the Baughman building remains. It was the largest, best supplied, and did the most business. At one point, it boasted a branch U.S. Post Office. Rob recalls going into it with Mom a few times to buy something she needed that didn't warrant a trip into Navarre where the big store was. It was disappointing when the store closed as it was a convenient place to get a piece of candy.

Grandma and Grandpa Jones' house in Harmon was right on US Route 62. Across the road and 100 yards east was Mrs. Kepler's store, a small one room building facing the road.

THE MCDONALDS

Rob recalls staying overnight at Grandma's when he was four or five. Grandma gave him money, a nickel, and allowed him to cross the road to go to Mrs. Kep's store. Grandma gave Rob strict instructions; he was allowed to go by himself IF he looked both ways before going across the road, crossing only if there were no cars in sight either way, going straight to the store, buy what he wanted – candy – and coming right back to Grandma's crossing the road only after looking both ways.

Being allowed to cross the road and make that journey alone was significant and Rob made sure he followed Grandma's instructions to the letter. The first time he was allowed to do this, Grandma accompanied him to the road but didn't cross it. After the first time, he was allowed to go completely alone. Although Grandma observed everything by looking out the window. Rob never saw her or knew he was being observed.

Mary recalls Mrs. Kep's store as well. She got to go there with her cousins, Sue, Sara, and Emily when staying with Aunt Eleanor. Mrs. Kep's store was right next door. All the girls had to do was cross the driveway.

ROBERT ALAN MCDONALD, KATHIE EILEEN MCDONALD COURTNEY, RICHARD EDWIN MCDONALD, MARY JO MCDONALD HELFRICH

THE MCDONALDS

Chapter Eight - Campers

Mo and Shorty Henley, a couple of older gentlemen, approached Dad, seeking permission to camp. The two men were brothers and were retired. They lived with their families in East Greenville, Ohio. Mo was the older of the two and was the tallest. Shorty's nickname amply defined him. Neither was married, but they both had children. The purpose of the camp was to get out in the country during the summer, enjoying the outdoor life, especially fishing in Sugar Creek, and drinking beer in the evenings. Shorty was more the beer hound, but they both could hold their own.

Dad immediately liked the two and agreed to allow them to set up camp. Dad charged them nothing. On the appointed day, the men arrived at the selected camp site on a bluff on the right side of Lawndell Road when heading west. The site overlooked the creek and was shaded by an enormous red oak tree.

When they arrived, they got right to work setting up camp. That first year, they had a large wall tent which served as sleeping quarters and living quarters during inclement weather. They also had a smaller tent to store supplies and coolers stocked with ice to keep perishables and beer cold. Of course, there was a campfire and a privy. Family members visited regularly and brought supplies.

The first year, they stayed about a month. Because they had a wonderful time, they approached Dad about doing it again the next year. Dad readily agreed.

Each year thereafter, Mo and Shorty camped. The time spent camping got longer and the gear more elaborate. Pretty soon, they purchased a travel trailer. Still later, they purchased a mobile home. The hygiene facilities were improved. Tents remained for storage instead of living accommodations. The length of time spent extended until they would arrive in the early spring, and they wouldn't leave until about Thanksgiving. Some gear, the mobile home for example, remained all year.

They would have family gatherings at the camp and had a wonderful time enjoying their retirement. They would come to the

ROBERT ALAN MCDONALD, KATHIE EILEEN MCDONALD COURTNEY, RICHARD EDWIN MCDONALD, MARY JO MCDONALD HELFRICH

farm and buy eggs from Mom, or we would take the eggs to them when taking the cows down the road to pasture. What Dad appreciated the most was their monitoring the part of the farm we couldn't see from the house. They would check the gates and close them if some careless person left them open. It would be hard to tell how often they prevented the cows from getting out on the road. Their presence may have kept other people from doing damage. It was a most satisfactory arrangement for both.

Shorty and Mo were good about sharing a beer or two with Dad and occasionally he would take a couple beers down to share with them. If we were along with him, he might share a sip or two with us. Mom didn't approve, but we would do it anyway. Rich recalls having his first beer at the camp.

Shorty was inclined to imbibe more than Mo, occasionally more than that was good for him. One of those occasions nearly got Shorty in serious trouble. Behind the camp was a steep bank dropping 30 feet to the creek. Shorty went over the bank one dark night, but somehow managed to get stopped before landing in the creek. Getting back up the bank took some doing. Mo recalled Shorty being nearly sober when he got back to camp.

Dad was having trouble with his knee. He stopped by the camp one morning as he often did and mentioned the knee problem to Mo and Shorty. One or the other of them immediately handed Dad a product called "Canned Heat." It was a liquid swabbed on the affected area. Dad put a liberal dose on his knee, but it didn't seem to do anything. With a little urging, Dad put on some more, and then some more after that. He wasn't impressed. Dad began walking up the road toward the house. The further he walked, the more the "Canned Heat" activated. By the time he got to the house, Dad needed ice! He couldn't wash it off. He had trouble getting a day's work done that day.

When passing by the camp, Rich discovered a Mail Pouch chewing tobacco pouch that wasn't quite empty. Mo must have discarded it before it was completely empty. Rich, being curious, decided to try it. Only a couple pieces of tobacco leaf remained. He carefully gathered the dregs and stuffed them in his cheek as he'd seen adults do. Rich describes the sensation as burning and tasting awful; the worst he'd ever experienced. He couldn't spit it out quick enough, but that didn't stop the burn, and the taste remained. Rich hurried to the house, went into the bathroom, and tried washing his mouth out using the running water in the sink. Mom heard the sink running and asked, "What's going on?" Rich's response was a typical boy's response, "Nothing, just washing up."

Rob recalls having a similar experience, only that time it was Ed Miller's discarded pouch of Cutty Pipe, allegedly tobacco that was good for smoking or eating, according to Ed. Rob also reports the taste being awful and wondering how anyone could stand the stuff. Both boys found this experience sufficient. Neither was ever tempted to chew after that.

After years, the inevitable happened. Mo and Shorty took one of their rambles southwest on the creek to a fishing hole they knew about. They were well off the farm and were both fishing. Shorty noticed Mo lying down and spoke to him. Mo didn't respond. Shorty went to investigate and discovered Mo had passed peacefully with a small smile on his face.

Shorty walked two miles to the house so that Mom could call emergency services. Rich recalls how distressed Shorty was. Dad went with Shorty to await the arrival of emergency services and family.

Shorty remained at camp for the rest of that season and attempted to continue camping the next year, but it just wasn't the same and, after a brief time, gave up. Shorty lived with his family until he, too, passed.

ROBERT ALAN MCDONALD, KATHIE EILEEN MCDONALD COURTNEY, RICHARD EDWIN MCDONALD, MARY JO MCDONALD HELFRICH

Chapter Nine – Farming Over the Years

Due primarily to technology, farming changed over the years. It went from human and animal labor intensive to mechanical and capital intensive. The equipment used became much bigger - requiring more power – and more complexity – requiring newer skills. Farmland increased in price and farming became specialized. These changes impacted us, but because Dad was reluctant to embrace change until the technology was proven and less costly, we often lagged behind. Eventually we got there.

A used Farmall F-20 was our first tractor. This model was manufactured from 1932 to 1939. These tractors weren't powerful, 19.6 horsepower at the drawbar, and were slow. Plowing was done with a trailing plow with one or two 14-inch plowshares. But it was faster than plowing with a team of horses that could only pull a single plowshare and who had to be rested frequently.

The Straw Stack

The straw stack occupied the center of the barnyard. Built around two posts set on end spaced 12 feet apart. The straw stack held all the animal winter bedding. It was about 30 feet in diameter, and 20 feet high. The barnyard was large, about 90 feet long–equal to the length of the barn–and 50-feet wide. Its size was because the farm was large, thus the barn was large and there were a sizable number of animals that used the barn yard, especially in the winter. The farm produced a quantity of small grain: primarily wheat and oats and later barley, and occasionally speltz or buckwheat.

Small grain was thrashed to separate the grain from the straw. The straw had to go somewhere once the grain was removed. Straw was valuable. It was used as animal bedding, after which it was returned to the fields in the manure enriching and providing structure to the soil.

Thrashing was a major chore when we first moved to the farm. Small grain is planted in rows by a machine called a grain-drill which had bins for the seed, fertilizer, and a smaller bin for grass seed. We planted timothy with the fall seeded crops—wheat and barley. Timothy wasn't seeded with oats planted in the spring because the oats ground one year became wheat ground the next.

We followed a four-year crop rotation: hay in year one, followed by corn in year two, oats in year three: and wheat or barley in year four. Corn needed the highest soil fertility. By planting corn after the hay crop the land 'rested' in that it wasn't plowed the year it produced hay, and the clover and especially the alfalfa affixed nitrogen in the soil that the corn needed. Oats followed the corn because it is a grass plant and isn't a heavy feeder, only limited fertilization was needed to produce a good crop. Wheat and barley are similar; both are grass plants. By having hay follow wheat the ground got a needed rest, and fertility was restored by nitrogen fixing and manure would be spread on the hay ground before spring plowing which added fertility and soil structure which helped water retention.

A side note on the seeding of the hay crop: in addition to timothy seeded in the fall while planting wheat or barley, hay consisted of clover and alfalfa, seeded separately. The small grain served as a cover crop to both the timothy and the clover and alfalfa. Planting clover and alfalfa was done on foot, walking the fields in the late winter or early spring while using one of two types of broadcast seeders: a fiddle or crank type.

At first, we had the fiddle type which had a bow that a person caused to move by sawing back and forth like the action of a bow when playing a fiddle. Dad used this type. Later, he got the other type which used a crank to drive the seeding mechanism. Seeding was done when the ground was beginning to thaw. In the early morning, fine cracks appeared in the surface of the soil, allowing the small seeds to penetrate, ensuring better germination. At first, Dad did the seeding. Later, when Rob got bigger, he helped. Still later, Dad did the seeding using a seeder mounted on a tractor.

Small grains like wheat, barley, and oats ripen in the summer. A reaper was used to cut the stalks and bind them into sheaves tied with binder twine. After cutting and binding, Dad, sometimes with help of a neighbor, would go through the field, pick up the sheaves, and shock them.

Thrashing was done using a machine called a separator powered by an endless flat belt run by a steam engine fired by coal or wood. These two pieces of equipment must have been expensive because there were very few of them. The owner, Mr. Glick, was paid based on the number of bushels of grain thrashed.

On thrashing day or the day before, the steam engine pulling the separator would come down Justus Avenue, turn right into Lawndell Road to the farmstead, and then up the driveway to the barn. The barn doors would be opened, and the Operator would maneuver the separator onto the appropriate floor using the steam engine. The separator would be pushed up the barn bank on the north side of the barn and through either the swing-out doors leading to the center barn floor or through the sliding doors into one of the other two barn floors. The stacker doors, which were opposite the north side barn doors, would be opened and the metal tube used to discharge straw would be pointed out one of the stacker doors towards the barnyard.

On thrashing day, a large crowd of men would gather. Some men would haul the shocks from the field, some would cut the binder twine and feed the sheaves into the separator, others would man the separator carrying bushel baskets of grain from the separator into one of the granaries, and others would work on the straw stack as the straw was blown out. Ed Miller always built the stack.

Ed worked continuously on the stack; he never got thirsty even though this was hot dry work. He would stay up there until noon. The stack would be about half of its finished height at that time and Ed would slide down the side for dinner. To get back up, he used a ladder, and in the evening, he would need a ladder to get down because the stack would be over 20 feet tall by that time.

There would be at least two teams of horses each pulling wagons used to pick up the shocks and haul them into the barn. There would be three or four men on each wagon. One or two men would be feeding the separator. Three or four men were needed to carry the grain into the granary and one or two to build the straw stack.

ROBERT ALAN MCDONALD, KATHIE EILEEN MCDONALD COURTNEY, RICHARD EDWIN MCDONALD, MARY JO MCDONALD HELFRICH

Inside the granary were three bins each with a doorway which was closed using one-inch boards which slid down from the top in rails built for that purpose. Each board was 8-inches wide or wider. At first, all the boards were removed from the bin door and the men carrying the grain would walk into the bin, dump the grain in the back filling the back of the bin first. As the bin filled, boards were added closing the opening, so the grain didn't run out. Eventually, all the boards were inserted, and the men had to lift the bushel baskets over the boards to empty them. The process was repeated filling each bin in each granary.

The hardest work was carrying away the wheat because each bushel of wheat weighed 60 pounds. Oats only weighed 32 pounds per bushel. But pushing wheat back into the bin was easier as the shape allowed it to roll instead of slide like the oats did. Barley was shaped similarly to oats, but it was heavier, 56 pounds per bushel.

The men carried bushel baskets filled with grain into one of the two granaries, depending upon the grain. The wheat granary was on the east side, and the oats granary on the west. Both granaries were lined with tongue and groove milled lumber. The doors were well fitted. The granary construction, fit and finish, assured that no vermin would gain entry. In fact, the granaries were also used to store smoked hams.

Small grain growing and harvesting was very labor intensive. A full crew was about 15 men including an operator simply known as the Thrasher.

Thrashing took a day, sometimes more. All that labor had to be fed, a chore that fell to the women. They often got help from the women on neighboring farms, which included kitchen assistance on thrashing day, and baked goods brought from their homes. It was something of a contest between the women to see who could put out the best dinner. None of the labor was paid, so a great meal helped ensure excellent quality help for the next year.

At our farm, the men were fed outside in the yard east of the house. Planks or an old door was laid over sawhorses forming tables.

Men sat on chairs brought from inside the house or on benches made of planks set on buckets or stumps. After dinner, the men would take a break with dinner lasting an hour to an hour and a half. At the end of the day, the men would return to their homes for supper.

Instead of being paid, each man worked for his neighbor helping with his crop. This way everybody had the necessary labor, and no money changed hands.

The wheat granary had a feature not found in the oat granary. Each bin in the wheat granary had a hole in the bottom with a wooden spout which protruded into the first floor. Each spout was fitted with a wooden slide, allowing grain to flow out when opened. Immediately below the granary, the barn's first floor, were two large doors mounted on tracks which would slide open allowing a truck to back in positioning it under one or two of the grain shoots. To load the trucks, all you had to do was open the slide. This was by far the easiest and least labor-intensive part of grain farming.

One can easily understand what a difference the combine made to grain farming. All the manual labor required to cut, shock, haul, and thrash the small grain was replaced by a machine that did all the work in the field with one operator and another to haul the grain to the barn. For that reason, Dad bought a combine in 1952 or '53.

Only one bin in the oat granary had a grain-shoot. It emptied into a purpose-built box in the feed way next to the horse stable. The horses could be given oats without having to climb up to the second floor. The other two oat granaries didn't have this feature.

Jing – Rob's Nemesis

Because there were two types of grain–wheat and oats–the straw stack was built on two different days, one to the east and the other to the west. In the center where the two types of straw met at ground level, there was a small hole between the two.

There were chickens in the barnyard. They liked to nest in the hole in the straw stack. It afforded protection. The chickens could eat the grain that made it into the straw stack, and they would roost and lay eggs there.

ROBERT ALAN MCDONALD, KATHIE EILEEN MCDONALD COURTNEY, RICHARD EDWIN MCDONALD, MARY JO MCDONALD HELFRICH

Getting eggs out of the straw stack was difficult. The hole wasn't much bigger than the size of a chicken and it went clear through, about 30-feet. That's where Rob came it. He was only four to six years old when we had a straw stack. He could crawl through the hole and out the other side. While going through, he could gather the eggs. Of course, he had to watch where he put his hands. Chickens relieve themselves wherever they happen to be when the urge hits.

There was another problem with going through the straw stack hole. The younger heifers would butt Rob when he came out. The one that really enjoyed doing that was Jingle Bells, Jing for short. For that reason, Rob never liked that cow and, of course, Dad kept her as part of the milking herd.

Making Hay

Hay making has changed a great deal over the years. A trend that has continued to this day. It has become more mechanized, allowing farmers to do more with less and less labor.

When we moved to the farm, hay was put into mows at either the east or west end of the barn. A description of making loose hay is included in Chapter 6 how Rob rode Bird when pulling the hay from the wagon into the hay mows and in Chapter 8, Harvest, which describes baling hay which we did every summer. But there was an interim step between loose hay and the balers that used baler twine. That was a wire tied baler. It used wire instead of twine.

Rob was young when this took place, four or five, and his recollection may be incomplete. To fill in the gaps, the internet was consulted, and the following was found:

By JD Seller posted Aug 10, 2019: *I studied up on this a few years ago. Around 1932 there was a small company that basically took a stationary hay press/baler and made a window (nee windrow) pickup for it. So, it did pick the hay up and bale right in the field. It took three people to run. One to drive the tractor pulling the baler and two to wire tie the hay bales. J.I. Case made the first commercially successful baler just right after the other one. I can remember some older case baler still being used when I was very little.*

Mr. Seller's description matches Rob's recollection very closely. Rob recalls Mom driving to a farm on Elton Road, between Brewster and Navarre, where Dad was working. Dad was sitting on one side of the baler helping run the wire tying operation. Rob thought, *Wow, my dad can do anything including run a machine he'd never seen before.*

After baling hay on Elton Road, they must have brought the baler to our place because for at least one year we had wire tied square bales.

The wire ties were removed when feeding. Not being one to throw out perfectly good wire, Dad kept it and stored it on the second floor of the old house. We used baling wire for all manner of repairs around the farm. It was handy stuff to have around. Rich even recalls using it, so it must have been years before we ran out.

But, run out we did. Then we had to use binder twine for those repairs, but it wasn't as good. It lacked strength and it would rot and break. But it was available, and it was free so…

Corn Harvest

The farm also produced a sizable corn crop. But instead of being seeded by a grain drill, corn is planted using a corn planter, a piece of equipment equipped with a seed bin and a fertilizer bin. The corn seed is spaced using a seed plate with allows one seed at a time to drop down a tube into the ground through a "shoe." The shoe is a length of metal with holes machined to allow the seed to drop through into the ground and a second hole that allows fertilizer to be placed 2-inches to the side and behind the corn seed. The fertilizer feeds from the second bin down a larger tube through the shoe.

Corn growing didn't require the intense labor that wheat and oats did as it was mechanized earlier. Initially corn was planted in rows about 42 inches apart with the seeds about 10 inches apart. Later this spacing was reduced to 36 inches, with a corresponding increase in fertilizer. Corn, when growing, would be cultivated at first using horse drawn cultivators, then by tractor mounted cultivators and now chemicals are applied to kill plants that aren't corn eliminating the need for cultivation.

Corn ripens in the fall. When we first began farming, corn was harvested by cutting the stocks with a corn knife. Some of these knives were swung by hand like a machete, but some had a corn knife that was strapped to a worker's leg. The worker would use his leg to cut the corn and his hands to catch the stocks and bind them. Later a machine called a corn binder eliminated the hand labor of cutting and binding, but the corn still needed to be shocked.

The shocks would be gathered by loading them on a wagon and taken to the covered corn crib where a machine called a corn husker, run off an endless belt, would separate the ear corn from the fodder. This was less labor intensive than wheat and oats thrashing but the operation was similar. The result was ear corn which would be stored in corn cribs. The result of the corn husking operation was ear corn and fodder. The fodder could be used as bedding or returned to the fields where it would rot and return to the soil.

The Barnyard

When we first moved to the farm, the animals were watered from a cistern located at the east end of the barn. The watering trough was in a three-sided building; the west side was open. Water was pumped by hand from the cistern into the trough. The cistern was filled by rainwater by way of a downspout off the barn roof.

There were problems with this arrangement. We would run out of rainwater especially if we increased the number of animals or the weather turned dry, or if the cistern developed a leak, which it did. And in the winter, the water in the trough froze solid making it impossible for the animals to drink. To solve this problem, Dad got a gasoline fired heater for the watering trough. He got it to work, most of the time, but it was dangerous and unreliable.

This heater was a remarkable contraption. It was built out of 4 inch metal tubes or pipe with a half-gallon gasoline tank mounted on the tallest pipe. The tall pipe was connected to another pipe at a 90 degree angle. That was the bottom of the heater that went in the trough. At the other end was another pipe, also connected at 90 degrees that went up like the first pipe. The joints were watertight. The way it worked was to insert the heater in the trough, so the bottom pipe was at the bottom of the trough. Then open the valve on the gasoline tank so that gas dripped into the upright pipe. Light the gasoline with a match and as the gas burned, the heat kept the water in the trough from freezing.

Since the watering trough was located in a wooden shed at the east end of the barn, there was a very real possibility of burning the barn down if there was any malfunction, which of course there was. We didn't use this heater very long, maybe just a year or perhaps even less.

We began watering the animals using a portable metal trough installed at the southwest side of the barnyard, filling it with a hose from the well in the milkhouse. This same well supplied water to the house. It was our only source of water. In winter, the hose would freeze solid. If we left water in it to prevent freezing, we would "walk the hose down." This involved detaching the hose from the hydrant in the milkhouse, then walking up to the barnyard, about 200 feet, and picking the hose up, hoisting it over our shoulder, and walking down to the uncoupled end at least three times. Once or twice wasn't enough. Any water left in the hose would freeze and prevent operation. If that happened, we had to pull the hose down the hill, wrap it in a wash tub, and pour hot water on it to thaw it. The easiest way of "walking it down" was to place it on your shoulder. In winter, this was cold work.

Years later, Dad concreted the inside of the barn, and the old trough was moved into the loafing pen where it was warm enough so it wouldn't freeze.

ROBERT ALAN MCDONALD, KATHIE EILEEN MCDONALD COURTNEY, RICHARD EDWIN MCDONALD, MARY JO MCDONALD HELFRICH

One of the common problems we had with both inside and outside watering was forgetting to turn the water off. We would get busy doing something else and let the water run. Then we had a large puddle of water either in the barnyard – added to the mess we already had – or inside the barn where it was hard to get the water out.

The early spring, particularly during the month of March continuing into April, the barnyard became a sea of muddy manure. In winter, the ground and the barnyard were frozen, and the cattle were clean. That all changed when the weather broke, and the thaw started. In those days, the barnyard wasn't paved so the soil got mixed with the manure.

The cattle had to walk through the muddy mess. Their udders, legs, and tails dragged in it, and they carried it into the barn where we milked. Getting the udders clean was an ongoing task. We cleaned them using old burlap bags. They would swish their tail and hit us with the nasty end which would get us filthy, too.

Sometimes getting the cows into the barn was an adventure. They might go out in the mud and stand there refusing to come in to be milked. We couldn't walk out and get them. The mess would be over our boots. We would resort to pelting them with rocks until they came in.

In the early years, the only way we had to clean the barnyard was with forks or shovels. Dad got a Templeton loader that mounted on the Minnie. That made cleaning easier, but we still took out soil with the manure. Later, Dad was able to pave the barnyard, described elsewhere.

Equipment Maintenance

Dad believed the equipment needed regular maintenance. After we finished plowing in either the spring or fall, we greased the plow shares to keep them from rusting. The grease came right off within a few feet the next time we began plowing, leaving the plowshares bright and shiny, allowing the ground to be turned easily.

We changed oil in the various engines, especially the tractors regularly and greased the tractors. Greasing and oil changing for most equipment wasn't difficult. But there were exceptions. The combine and the baler were harder to grease, especially the combine. Both these pieces of equipment had Wisconsin VE4-cyclinder air-cooled engines. These engines needed maintenance, meaning oil changes and tune-ups like new spark plugs and other electrical parts.

The reason these two pieces of equipment had engines, even though they were not self-propelled, was because the Minnie didn't have live-power take-off. Disengaging the clutch not only stopped the tractor's movement but also stopped the PTO from running the attached equipment, thus auxiliary power – the Wisconsin engines were needed.

Both Wisconsin engines were prone to what Dad called vapor lock, which occurred when the engines were shut down when hot. The baler engine was the worst. And it was worse on hot days. But of course, these engines were used in the summer when it was hot. The only solution was to keep these engines running until we were finished for the day. Once the engines sat overnight, starting them the next day wasn't hard. As Rich points out, occasionally these engines got a valve job and for a year or two, starting was much easier. But Dad wasn't going to pay for repairs every two or three years.

The baler was particularly troubling because we tried hooking the wagon to the baler so the bales could be delivered to the wagon right out of the chute. When we baled enough hay to fill the wagon, it would be taken to the barn for unloading. This meant shutting down the engine. Leaving an air-cooled engine running when not moving built up heat and used fuel – neither being a good thing. When we came back with the empty wagon, we had to re-start the engine. Sometimes, because of vapor lock, the engine wouldn't start. We did all kinds of things including pouring cold water on the intake manifold to get it to run. Cranking the engine wasn't much fun either. It could wear us out. It wasn't unusual for Dad and Rob to crank it many times before it would start.

Finally, Dad made the executive decision that instead of loading the wagon off the baler, we would drop the bales and pick them up by hand. This practice allowed Dad to start the baler engine and bale until finished for the day, then would join us to help load and unload the wagon or trailer. This meant we had to pick the bales off the ground to load the wagon or dual wheel trailer.

We used the combine to harvest small grains – oats, wheat, and barley. The combine was greased every day before it was used. The baler was greased daily as well but it was an easier job. Greasing the combine usually fell to Rob, it was a dirty, difficult job requiring acrobatic contortionist skills. Rob recalls having to crawl into the space under the grain bin next to the big flywheel behind the motor, 30 inches off the ground backwards, face up, while holding the grease gun. Rich says that each time Rob did this he wasn't sure he was going to get his brother back. Rob would start the greasing job in the morning when he was clean and by the time he finished, he was filthy. Finally, he started taking off his shirt and washing his upper body after finishing so he didn't catch it from Mom about his shirt being greasy.

There was an abundance of grease fittings – zerk-fittings. Dad and Rob went over the locations to be sure none were missed. One year, Rob forgot one fitting every time. It was in a difficult location next to the body of the machine behind a pulley. Half-way through the harvest, the bearing burned out and repairs took a couple days to complete. Rob was worried that Dad would be upset due to his mistake. But surprisingly, Dad took it in stride and got the repairs completed.

The grease gun had a metal tube with a bend which allowed it to be positioned so that the female and male fittings lined up in a straight line, which minimized waste. Filling the grease gun required unscrewing the endcap thus removing the pump, leaving the empty tube. The tube would be filled by inserting it into the 5-gallon grease bucket. The grease was drawn into the tube by pulling up on the charging handle. Once full, the charging handle would be locked open and the top screwed back on. Then the charging handle could be released, and the internal spring would force the grease into the pump.

Rob recalls trying to convince Dad to buy a greasing outfit, run by compressed air, which would eliminate filling the grease gun and would be easier to use. That didn't happen. Dad did get a new grease gun with a flexible tube. It was an improvement, but we still had to load the grease gun out of the 5-gallon bucket – no pre-filled tubes for us. Dad didn't wish to spend money foolishly.

Repairing the web on the manure spreader wasn't Rich's favorite job. The web consisted of two flat chains, one on each side of the bed with angle iron spaced about 18 inches apart, connecting the two sides. There were toothed drive sprockets at the front and rear of the bed which were used to move the chain in sync, thus moving the manure toward the rear where a series of beaters tore the manure to small pieces and spread it on the field.

Over time, the flat chain links stretched and could twist and disconnect. When this happened, the manure spreader had to be unloaded by hand using a pitchfork, then the chain links had to be reconnected or sometimes replaced. It was hard to get the links reconnected because the chain had to be held at an angle of about 45 degrees against a hammer while hitting it with another hammer. It was very easy to hit your fingers, plus it was dirty.

Cultivating Corn

Keeping weeds out of the corn to maximize yield required manual cultivation. In the early years, there were no chemicals available to kill weeds. Battling weeds started when the corn ground was plowed and ended when the corn got big enough to shade the ground blocking sunlight from the weeds.

After planting using a two-row corn planter before the corn plants emerged, we went over the corn fields with a spike tooth harrow set at a shallow depth. The purpose was to expose the weed's roots to the sun, killing them, giving corn a head start.

After corn plants emerged, when 6 inches tall, 4 or more leaves, we would cultivate for the first time. We tried cultivating twice during the growing season, the second time when the corn was 12 to 18 inches tall.

This meant we had to mount the cultivators on the Minnie. Cultivators were in three pieces: one on the left and one on the right side of the tractor beside the engine and in front of the rear drive wheels, and one on the back. The front units were spaced to match the width of the corn rows, thus only the ground between the corn rows would be worked which removed weeds growing there. Each side consisted of a steel square tube frame on which steel shafts ending with "shoes" shaped like spades in a deck of cards. The rear cultivator was a single steel square tube with three gangs of spring teeth attached. All three units were lifted simultaneously. The cultivator was mounted to specific brackets strategically located and bolted in place. Once installed we left the mounting brackets in place. The cultivators were heavy. Mounting them was all manual labor. Care had to be taken so that pinched fingers didn't occur, but even taking care, pinches did happen.

Before mounting the cultivators, we had to widen the rear wheels on the tractor. Dad elected to jack-up the tractor, unbolt the lug-nuts, slide the wheel off, turn it around and re-bolt it. Thus, the dish in the wheel moved the tire out about 8 inches on each side. The other choice would have been to jack-up the tractor, loosen the bolts that clamped to the wheel to the axle, and slide the whole assembly out 8 inches. Dad thought our way was faster. After we were finished cultivating, we would dismount the cultivators and remount the wheels in the correct position.

The Minnie had a hydraulic slave cylinder that we used to raise and lower the cultivators and raise and lower the 7 foot sickle bar on the semi-mounted hay mower. This slave cylinder was an innovation for the time as only Ford or Ford-Ferguson tractors had 3 point hitches.

When Dad cultivated corn, he frequently found arrowheads. He had an uncanny knack for spotting them when working ground or cultivating. Rob and Rich both say they always looked for flint and neither ever spotted any flint or arrowheads. Kathie may have inherited Dad's eyesight as she could spot 4-leaf clovers. Neither of her brothers could do this either.

Cultivating corn could be difficult. Not because the work was hard, but because watching those rows of corn coming at you while you tried to stay focused so you didn't plow it out, could put you to sleep. Dad used to get off the tractor and sit down on the ground with his back to one of the rear wheels and catch 40-winks.

Cultivation seemed good for the corn plants. It aerated the soil. We always thought we could almost see the corn growing after it had been cultivated.

Plowing with Trailing Plows

Dad did all the plowing initially, but over the years that changed. Purchase of the Minnie meant plowing got done faster than with either the horses or the F-20. As Rob grew up, he could operate a tractor, so Dad bought the Case DC at a farm sale. Both the Minnie and the Case were rated 2-3 plow tractors. We had two 2-bottom trailing plows, one for each tractor. Having two tractors plowing cut the time in half, a major improvement.

Trailing plows were made so that at the beginning and end of furrows, the plows were raised and lowered via a trip rope. When starting a furrow, a pull on the trip rope dropped the plows into the ground and at the end, a pull raised it to make the turn. We always sat on the plow rope. To prevent breaking plow points, the plows were equipped with a spring-loaded break-away hitch. If a hard obstruction were encountered the hitch would unlock, and the plow would be detached from the tractor.

When an obstruction, such as a rock, was struck, two things happened – fast. First, a loud BANG occurred, when the hitch detached, and second, you stood up quickly and pulled the clutch – both the Minnie and the Case had hand clutches – to stop forward motion. You stood up because the rope, which was between your legs with a knot in the end, came back through your legs quickly. That knot would strike a delicate area of the male anatomy when seated, so you learned to stand up when you heard the BANG. Usually, one lesson was all that was required.

The Silo

Dad decided we needed a silo, something the farm didn't have. After shopping around and talking to other farmers, he decided a Michigan stave silo was what he wanted. He conferred with the Michigan dealer to determine the size and price. As with everything Dad did, price took top priority. He started out with a 10 foot by 40 foot model. The dealer explained that for an upcharge he could significantly increase the storage capacity if he went with a 12 foot by 40 foot model instead, and even better would be going with 14 feet. Dad didn't like the price increase but realized increased volume was needed so he opted for a smaller up-charge and went with a 10 foot by 45 foot model, he added 5 feet to the height. This was the first mistake. The addition added 13% to the capacity, but the 2 foot width increase would have added 20%. The 14 foot model would add 40%. And the fill height would have been lower with either of the wider models.

The second mistake was the silo location: the northeast side of the barn. Although convenient to the milking parlor where silage would be fed to the dairy cattle, this location put the silo in the coldest spot. Being in the coldest spot meant that in winter, silage froze to the outside walls. Unloading by hand was difficult, in fact at times impossible. A larger diameter could have prevented this difficulty and may have resulted in adding a self-unloader, which would have been able to limit or even eliminate the freezing problem. In Dad's defense, he had no idea of these problems when he made the final size and location decision.

The third mistake, which could be easily rectified, was no electrical wiring included in the silo. Thus, there was no light. This mistake was taken care of when the boys grew up and left home leaving Dad to climb the silo in the dark of winter. At that point, having a light in the silo became a priority and was installed. The freezing problem was never resolved.

The fourth mistake was feeding silage when milking. This added significantly to milking time. We were milking 20 to 24 head, which meant that some stalls had to be used twice. Instead of just feeding grain – chop – we fed grain and silage in the winter. We didn't feed silage when the cows were on pasture. So, the silage had to be put in front of the cows when each round came in to be milked. Since the stanchions were on both the north and south sides of the milking parlor, bushel baskets of silage had to be hand carried from the north side to the south side during milking. This extra work added to the time needed to milk.

Initially, Rob got the job of climbing the silo and throwing out the silage using a silage fork – a wide fork with multiple tines. Not long after, Rich got the job part of the time and later, when Rob went to college, he got it full time. Light didn't penetrate the silo very easily, and it got dark early in Ohio winters. To see what they were doing, Dad got a railroad lantern from one of the Railroad employees. Dad knew everybody and was well liked. He prevailed upon these "friends" to get him a railroad lantern and the 6-volt batteries that they used. These lanterns had two bulbs in the bottom. One provided a concentrated beam and the other more of a flood light.

Even though the lanterns and the batteries didn't cost Dad anything, he continued to let the railroad supply them. He didn't like the constant replenishment made necessary by battery wear out and damage to the lantern caused by dropping or banging them on the sides of the crawl space when climbing into the silo every day. Both Rob and Rich heard about it when they needed new batteries or lanterns. Dad tried to have Kathie do the climbing, but she couldn't manage the weight and frozen silage, so he had to do the job himself. That's when electric light was installed, thus solving the lantern problem, but the freezing problem remained. We used a mattock to chop the frozen silage but had to take great care lest we hit and brake one of the concrete staves.

Before constructing the silo, we had to dig the footer. It had to be at least three feet deep – below the frost line – and fully cured concrete. To mark the boundary Dad used a two by four with a spike which functioned as the center point and nails that marked both the outside and inside of the circle. Then all Dad had to do was dig out the soil between the two marks. Once dug, a ready-mix truck arrived and the footer was poured. After pouring, Dad worked the concrete getting it level. It was left to cure for over a month.

On the day scheduled for construction, the Michigan Silo company truck arrived with all the staves, the hoops which encircled the silo along with other hardware which included the exterior steel ladder, crow's nest which would be placed at the top of the silo ladder, and the metal roof. The silo builder remarked after backing over the footer, "Good work, that footer didn't move." Dad, a bit taken aback, responded, "It wasn't supposed to, was it?"

Dad recruited Bob Kuehner and Gene Jacobs to help with the construction. It was Dad, Bob, and Gene's job to get the staves to the Michigan Silo builder and to bolt the hoops in place. Gene got the job of running the machine that hoisted the staves. It was a four-man job, but it got done in one day.

From Dairy to Beef Production

Dad never intended to be primarily a dairy farmer. In the '50's, Dad encouraged Rob to buy beef brood cows. Eventually, these conversations led to Rob purchasing two Polled Herford brood cows. (Polled means the cattle do not have horns.) To make the purchase, Rob used the money from his college fund. These two cows became the foundation for a larger herd that would eventually replace the dairy cattle. By this time, the entire family, Dad included, were tired of milking. A twice a day everyday operation.

If Dad would have wanted to be a dairy farmer, he would have upgraded the barn to produce Grade-A milk. Grade-A is milk that, after pasteurization and homogenization, could be sold for drinking. As it was, the milking area had a dirt floor which would have had to be concreted, and the milk handling system would have required better refrigeration and better sanitation. Dad would have had to submit to inspections by a third party. That would have violated his oath to "take no more orders." As configured, we sold manufacturing milk. The price was lower than Grade-A, which meant lower income but less investment and no inspections.

The floor in the milking parlor (using the term parlor very loosely) was uneven. There were holes behind some stanchions which resulted from cleaning up manure and urine when the cows urinated or defecated. In some cases, the holes were pronounced to such an extent that it was difficult to place the 5 gallon bucket, used as a stool when milking by hand, so that it could be level enough to be used.

Our cousins, the Labs, lived in Canton. They were city people and may have told tales about farm living to their friends and acquaintances. Rob recalls one of these friends asking him if we had electric lights and running water in our house. Tom, our oldest male cousin, became engaged to Lynn, so the Lab family brought Lynn to the farm to meet us. What they told Lynn on the way must have been wild. They got to our house at supper time. We were all seated at the table in the dining room. They put Lynn at the head of the line, knocked on the door, and when Dad said, "Come in," Lynn peaked around the door, obviously not knowing what to expect. She had an expression of total apprehension mixed with consternation. Dad, of course, seized the moment and really laid it on thick. Lynn was a city girl. She had no idea what farm life was like. After we finished eating, we took her to the barn so she could watch us milk. One of the cows decided to do what cows do and raised her tail in preparation for defecation. So, Rich did what we usually did when this happened; he grabbed the scoop shovel which we kept hanging on a nail embedded in one of the posts and caught it in the shovel then disposed of the waste. This was better than having to scoop it up off the dirt floor. Lynn was shocked. This was more than she could believe. Her comment was, "Oh my god, he caught it." The expression on her face was "priceless."

A lesson that we all learned early was that getting behind cows and horses could be dangerous. These animals kick, especially when surprised or disturbed, and they defecate and urinate suddenly. For example, a cow might cough which may cause sudden defecation. Rich recalled learning this lesson by being directly behind a cow that coughed and when she did, she promptly filled his pants pocket. We learned to stand slightly off to one side. If we needed to be behind a cow or horse to be either close, so if they decided to kick, their action would have little power, or far enough away that the kick wouldn't reach us. Dad would tell us, but sometimes a single lesson was needed to reinforce the message.

The farm had plenty of pasture and beef cattle were more docile than Holsteins thus they could be pastured side-by-side with no difficulties. Since there were but two cows keeping a bull just for them didn't make sense, so the services of NOBA (Northern Ohio Breeders Association) were used. When one of the beef cows was in season, Rob called NOBA, and a representative came to the farm and serviced the cow. It was a way to have access to higher quality, full-blooded bulls without having to buy one. Rob picked the sires from the NOBA breeding book. Rich remarked that he was fascinated by the breeding book and the opportunity to upgrade the stock without having to buy a bull which would have cost thousands of dollars. Money we didn't have.

Usually, the heifer calves were kept and became brood cows, while the bull calves became steers which were fed out then sold for slaughter. The steers were sold after reaching a finished weight, which was around 1000 pounds.

To accommodate the beef herd while still milking, the house stable was used during wintry weather. The dairy bull continued to occupy the large stall in the northwest corner of the barn. As the beef herd increased, additional space was needed so the horse stall at the southwest corner of the barn was closed in and the dairy bull moved there. There was no water in the horse stable, so the dairy bull, Bill, and the beef cattle had to be watered by letting them out to go to the watering trough, a task that initially Rob handled, but got turned over to Rich and Kathie when Rob went to college.

Over the years, the number of brood cows increased until there were over 20 of them. By this time, Rob began college, so the herd was sold to Dad. Rob used the proceeds for college. As the number of beef animals increased, Dad decreased the number of dairy cows. In 1969, at the time of the July 4th Flood, Chapter 18, there were about 15 head of dairy cattle left, but the beef herd totaled 50 head, including cows, calves, and feeder stock and by then a herd Hereford bull had been added.

Buying the Minnie G750

Over the years, additional equipment was added. Most notably were tractors. When Rob was old enough to operate a tractor, Dad bought a 1939 Case DC at Mr. Stringfellow's farm sale. Later, Dad bought a Massey-Ferguson 65 and a 3-bottom 3-point hitch mounted plow.

But Dad was looking for a tractor with more power compared to the Massey 65 – a 3-4 plow rated tractor – which was the largest tractor on the farm. He learned of a farmer near the Pennsylvania line who was retiring and was auctioning his equipment. That farmer had two Minneapolis Moline G 750 tractors – 70+ horsepower diesels. A significant upgrade from the gasoline powered Massey. Dad always liked Minneapolis Moline tractors.

ROBERT ALAN MCDONALD, KATHIE EILEEN MCDONALD COURTNEY, RICHARD EDWIN MCDONALD, MARY JO MCDONALD HELFRICH

On the sale day, Dad and Rich made the trip. Rich recalls Dad being extremely nervous. When the first Minnie came up, Dad bid it up to $7,000 and won the bid. Next, the second one came up and he asked Rich if he paid too much and if he should bid on the second. Rich didn't really know if Dad overpaid and really couldn't advise him on the second. Rich was out of school and working as a carpenter. Not wanting to discourage him, Rich told Dad he had made a good buy. Dad didn't bid on the second and it sold for $5,500. In addition to the tractor, Dad also bought the 5-bottom Oliver plow that went with it. Overall, Dad spent a lot more money that day than he was used to spending. And to top it off, he didn't have that much cash in his checking account. He had to go to the Navarre Deposit Bank and arrange a loan to make the check good that he wrote.

Of course, the loan wasn't a problem as there was no debt on the farm, but Dad hadn't spoken to the bank before going to the sale. He walked in and spoke to his brother-in-law, our Uncle Don, who was the bank president. He got the loan. The big Minnie was everything Dad hoped it would be. It was rated as a 70-horsepower 4-5-bottom tractor. It managed the 5-bottom plow in the farm's sandy loam with ease. On the dynamometer, a machine used to measure power, the engine in the Minnie produced 83 horsepower. Dad really enjoyed operating that tractor. It was too bad he didn't buy it earlier.

Chapter Ten – Farm Work and Chores

We worked because that's what we did, not because there was a paycheck or money involved. We got money when we needed it, but it didn't relate to the work we did. We knew people worked and were paid for it, but that was other people. It didn't apply to us until we got jobs away from the farm. Then we had to learn how to relate the two.

Every one of us had chores. For Rob and Rich, regular daily chores began upon entering the first grade; our school system didn't have kindergarten. We fed animals, cleaned up and disposed of animal waste, milked, gathered eggs (on those occasions that Mom didn't do it), helped with land cultivation, and fixed equipment, fences, and buildings.

Kathie and Mary started with Mom doing housework, but they got into outside work as they grew up. The boys got a bit of housework working with Mom. Chores didn't have a gender. In winter, we worked in the barn and in the woods cutting wood for heating and turning trees into lumber.

Our year was mandated by the farming season and the school year. We always had chores which had to be accomplished every day. Every day meant just that, 365 or 366 days a year. As Dad said, "Cows don't know when it's Christmas." And hogs got hungry every day just like we did. Twice each day the hogs had to be fed, and the cows had to be fed and, until 1969, milked.

Planting season began in March or April and lasted into May or occasionally June, except for wheat or barley, which was planted in September. Harvest began with first cutting hay in June, then the second cutting in August, and finally September or October for the third cutting or occasionally stubble hay.

During the summer, at Mom's direction, food was canned and preserved. This meant planning the garden, weeding it, and gathering the produce.

ROBERT ALAN MCDONALD, KATHIE EILEEN MCDONALD COURTNEY, RICHARD EDWIN MCDONALD, MARY JO MCDONALD HELFRICH

Wheat and barley were harvested in July followed by oats finishing in early August. Finally, corn would be harvested in September, October, and sometimes even into November.

September through April, we had to make sure there was wood on hand to keep us warm. Butchering was done during cold months. That way the meat wouldn't spoil during the process

In those days, the school year started after Labor Day and ended before Memorial Day. It was a good thing it did because summers were busy.

Feeding the Animals

We ground a week's supply of cow, hog, and chicken feed on Saturdays during the school year.

Grinding feed involved grain hauling: corn, oats, barley, feed supplement, and even third cutting alfalfa hay. Ear corn was stored in a corn crib across the driveway east of the barn. The hammer mill, used to grind grain, was next to the sliding doors on the northeast side of the second story barn floor.

Oats and barley were stored in the granaries and had to be carried to the grinding area. To get a uniform mix we layered the grain in a three-sided container made from 1 inch by 10 inch hardwood boards two boards high. The overall dimensions of the container were 5 feet wide by 10 feet long. The open end faced the grinder. Grain was placed in the container in layers starting with the corn. We did it in layers so as we shoveled the grain mixture in the grinder, the mixture would be uniform. All the ground feed was sacked in burlap bags. Later, after making improvements for ground feed storage, it was no longer necessary to sack all the feed.

Corn was used in all animal feed. At the corn crib, we shoveled it into a wheelbarrow, which we pushed along the driveway and up the barn bank. Wheelbarrow load after wheelbarrow load of ear corn was required. Moving and shelling corn claimed most of the time. Ear corn was ground for the cattle, as their digestive systems could process the cellulose in the cob. The cattle feed was ground corn on the cob mixed with oats.

We used shelled corn for hog and chicken feed because of their digestive systems. Since all the stored corn was on the cob, we had to shell what we used for hog and chicken feed. We filled and pushed wheelbarrows of corn up the barn bank to the second floor where the corn sheller and hammer mill were located. Then we ran the ear corn through a hand cranked corn-sheller one ear at a time.

Hog feed was a layer of corn, a layer of oats, a layer of barley, and sometimes second or third cutting alfalfa for additional protein run through the hammer mill.

Chicken feed also required shelled corn mixed with oats and supplement purchased from a feed mill in Navarre.

Oats and barley had to be carried from the granaries on the second floor of the barn.

We powered the hammer mill used for grinding by a flat belt driven by a tractor. We would place the tractor outside the barn so it would be outside, but close enough that the flat belt would reach the tractor. Using burlap bags, we bagged all the ground feed to make handling ground cattle feed—what we called 'chop'—easier. Dad had Bob Kuehner built a metal storage bin and installed it in the corner of the east hay mow next to the hammer mill. Thus, the bin was loaded from the top, the second floor, and unloaded on the ground floor. The bin had a slide at the bottom, allowing the chop to flow into a bucket. To keep hay out of the bin, we put an old door over it so we could still use the space above as part of the haymow. We should have put a top on the bin so that the rats couldn't get in, but we didn't think to do that when it was built. The bin eliminated handling bagged feed.

Before too many years, Dad bought a corn sheller that ran off the flat belt. We thought that was the greatest thing. No more cranking the hand sheller. We could even take the sheller and place it next to the corncrib and not have to push the wheelbarrow up the bank. Years later, Dad bought a sheller mounted on a three-point hitch and powered by the tractor's power-take-off. And, finally, he bought a Brady feed grinder-mixer also powered by the tractor PTO.

It reduced manual labor because we could move it to the grain storage locations and unload when and where needed. Mechanization made the work easier, but the greatest impact was that we got more done in a shorter amount of time, allowing us to manage a larger number of animals.

This was powered by the tractor PTO and had an unloading auger we used to place the feed in the bin in the barn and in the self-feeders in the hog finishing pens. This was a vast improvement.

Sanitation

The hog house, the converted sheep barn, was cleaned twice a week, every Saturday and Wednesday. Hogs had to be kept clean. Contrary to widespread belief, hogs are not dirty animals if given a choice. And they grow better when kept clean. Also, butchering hair removal by scalding is much easier. Rob recalls being judged about how clean the hogs were at butchering time.

During the school year, Dad usually milked and did the morning chores by himself. The evening chores of feeding all the cattle and hogs the children usually did along with milking. This changed when we were out of school for the summer. Then we helped with morning and evening chores and did other farm work. However, Rich helped with the morning milking during his junior and senior years.

We did land preparation; harvesting: hay, small grain, corn, silage, and garden produce; butchering; fence building and repair; construction; and repair. The work involved equipment use and hand labor. We did about anything that needed doing.

The Young Holstein Bull

Dad had purchased a young Holstein bull that was going to take over as herd bull. At the time, we still had the old bull who was kept in the bullpen at the north end of the horse stable. The plan was to sell the old bull and then put the young one in the bullpen. In the meantime, the young bull was chained in one of the horse stalls. One of Rob's chores was to water the stock and that included Bill and both bulls, one at a time. Bill was no problem, and neither was the old bull, as there was a door to his pen.

But, as the young bull grew, he became more aggressive. It was getting harder and harder to untie him, and he didn't much like being re-tied after getting his drink. Rob had to go up beside the young bull when un-tying or re-tying him. Rich recalls Rob telling him to stick around just in case. It finally happened. Rob had just gotten the young bull re-tied when the animal swung his rear, knocking Rob forward. Rob went over backwards into the manger with one leg tangled in the chain draped over the top board.

The young bull took this opportunity to gore Rob but couldn't because the chain restricted his movements. But the young bull had Rob's leg pinned, and he slammed his head into Rob's leg, pinning Rob in place. Rob yelled for Rich, who quickly figured out what to do. Rich grabbed the straw fork, came over the top of the manger from the feed-way where he was. He hit the bull with the fork, sinking the tongs into its neck. The bull backed off enough for Rob to untangle his leg and get out of the manger.

Fortunately, Rob wasn't badly hurt, just bruised. But when Dad was told, he let Rob know it was his fault that this happened. But it wasn't very much longer before the old bull was sold and the situation resolved.

For a brief time, Kathie got the job of watering the Holstein bull. When Mom found out, that decision was promptly changed and one of the boys or Dad let the bull out of his pen and made sure he got back in.

Even after being excused from watering the bull, Kathie did get stuck feeding hay to the herd. One bull took delight in tearing up every hay bale he could. Kathie recalls him making extra work for her because he'd tear open the bale before she could get the strings off and in the proper manger. This meant she had to hunt the strings and move the hay.

ROBERT ALAN MCDONALD, KATHIE EILEEN MCDONALD COURTNEY, RICHARD EDWIN MCDONALD, MARY JO MCDONALD HELFRICH

Tire Repair

The farm equipment had rubber tires which wore out, became damaged, or just lost air pressure. We fixed tires regularly. The tools we used were rudimentary. We had tire irons – pieces of flat iron ground or beaten into the proper shape for removing tires from wheels, a 12-pound sledgehammer, a 5-pound hammer and an old worn-out hand air pump. We tried for years to get an air compressor, but the cost got in the way.

Dad kept a supply of spare tires, some of which even had tread left on them. When we had a tire problem, we would remove the wheel from the piece of equipment, lay it on the ground, and beat on the tire with the sledge to loosen the bead from the rim. We had to be careful not to hit the wheel rim with the sledge because that could damage the wheel. So, we learned to remove the tires by running over them with one of the tractor front tires near the rim to break it loose from the rim. Then we could use the tire tools to finish removal. Next, we would determine the problem, perform the repair – usually this meant patching the tube - and reinstall the tire on the wheel.

The final problem was re-inflation. All we had was the worn-out tire pump. We could pump on that thing for hours until our strength was gone, and the tire remained uninflated.

Fortunately, Grandpa Dan, years before, purchased a Sears paint spraying outfit. Part of which was an air compressor. It didn't flow a great deal of air, but it sure beat the hand pump, so it was our go-to. Dad acquired – we can't remember how or where he got it – a piece that converted one cylinder of the Minnie into an air compressor. To make it work, we removed one sparkplug, screwed the device into the sparkplug spot, and started the tractor which would run on three cylinders. Voila! An air compressor right where we needed it. Another example of make-do and conservation of capitol.

The hay wagon was built from the frame of a Model A Ford. It had spoke wheels, which used 6 by 16" tires. When Ford built Model A's, the tire size was common, but by the 1950's, those size tires were hard to find, unless of course new ones were purchased—something Dad wasn't going to do. Finally, it happened. The tires on the hay wagon all needed to be replaced. The wagon had been out in the weather for years and the lug nuts were rusted so badly that removal of the nuts was no longer possible. We considered cutting them off with a hacksaw or a torch. But, if we did, we would need to buy new lugs AND replace the ones we cut off with new ones. Or, we would have had to replace the entire wheel assembly. So, we took off the old tires and installed replacements while the wheels remained in place. It certainly wasn't easy, but we sure weren't going to scrap the wagon. Rich and Rob remember spending hours beating on those tires to get the beads loose. When the hay wagon was sold, those tires were still on it.

The best use for most of the tires Dad kept was starting a fire. Most of them were completely worn out or were the wrong size for any of the equipment. Although a burning tire generates black smoke, it burns hot. An ideal method of starting green brush burning, something we did occasionally.

Trash Disposal

Behind the butcher house, we kept a couple 55 gallon drums that we used for trash of all kinds: tin cans, glass, cardboard, and even a small amount of spoiled food. These drums would get full and had to be disposed of once or twice a year. We used the swamp located at the edge of the 8 acre field next to the railroad right-of-way as a dump site. We'd load the barrels on the hay wagon, pull it down to the cut, just off the old streetcar right-of-way, dump the trash, and bring the barrels back for re-use.

Mom had a bunch of old canning jars that were obsolete. She decided those jars needed to go to the dump. So, Rob and Rich loaded them on the wagon and took them away. Since the jars were of no use, we thought, we took care to smash them as we unloaded. It was great fun!

Years later Mom learned that those obsolete jars were collector's items and could be sold for money—a good sum of money. She told Rich it would be a promising idea to go to the dump and gather up those old jars and bring them back so they could be sold, figuring she might get several hundred or even a thousand dollars for them as she recalled there were quite a few. Rich told her it was no use even looking, we had broken them all. Mom's response was classic, "Why did you do that, you dump yaps?"

Other Chores

We didn't have a root cellar. One of the few things the farm didn't have. To keep potatoes and sometimes apples, we used an old cistern on the west side of the house. When we needed potatoes, one of us, at first it was Rob, got the job of climbing down a rickety metal ladder after taking the concrete lid off, and loading a couple buckets with potatoes or apples, which Dad would pull up using a rope. Climbing down into the cistern just wasn't a fun job, but it had to be done so…

The cistern cover was heavy. It took both Rob and Rich to move it. Dad made it out of a metal wagon or implement wheel, 42 inches across, filled with concrete. Once in place on top of the cistern, it didn't move.

Another job we didn't care for but had to do was washing the milking machines. It was hard to get the milk stone out (calcium build-up due to milk drying), and then they had to be carried to the barn. Kathie recalls this being especially difficult in the winter with one in each hand, then falling on the ice and snow.

THE MCDONALDS

Harvest

In the late spring and summer, we made hay; at least two cuttings and usually three. Altogether we put about 10,000 bales of hay in the two mows, about 2,000 bales of straw – wheat, oats, and barley – on one barn floor and in the hog barn, and a hundred bales of alfalfa, the third cutting on top of the straw. All of this was fed to the cattle and horses in the winter. The cattle were pastured in the spring, summer, and fall until the grass was no longer growing.

As we got older, Dad usually did the baling and Rob, Kathie, and Rich picked up and loaded the hay onto the trailer or the hay wagon. After finishing baling, Dad would join. At first, Rich drove the tractor, but after he got bigger, he and Kathie switched jobs and she drove, and Rich loaded. Rob's job was to pick up the bales and toss them on the trailer or wagon. The bales weighed 40–50 pounds and tossing them on when fully loaded took a good heave. While driving, Kathie recalls Rob fussing at her because of the pace and stalling the Case tractor that had to be hand cranked.

From the left: Grandma Julia, Aunt Hattie & Uncle Charlie McCorkle (Grandma Julia's sister and brother-in-law), Rob, Dad, Mary & Rich. The tractor was the Minneapolis Moline pulling the dual wheel trailer.

ROBERT ALAN MCDONALD, KATHIE EILEEN MCDONALD COURTNEY, RICHARD EDWIN MCDONALD, MARY JO MCDONALD HELFRICH

Hay making season rolled around every year and Kathie's sophomore year of high school was no different. Hay needed making. But this year, neither of the boys were home, which left the crew at least one member short.

Dad, as usual, did the mowing, conditioning, and, when ready, raked the hay into windrows for baling. Mary, seven years younger than Kathie, got drafted as the tractor driver when picking up the baled hay. Kathie could do the loading riding on the dual wheel trailer, but there was no-one to toss the bales onto the trailer. Waiting till Dad finished baling wasn't a good option because it slowed down the process.

Dad asked the girls if they knew anyone from school who he might hire to help with haying. Kathie suggested Red Washler, a boy in her class. Red was contacted and he agreed to help. The wages were agreed to and on the appointed day, Red began working on the haying crew.

Red's job was to pick up the hay bales and throw them on the trailer where Kathie would place them so the load would ride to the barn. In the barn Kathie unloaded onto the elevator. Red and Mary did the mowing with Red placing the bales in layers with each layer crossing the layer below at right angles. Mary helped by rolling the bales toward Red as they came off the elevator. The bales weighed 45-50 pounds. Mary was skinny, weighing just a bit more than the bales, so her only choice was rolling. Fortunately, this crew structure was temporary, usually only lasting one load.

When Dad finished baling, he joined the crew. In the field, Dad and Red threw the bales onto the trailer with Kathie loading. Dad, being strong and experienced, would place the bales when he tossed them, so Kathie didn't have to strong arm those bales. But Red, being younger, less experienced, and not as strong, did the best that he could, but Kathie had more work with his bales. A normal day's work was 600 to 750 bales, four or five trailer loads as a full trailer load was 150 bales.

The mowing changed also with Dad unloading and Kathie and Red in the mow. Kathie, being older and stronger, could move the bales to Red for final placement. Mary could get a break. After all, she was only seven or eight years old.

After the first day, the crew went to the house and had supper. They had a good dinner earlier in the day and a short rest after dinner. Dad then took Red home. The girls finished up in the house with Mom and, when Dad got home, helped with the evening chores: milking and feeding the hogs.

The next day, Dad went to Red's home to pick him up for work. Red's dad met Dad and proceeded to berate Dad for being a "slave driver." According to Mr. Washler, Red was very tired when he got home because Dad worked him so hard. Dad was perplexed. After all, what they done that first day was a normal day and the girls did as much work haying as he had, and had done chores in the morning, evening, and had helped Mom with the meals. And the girls weren't complaining.

But to Red's credit, he put in another day and again went home tired. On the third day, Dad went to pick up Red. Dad wasn't looking forward to this visit. But this time, Mr. Washler met Dad with an apology. Red told his father that the girls had done everything he had done and, in addition, they had helped with the meals and did morning and evening chores. Red told his father that he'd have to quit school if it got out that he couldn't keep up with girls, one his age and the other seven years younger. He would be the laughingstock.

Red helped with haying for the next several summers.

Dad bought a combine to harvest the small grains: wheat, oats, and barley. At first, he tried hauling the grain with the truck, but that wasn't satisfactory as grain had to either be pushed or shoveled off into the elevator used to fill the granaries. Had the truck been equipped with a dump bed, it would have been fine.

Dad enlisted Bob Kuehner's assistance and expertise. Between Bob Kuehner and Dad, they designed a gravity bed mounted on a 1941 Mercury car that Dad bought. They cut the back half of the body off, leaving a cab over the front, which included the front seat, leaving just the frame and running gears in the back. Then they fabricated a gravity bed and installed it. Total capacity was about 50 bushels, which would hold two of the combine's grain hopper loads. The Mercury had adequate power as it had a 239 cubic inch flat head V8 engine with a three-speed manual transmission.

At 12, Rob got the driving job. He got to drive all over the farm, including on Justus Avenue, the eastern border, the road through the farm and across the fields. Rob's primary companion was Rich, then about 5 years old. Rich was an especially important team member because he watched and directed Rob when backing up to unload. There were no mirrors and the view from inside the car wasn't adequate, so Rich got out and directed, while Rob backed up to the elevator for unloading. from the back. When they'd get ready to take off, you could hear Rich say, "Peel it, Rob!" And off they'd go.

Overall, the set-up worked well. But due to lack of maintenance, after a couple years, the flat-head engine seized and could no longer be used. They cut away the back end from the front and converted it to a trailer, which we pulled with a tractor. It worked very well but wasn't as much fun. Tractors don't peel out.

Animal Care

A steer got loose and ended up in a neighbor's barn. They penned him up and called us to get him. Rob and Dad walked west on Lawndell Road to the neighbors. The only thing they brought was a rope. They put the rope on the steer, who weighed over 400 pounds, and Dad said to Rob, "Lead him home."

The steer never had a rope on him before and wasn't of a mind to be led anywhere. But Dad said, "Do it," so…. Rob got the steer out on the road which had been chip & sealed. This meant the steer's hooves wouldn't get a good grip if Rob could keep him in a vulnerable spot. The steer took off; Rob dug in his heels and yanked the rope. Sure enough, the steer's hooves didn't hold, and he hit on his side—hard. The steer got up, took another run, and got the same treatment. After that, Rob led him home about a mile up the road.

Dad fabricated a makeshift shelter, a pit cut into a bank with railroad ties over the top. It was used to provide shelter for the sows and boar hog. There was an opening in the front that the hogs used and which a person could enter. This pit was nasty; wet and muddy because the roof allowed rain or snow melt to enter. Dad wanted the sows and boar out of the pit. Rich got the job of going in and chasing the hogs out. The pit was warmer than the outside, so the hogs were reluctant to leave, especially the 500 pound boar. Rich didn't want to allow that hog to get between him and the door, as that old hog was scary.

One day, Rich couldn't get the boar to leave the pit. That old hog had Rich buffaloed. Rich came out and told Dad, "You can call me chicken or whatever you want but I'm not going to get that boar out of there." Dad gave Rich a look that said, "What's your problem?" Or more likely using one of Dad's favorite expressions, "What's the matter, have you got shit in your blood?" Dad went into the pit himself. Rich says that old boar came out of the pit like his tail was on fire. Dad scared that old hog.

Fall Grazing

Kathie and Rich got the job of watching cows one evening but weren't using Bill. Rich says he was up late the night before. He thinks they were at Kuehner's in Canton. Rich suffered with sleep apnea and could go to sleep standing up if he were tired. That was his condition this time. He said he told Kathie he was going to lay down in the grass which was over two feet tall. When he laid down, he disappeared, and Kathie lost track of him. When it was time to bring in the cows, Mom asked, "Where's Richard?" Kathie says she waved in the direction where she'd last seen Rich while saying, "Over there." At the time, Mom was expecting Mary, but we had no idea if the baby was a boy or girl. Kathie was seven and Rich was five. Mom and Dad started looking for Rich and were not having any luck. So, Kathie said, "Well, if we can't find Rich, maybe you'll have another boy." Rich recalls they woke him up when they found him, and he couldn't figure out why they wouldn't let him sleep.

Milking

Milking was a year round, seven day a week, twice a day responsibility. It didn't matter if it was summer or winter, the cows had to be milked. All that changed was how the cows were fed. In the spring, summer, and for part of the fall, the cows were taken down the road to the pasture. In the late fall, winter, and early spring, they were fed in the barn.

Dad milked in the morning, but when we were bigger, we milked at night. First, Richard and Robert milked and did the barn chores. After Robert went to college, Kathie helped with the milking and chores. Rich milked in the mornings when he was in high school. By doing so he got to drive to school.

In the dead of winter, it could get extremely cold in the east end of the barn which we used as the milking parlor. It got so cold that, at times, the air vacuum lines froze due to the water that had condensed in them. To thaw them out, we soaked corn cobs in kerosene, lit the kerosene, and used the resulting heat to thaw the lines. Looking back on this practice, we realize we were fortunate not to burn the barn down.

The milking equipment was made by Hinman. Each machine was operated via a pulsator, through which the vacuum operated. In the winter, the pulsator, which used a light grease as a lubricant, would freeze even while in use. To thaw them, we had to take the top off and place our hands around the mechanism. Sometimes one thaw out was enough, but sometimes it had to be done repeatedly. Holding that cold metal nearly froze our hands. We learned to warm our hands by holding them in the space between the cow's udder and hind leg.

Chores included feeding and watering the animals. Kathie hated watering inside the loafing parlor. The water trough was in a dark corner and frequently there were rats around it.

The boys usually threw the silage out of the silo. In the winter, it would freeze to the silo walls and Kathie was not strong enough to get it loose. She tried throwing silage down a few times. Instead, she would put the silage out in front of the stanchions where the cows stood for milking. This also included the chore of putting ground feed, chop, on top of it. Rich and Kathie did this frequently together.

One day, Kathie was filling a bucket with chop from the storage bin when the grain stopped flowing. A piece of what looked like timothy was hanging out at the bottom. When Kathie grabbed the timothy to remove it and unblock the obstruction, the timothy did not pull out; instead, it went up! It was not a hay obstruction. It was a RAT's TAIL. Kathie slammed the bucket up to block the rat's exit and yelled for Rich. He came and helped kill it. Actually, Rich did the killing. Kathie removed the bucket and got out of there. Way to go. Richard to the rescue!

Kathie sometimes milked by herself when Richard was playing ball. Dad faithfully attended the ball games. Mom would come up to help, but she was moral support. Mom had trouble even taking the milking machine off a cow. Sometimes if it was heavy, she had trouble carrying it to the milk can and pouring it in.

We used to tease our Aunt Dudy (Julia) by telling her she didn't know how to milk. To show us she did, she went to the barn with us and said, "Okay, I'll show you I can milk." We gave her a cow with the largest teats to milk. Her teats were so large, she was almost impossible to milk by hand. Aunt Dudy gave it her best and could get a little milk. She was a good sport about it, even though we pulled a prank on her.

We milked a few cows by hand. Occasionally, we would have milk fights–squirting milk at each other across the milking parlor. We got pretty accurate squirting milk. Our cousin, Debbie Bartko,

ROBERT ALAN MCDONALD, KATHIE EILEEN MCDONALD COURTNEY, RICHARD EDWIN MCDONALD, MARY JO MCDONALD HELFRICH

was sitting atop a box stall while we milked. She was talking – meaning her mouth was open – Rob was milking Nellie close to Debbie's perch. He turned quickly and unloaded a full stream right into Debbie's open mouth. She sputtered quite a bit but didn't fall.

One cow delighted in stepping in the bucket when we were about to finish milking her and the bucket was full. She wouldn't do this for days and just when we thought she wouldn't do it again, she did.

We used stanchions for some cows, and on others we used chains. Rob was securing one of the chained cows who had a good set of horns, when she suddenly pulled out and swung her head toward Rob, hitting him a good wallop alongside his nose. The cow got away, and Rob went to the house to work on his nose or get a gun to shoot the cow. Rob wasn't sure which he was going to do. When he got to the house, he looked in the mirror and found the cow had straightened his nose that had been knocked crooked when playing football when he was 12. Since she fixed his nose, Rob decided not to shoot the cow. He really wouldn't have anyway.

We built the machine shed before building the hog pens. We installed a wood burning furnace in part of the machine shed. For a brief time, a year or two, we put farrowing pens in the machine shed heated area. This arrangement enabled larger litter survival sizes and better growth. Kathie remembers finding a dead two-headed pig which she disposed of in the furnace.

In warmer parts of the year, sows continued giving birth outside in the boar and sow lot. Kathie remembers finding one newborn pig in a mud puddle. She had to clear its airway so it could breathe.

Bringing the Dual Wheel Trailer Home

For years, we "borrowed" the dual wheel trailer from George Gonner. But like all good things, the "loan" was called in when Mr. Gonner sold the neighboring farm and auctioned off the equipment. Dutifully, Dad took the trailer and placed it with the rest of the equipment being sold.

THE MCDONALDS

Mr. Gonner must have custom built the trailer because we had never seen another like it. The bed was sixteen feet long and about 8 feet wide. The bed was heavy wood planking framed with 2 inch angle iron on all sides. There were 4 inch by 2x4 inch pockets in the angle iron to hold side boards. At the center front was a roller over which a ½-inch wire rope spooled. It was long enough to reach completely over the bed. It was operated by a hand operated windless. The bed would tilt to the rear with the back reaching the ground. By using the wire rope and tilting the bed heavy equipment could be loaded for transport. On one occasion, we hauled the Minnie Z to the shop for repair. The running gears and hitch were heavy duty. The bed was about 30 inches off the ground making it ideal to haul hay and straw. Being dual wheel single axle, it was easy to back into tight places where putting a four-wheel wagon wouldn't go. Overall, a fine piece of equipment.

Dad bid on the trailer on sale day and bought it. Now all he had to do was take it home. Rich was with Dad, and they had the Minnie so they could bring the trailer home. Dad pulled the Minnie up in front of the trailer after coming up the road in fifth gear (road gear). Dad got off the tractor and opened the gate. He told Rich, who was 6 or 7 years old, to drive the Minnie through the gate. Rich was so small that he had to leave the tractor seat to work the hand clutch, which was engaged by pushing forward. Rich, who was watching closely, said to Dad, "Did you take it out of road gear?" Dad responded, "Of course I did, just pull it through." Rich didn't think it was in the correct gear, but he did as he was told.

After being assured it was in the right gear, Rich left the tractor seat and pushed the clutch in while hanging onto the steering wheel with his left hand. To complete the maneuver, Rich had to push forward and then get back to the seat to steer. He pushed forward, but just as he suspected, the Minnie was in road gear. It leapt forward while Rich was trying to get back to the seat. He then had to reverse the process, going against inertia to pull the clutch to stop the forward motion before any damage was done. Try as he might, Rich just wasn't fast enough. The Minnie hit the hitch on the trailer full force. The impact ruined the tire bending the rim making it unusable.

ROBERT ALAN MCDONALD, KATHIE EILEEN MCDONALD COURTNEY, RICHARD EDWIN MCDONALD, MARY JO MCDONALD HELFRICH

Rich thought he was in serious trouble, but Dad remarked, "Well, I guess I did have it in road gear." From then on, the Minnie only had one wheel on the front.

Passing the Chores

One chore that got passed around was mowing the lawn. When we first moved to the farm in 1947, we had a reel type push mower. Only Mom or Dad could operate the thing. This chore usually fell to Dad because he was much stronger. A power reel mower was purchased. It was an improvement, but it had its drawbacks. It didn't cut very well because it was hard to sharpen. It required constant adjustment. And it was difficult to start. Initially, Rob got this task because he was older. Pretty soon rotary mowers became popular, and we got several of them. They worked well and the yard expanded, which expanded this task. Each of the children got this task. Lawn mowing got passed around because none of us really enjoyed mowing. We did like the place to look nice so whoever had time mowed the lawn.

As time passed, the older siblings left the farm. The chores didn't go away but got distributed to those that remained. Mary, being the youngest, ended up having chores with Mom in the house and with Dad outside.

Other things changed that modified the work, but it still needed doing. Mom went to work at the school and wasn't home during the day. Dad got older and couldn't climb in and out of the hay mows and do all the work he did when younger. But they did buy equipment and change the farm operation, which improved efficiency. One substantial change was conversion from milking to beef cattle and expansion of the hog operation. This change required even more ground feed, but a PTO driven grinder/mixer made this chore easier, and a new corn crib was built making it easier to get corn into the sheller and the grinder/mixer. The grinder/mixer was pulled behind a tractor making it easier to get close to the grain storage areas and distribute the ground feed around the farm.

Mom insisted on a clean house. Baseboards dusted every week, furniture moved out each week and cleaned behind. Mary remembers that she and Mom took turns cleaning the bathroom daily. Mary got to help on Saturday with the wringer washer. Mom ironed on Saturday. A portable dishwasher reduced this chore, but it had to be loaded and unloaded. Each night, Mary helped load the portable dishwasher which Mom usually emptied in the mornings so Dad could put his lunch dishes in it.

Mary did all her homework in a one-hour study hall at school because by the time she completed inside and outside chores, there was no time for homework.

The farrowing house was cleaned daily. Mary's job was to clean each farrowing crate and replace the bedding with ground corn cobs brought down from the second floor, one five-gallon bucket per crate. Mary was excused from milking but got to smell like a "peach." She threw down all the hay to the barn floor to feed cows and horses. Dad would climb the silo in the morning and loosen the silage with a pick and throw out enough for the morning but sometimes would have Mary climb again at night to throw down more. Mary fed the horses: Ginger, Janey, Jonny, and of course Bill. She watered them in the winter. Several times a week, the horses were groomed. At times, Mary helped Dad grind feed or empty the granary to sell wheat or buckwheat. Once the buckwheat was so weedy that Mary coughed up yuck for a couple of weeks until her lungs cleared. When the cows were in the barn, she bedded the cows with straw thrown down. She carried hay out under the overshoot to feed the Herefords.

That's not to say that we worked all the time, but Mom and Dad could find something for us to do if they thought we might get bored.

We grew up being proud of ourselves and each other. No task was too large, and no task was meaningless. It was our responsibility to accomplish each task assigned and to do it right and on time. Work ethic was ingrained. We worked together so much that we didn't need words to coordinate the tasks. We were an integrated unit, watching each other, and adding help when and where

ROBERT ALAN MCDONALD, KATHIE EILEEN MCDONALD COURTNEY, RICHARD EDWIN MCDONALD, MARY JO MCDONALD HELFRICH

necessary. This made everybody's load lighter, and we got a lot done. We didn't always get detailed instructions. Often, we had to figure out the best way of completing work. These were the best lessons as we learned how to be self-sufficient.

As Mary relates: Mom and Dad had a hard life, but they found joy on the farm. Both were independent spirits, and it was the life they wanted. Near the end of her time on earth, Mom was sitting on the porch facing south and commented, "I'm king of all I can see." She was looking over the farm.

Rob notes Mom was so happy that she could remodel the house, have the barn restored and painted, and have the farm well ordered. She was so pleased that Rich did the remodeling. She felt he had the skill and did outstanding work. Mom was proud of his ability, but she might not have told him in words.

Rob got the job painting the barn the last time we did it. The job required priming and then top coating. To ensure a good lasting job, Mom wanted the paint brushed on, which is the way Rob did it. It took 70 gallons of paint all put on with a 4 inch brush. The paint job was done before Mom had cataract surgery. After having it done, she remarked, "Well, it looks pretty good." She couldn't see the barn very well before.

Chapter Eleven – The Woods

We loved the trees. Some we climbed, some we didn't. All were special. And we had favorites. We only climbed those trees that offered a branch or low limb to get started. We didn't cheat by nailing cleats into the trees, somehow that just wasn't fair. Most of the large trees didn't have limbs close to the ground so they were for admiring, not climbing.

Around the house were the buckeyes lining the driveway entrance, that threatened to scrape us off the hay load when we passed under them. The acorns shed in the fall by the chestnut oak that brought the deer into the yard, the two huge sassafras trees with a tire swing hung in the one in the middle of the yard, and the other shading the gas tank. The persimmon and pine where the hammocks hung and the enormous weeping birch with its white bark shaded the north side of the house. And the four maples that lined the road which produced a crop of leaves in the fall that we raked into huge piles that we jumped in many times before a match turned them into fertilizer.

On the west was the giant maple that shaded that side of the house and that we climbed. It must have been five feet through the stump. Its huge limbs allowed us to climb all over with no fear that one of them would break. Sometimes there would be one of us in it. At other times, two or three. Getting a climb started was hard. We would jump up and grab one of the lower limbs, swing our legs over, ride it like a horse, balance on that limb while grabbing another higher one with one hand, then pulling ourselves up. But once we were on that limb, the rest of the climb awaited. We could go up into the canopy and look down on the world or go out on a series of limbs leading westward over the adjacent field, where we could hang suspended by our hand griping the limb until we tired and put our feet on the lower limb.

The mature trees sheltered and protected the house. One of the most unusual occurrences was a lightning strike on the weeping birch. One day when Rob was five or six, a thunderstorm was raging.

ROBERT ALAN MCDONALD, KATHIE EILEEN MCDONALD COURTNEY, RICHARD EDWIN MCDONALD, MARY JO MCDONALD HELFRICH

Rob was in the house with Mom who happened to be looking out one of the north facing windows toward the birch. Just then came a CRACK, and a ball of fire lit up one of the birch's stems about ten feet off the ground. Mom jumped and cried out. It scared her badly. She had been looking right at the spot the lightning hit. Rob, wanting to see what scared Mom, came running toward the window. Mom grabbed him and wouldn't let him near the window. Mom described what she had seen as the fireball just hanging in the tree. There was minor damage to the bark, but, otherwise, the tree didn't seem to be hurt.

Going westward, we would pass the big red oak under which the campers set up. That tree had been there a long time. When it was much smaller than when we knew it, the fence had been nailed to it. Over the years, many handbills had been nailed to it by politicians running for office, or by others giving notice of one thing or another. The tree continued to grow from a fine young tree holding up a fence to a tree of commanding presence with the fence running through the middle with the nails that held the handbills completely buried within it, protecting a campsite.

Further along near the bridge grew a tremendous sycamore specimen. Mary's painting of it can be found in the art chapter. Other similar sized sycamores grew in the north pasture woods. One of them caught the oak Dad was felling, and since it was so large, it couldn't be cut down. We had to resort to blasting to get the oak to the ground. A story found elsewhere.

Trees, like all living things, have a lifespan. Some of the trees described are still alive, like the sycamores by the creek and in the woods and the maples by the road. But others' lives have ended. The red oak that sheltered the camp was struck by lightning. The maple to the west of the house and the weeping birch began to weaken and had to be cut down to prevent them falling on the house. The saffrasses also weakened and had to be removed as did the persimmon and the pine. We didn't like losing any of the trees, it was like losing a friend, but we understood the cycle of life. It's one of the lessons that farming teaches.

Hammocks

Seeing two trees, an old persimmon and a large pine, ideally spaced for hanging a hammock, Dad decided to make one. Somewhere he got a wooden cider barrel. He took the barrel apart, laid the staves out flat and wired them together like links in a chain using no. 9 wire.

No. 9 wire is hard to work with. It doesn't bend easily, but once in place it stays that way. Dad worked several days painstakingly connecting the staves. Once connected, it made a sturdy hammock. All he had to work with was fencing pliers, slip-joint pliers, and a hammer. Next, he used the wire to connect a strong steel ring at each end, which he tied around the trees. Once in place, and with the addition of a pillow, it made a great place to take an afternoon or evening nap. Bob Kuehner tried it out after it had been in use for a couple years. Unfortunately, during those years, one end which connected to the supporting tree had rusted, it broke, dropping Bob to the ground with a thump. Bob initially thought somebody untied it. He was HOT! We hadn't of course, and he eventually calmed down.

Bob Kuehner ran across a WWII jungle hammock in a military surplus store and brought it to The Farm. But we only had two trees properly spaced. That didn't deter Dad and Bob, they hung the jungle hammock above the barrel stave one in the same two trees.

The jungle hammock was designed to be slept in. It had a canvas bottom, a water-resistant top which served as a roof, and sides of mosquito netting. Nothing would do but for Rob and Rich to sleep outside. They used it several times. It worked fine.

Woodlands

Most of the Woods were in the north pasture with some located on the east bank of Sugar Creek accessible through the night pasture.

ROBERT ALAN MCDONALD, KATHIE EILEEN MCDONALD COURTNEY, RICHARD EDWIN MCDONALD, MARY JO MCDONALD HELFRICH

The Woods constituted a substantial portion of The Farm, approximately 25 acres. Swamp land consumed another four acres.

During the warm months, the Woods provided pasture for the cattle and shelter for them during rains and hot or cold days and nights. During the cold months we harvested wood for heating and timber for construction projects. And it was a fun place to go to play. There were wildflowers, blue bells, dog tooth violets, and other blooming plants. There were grapevines in the area surrounded by a meander scar. And just beyond the Woods in the meadow bordered by the creek, bluebirds were plentiful.

On the north, there was an open meadow area which provided pasture, and on a few occasions a spot for a picnic or other activities.

One spring day, Dad was plowing the field south of the road along the creek. The west side of that field is made up of a steep bank making it difficult to manage the tractor and the plow. That bank overlooked a widened area in the road where couples liked to park. Usually parking occurred during the evening, but this day a couple parked and began doing what people attracted to each other often do. Dad couldn't help but notice. After a trip or two, he stopped and called to the man and asked him to come over to where Dad had stopped. The man approached and Dad said to him, "I can't help but notice what you two are doing. I can't watch you and plow this field. So, tell you what, I own the field on the other side of the creek. You drive your car over there, go through the gate, and drive to the back of the field beyond the Woods. That way you won't be bothered, and I won't get hurt either." That's what the man did. Dad enjoyed relating this story.

Various animals lived in the Woods: birds, squirrels, raccoons, opossums, and occasionally deer. If we were quiet, we might spot forest dwelling animals, but we were usually boisterous so we didn't see everything that we could have. There were pests, too. Mosquitos could be plentiful, and the fence rows always had poison ivy.

Prior to our owning the Farm, framing timber for two barns had been harvested from the Woods. Since that time, the trees had replenished themselves, some of the younger trees had grown and matured.

Primary species were elm, hickory, beech, butternut, sycamore, oak, and maple. The largest were the sycamores, which in several cases were so large that their diameter and overall immense size prevented them from being harvested. Many of the largest remained in the Woods, near the creek, and one great tree near the bridge in Lawndell Road remained when we sold the Farm.

Beech trees were found on the ridge overlooking an ancient meander scar (old stream beds that the creek abandoned) where Sugar Creek had reached its farthest westward movement, and a single specimen with several instances into which initials were carved. It was located at the north edge of the Woods. The hickories were in the middle of the Woods where another meander scar, which sometimes still held water, was located. Elms, the oaks, and maples were scattered throughout. Sycamores were on the creek banks.

There were two types of hickory: shellbark and pignut. The shell bark type produced edible nuts. Pig nuts also produced nuts, but smaller, extremely hard to crack and bitter – not edible. All the Woods was creek-bottom land; well-watered sandy-loam. The hickories grew tall and straight, reaching for sunlight. The older larger trees were vulnerable to wind. Those winds would sometimes catch a treetop and over the tree would go. We'd find them lying on their sides with a large root ball. Because the growing conditions were so favorable, the trees didn't need an extensive root system making them susceptible to wind.

Timber on the east side of Sugar Creek wasn't commercially viable but did supply a small amount of firewood.

Willows grew along Sugar Creek when its path took it out of the dense woods. Willow didn't grow well under other taller trees. Willows weren't harvested for either lumber or firewood. But they provided nesting places for bluebirds, which before the flood of 1969, were plentiful in the meadow area of the north pasture.

Swamp land was found in the night pasture west and north of the farmstead, and adjacent to the railroad south of the farmstead and forming the border between the field south of the farmstead across

ROBERT ALAN MCDONALD, KATHIE EILEEN MCDONALD COURTNEY, RICHARD EDWIN MCDONALD, MARY JO MCDONALD HELFRICH

Lawndell Road and the field we called Gobbler's Knob further south. The swamp contained peat which we occasionally harvested for our own use and trees that weren't adequate for commercial use. From time to time, trees in the swampy areas could be used for firewood as could trees that grew in fence rows in various places.

To aid peat harvesting Dad bought a 10 inch hammer mill, cut the bottom out to eliminate the screen, and put the peat in as the hammers rotated. The result was fine shredded peat moss as nice as that sold by any of the garden supply stores.

When we first moved onto the Farm, the swamp next to the railroad across from the farmstead held water. It wasn't deep, less than a foot, which allowed it to freeze clear through. On this pond, Rob learned to skate. Over the years, cattails and other swamp-loving plants grew until there was no standing water left. Nature did what nature does, reclaimed its territory.

Keeping Warm

In the early 1950s, Dad bought a chainsaw from Sears Roebuck and Company. His justification was making firewood and harvesting lumber. Trees have a life cycle and every year trees came down. Instead of allowing them to rot away, we cut them into firewood.

The house was heated by a convection furnace which used either coal or wood for fuel. At first, coal was the primary heat source. There were coal mines not far away located in Tuscarawas and Holmes counties. Dad used the old truck to haul the coal, or he could have it delivered for a fee. One of the mines was reached by going through Dundee, Ohio. Rich recalls our counting the outhouses along the route, which got hearty chuckles out of Dad.

Coal would be stored in the cellar next to the furnace. Access to this area was on the west side through a window size opening in the foundation. Before unloading, coal had to be "washed." Not to clean it but to reduce or eliminate coal dust.

There were drawbacks to hosing down the coal before it entered the house. One, the water, when it drained off the coal, puddled on the cellar floor resulting in a mess that the person who fired the furnace, usually Mom, had to walk through or around. And two, in freezing weather, the water would freeze, turning the load into frozen chunks too big to shovel.

Rich recalls that one frigid winter day, Dad decided to skip the wash. Freezing was prevented, which was Dad's aim, but coal dust went all over the house. Mom was very unhappy and let Dad know. As Rich remembers, that never happened again.

Firing the furnace was a manual effort which very often fell to Mom. For one reason, she was usually awake and up before Dad and during the day she was in the house while Dad was outside working so she knew when it needed fuel. That isn't to say that Dad never fired the furnace or that us kids didn't get a turn now and again. If Mom had problems, say with a large clinker, Dad got the task of getting it out and starting the fire. On cold winter mornings, we listened for Mom shaking the furnace grate so heat would start coming out of the register at the foot of the stairs where we got dressed. When we heard the shaking, we knew there soon would be heat.

One job the kids got was hauling out the ashes and clinkers. Coal ash was much heavier than wood ash. Often coal ash was used on the driveway to cover icy spots and to melt snow and ice. Coal ash was also tossed into the boar and sow pen. The hogs ingested it. Perhaps it supplied minerals that they needed.

There were ways of keeping a coal fire burning besides making a trip to the cellar each time the fire got low. There was a device called a stoker. It required the use of coal crushed so the pieces were of uniform size with no chunks to form clinkers. Rob recalls visiting Aunt El and Uncle Pink during the winter and hearing their stoker automatically charging the furnace. They used coal for heat but only had to load the stoker once a day. Their house had a uniform temperature, and their furnace had a blower which got heat more uniformly all over their house. Rob thought they really lived well.

ROBERT ALAN MCDONALD, KATHIE EILEEN MCDONALD COURTNEY, RICHARD EDWIN MCDONALD, MARY JO MCDONALD HELFRICH

In winter, we cut wood for heating. The house was large, the walls hollow, the attic uninsulated, and the convection heating system inefficient. We burned a lot of wood. We used the large trailer when cutting and hauling wood. The trailer was 16 feet long and about 8 feet wide.

Kathie was often the loader. She had to build a wall around the outside perimeter, about 2 feet high, and then fill up the middle and put more on the outside. A full load was more than half a cord and could be a full cord.

The first chainsaw was a David Bradley from Sears. It was an early model and very heavy. Chain saw technology hadn't progressed to having an all-position carburetor, and the chain had to be oiled by way of a hand operated plunger. So, the saw worked well for bucking, but not so well for felling. Rob and Rich did the splitting while Dad used the saw.

We worked hard and fast. Never had much of a break. Then we took the wood to the house and filled the coal cellar. Kathie recalls how hard Mom had to work. We used coal to hold the fire overnight, which caused heavy clinker formation, which Mom placed in five gallon buckets for disposal outside. Mom carried those ash buckets, which were a lot for her slight frame to carry. We don't understand how Mom did all that work. We did help when we got bigger.

To use up the elm killed by the Dutch Elm Blight, we turned much of it into firewood. Most of that wood needed to be split so it could fit through the furnace door. All we had for splitting was a double bitted axe. No splitting maul for us; mauls cost money. Elm is what we called curly grained – interlocked grain – making it extremely attractive for furniture and shock resistant. However, it doesn't last in contact with the ground, so we left the firewood trees standing as long as possible. Between Rich's freshman and sophomore years of high school, he split elm all winter. Curly or interlocked grain is extremely hard to split. That spring when baseball season rolled around, he had developed unusual strength in his back and legs from all that wood splitting. He had a terrific season pitching Fairless into a long run at tournament time.

Fence rows are prone to trees growing in them and from time to time needed cleaning out. When Rich was about six, Dad was working on the fences adjacent to the railroads in the field across the road, south of the house. Most of the trees were wild cherry, good firewood and easy to split. It wasn't going well. Dad needed a tractor driver because instead of cutting all the trees down, he pulled some out by the root using a tractor. After the tree was out, Dad would cut it into firewood. By pulling out by the root, the tree would take longer to re-grow. Rich, six years old, was in the house, so Dad went in and told Rich to get his coat on and that he was going to drive the tractor – the Minnie – and pull the trees out. Dad was going to hook and unhook the pulling chain. Mom strenuously objected. According to Mom, Rich was too young. At six, she was right. Mom and Dad got into a heated exchange. In the end, Rich went out with Dad, and as Rich found out later, Mom watched from the boy's second floor bedroom window.

Rich says Dad showed him where reverse and second gears were on the Minnie, one to the far right straight up and the other straight down. The Minnie had a hand clutch that engaged by pushing it in and disengaged by pulling back. Rich, being small, had to stand up to operate the clutch in either direction. This meant he had to hang onto the steering wheel with his left hand while operating the clutch with his right. The tractor seat was of no use to Rich at all.

Sometimes the tree would come out of the ground on the first pull. When the tree came out, Dad would holler, "WHOA." If Rich didn't WHOA fast enough, Dad, still angry about the exchange he had with Mom, would add, "G__D___ IT, WHEN I SAY WHOA, I MEAN WHOA!" Other times the tree wouldn't come out and the tractor would start bouncing up and down. At that point, Rich would be hanging on for dear life with his left hand while trying to work the clutch with his right to get it stopped and stop the bouncing. He remembers seeing that rear drive wheel bouncing as it turned and thinking, *If I fall under that wheel it's going to hurt. I better hang on!* When the tree didn't come out on the first pull, Rich would have to back up a little then hit it again until it did come out. Fortunately, Rich didn't fall and survived the experience. But it was something that stuck with him. He did think that he and Dad got a little closer because he was able to get it done. While it was going on, he was worried because Dad was mad at him, and he couldn't understand why he couldn't do what Dad wanted no matter how hard he tried.

Thorn Trees

One day while we were in the woods, Rich spotted a honey locust tree loaded with wicked looking thorns. Honey locust thorns can be either single spikes or have multiple points. This tree was covered with the multiple spike type. It interested Rich, who was around five at the time, so he picked one off the tree and took it with him. This was very likely the first time he'd seen a honey locust thorn.

Rich headed back to the house; the thorn still clutched in his hand. What exactly he planned to do with it, he very likely didn't know, but it was interesting, so he brought it along. After admiring it for a short time, something else caught his attention and he put the thorn down on a convenient flat surface, the seat of Dad's chair.

It wasn't long until Mom had supper ready, so everybody gathered around the table taking their customary places. Dad's chair was shorter than the others, and dark brown which did a good job of hiding the thorn. Dad sat down and immediately shot straight up with an oath, "Damn! What was that!" He reached behind and located the thorn and raised it to see what it was. He recognized it immediately. "Who put that on my chair?" Dad exclaimed. Rich immediately owned up. Not to surprisingly, Dad realized it wasn't intentional, so all Rich got was scolded.

Little did we know that this was just the beginning of our misadventures with thorn bearing trees.

Honey locusts started growing in the south pasture. We didn't realize what a problem they could become so instead of grubbing them out, we let them grow. And grow they did. In just a few years, we had a nice crop of honey locusts with beautiful thorns all over them. Then we decided to do something about them.

Our solution was to hook a chain around the trunk near the ground and pull them out by the roots, which would hopefully kill them and prevent spreading. By this time, Dad had purchased the Massey-Ferguson 65. It had sufficient power, provided the trees weren't too big. So, we began hooking and pulling.

Things were going pretty well until the tractor operator, we think it may have been Dad, but we can't swear to it, pulled in toward the trees instead of backing up to hook on. It was possible to hook the chain to the front or the rear of this tractor.

We hadn't pulled many trees till both front tires were flat. Those honey locust thorns went right through the tires and let the air out of the inner tube. We dismounted the wheels, got the tires off the rims, located the hole and patched it using self-vulcanizing patches, then reassembled it, and remounted it. We got both tires back on the tractor and drove the tractor a couple feet, which is when we discovered we had two flat tires. Two more thorns we figured. So, we repeated the process, fixed the tires again using self-vulcanizing patches, and started again.

Again, we drove a few feet, and the tires were flat. We thought we knew where the thorns were, but we discovered we either weren't finding them all or another thorn would penetrate and cause another hole. We ran out of self-vulcanizing patches. It finally occurred to us that the only solution was going to be to buy and install new tires for the 65. The old ones had so many thorns we couldn't find them all. Having to buy new tires didn't sit well with Dad, but he realized we were never going to get the job done if all we did was fix flats.

After the experience with the honey locusts, a person would think we wouldn't make that mistake again, but we did. But this time it was the north pasture, and the thorns were on the wild crabapple trees. And the tractor this time was the Minnie G750.

The big Woods always had a few wild crabapples in it, but they were in just a couple spots and at first didn't cause problems because we knew where they were and stayed away from them. The thorns on crabapples are single spikes, but they're very sharp, and can be nearly three inches long. Unfortunately, the crabapples began spreading.

Again, we let the wild crabapples spread and by the time we got around to dealing with them, there were clumps or single trees scattered all over what had been open pastureland. And to make matters worse, the trees had gotten big. We surmised that the spreading method was animals or birds eating the crabapple fruit and spreading seeds through their droppings or by simply dropping the crabapples.

The G750 was a good choice for pulling as it had plenty of power. It was a two-man job with one guy, Dad, operating the tractor and another, Rob, hooking the chain or wire rope. Things were going pretty well until we ran over a spike and flattened one of the front tires. But this time we knew what the problem was and how to deal with it. As a result, we got back into business fairly quickly. After a couple days, Rob noticed a pain in his leg just below the knee. He squeezed and a thorn about ½ inch long popped out. It was so sharp it had penetrated, and Rob didn't realize it had done so. Although we spent a fair amount of time pulling the trees out by the roots, we certainly didn't get them all. There are probably groves of crabapples remaining.

Construction

Since there were so many dead elm trees, one of the mainstays in our Woods, and because we could make sheathing lumber from it, some were harvested. There were so many that it took years before we could harvest all the dead trees. Many stood dead and upright for years before falling.

As farming technology advanced and the equipment became larger, storage became more important. Dad's army buddy, Bob Kuehner, was running a side business – ornamental iron work – he

THE MCDONALDS

hoped to turn into a full-time occupation. At the time, we wanted to expand hog production and add machinery storage. Dad and Mom discussed which building project should be first. We children were privy to the discussions but weren't decision makers. It was agreed we couldn't do both at once. Since Bob needed space for his business, it was decided we would build a 30' by 70' machine shed. Bob could rent the 30' by 30' shop, thus generating income, and farm machinery would be stored in the 30' by 40' end. We were going to do a lot of the construction ourselves. It was decided to build the machine shed on the north side of the driveway, where the garden had been.

The building was to be cement block with a second floor accessible for storage. A hip roof would maximize storage space as there would be no roof support as the rafters attached directly to the second-floor joist. Lumber needs included floor joist, rafters, support beams for the center of the 30' by 40' machinery storage, and beams over the doors on the south side, one a 12' foot overhead door and the others sliding doors on overlapping tracks.

Construction began in the fall after most of the harvest was over. We leveled the building area and began digging the footers, by hand of course.

Each winter we went to the Woods. We cut firewood and trees for lumber. We engaged the services of local sawmills who cut the trees into rough sawn dimensional lumber. Most were 2" by 8" or 10" which were for the rafters and joists. Some were cut into beams necessary to span the door openings and as support for the centers. The rest was cut into 1" by whatever length and width the sawyer found appropriate. The 1 inch boards would be used for roof sheathing. After the sawyer was done with his part, we hauled the lumber home and racked it so it would dry without warping. We air-dried all the lumber because we weren't going to use it right away, so it had time to dry, and because kiln drying involved would add hauling and drying cost.

One of the trees Dad marked for lumber was a large white oak. Dad remarked that given the size of the tree, it must have been virgin timber. We knew there was considerable lumber in the tree. Besides

ROBERT ALAN MCDONALD, KATHIE EILEEN MCDONALD COURTNEY, RICHARD EDWIN MCDONALD, MARY JO MCDONALD HELFRICH

the butt log, we estimated it to be a 16 footer. We thought there was another 16 footer and another shorter log. Dad felled the tree, and we cut it into three large logs.

To get it out of the woods and on to the sawmill, we needed to load it onto the dual wheel trailer. We didn't have any equipment that would lift the log, so we needed another way to get it on the trailer. That butt log weighed four to five tons.

Dad cut down two smaller trees that were 6 to 8 inches through. We placed those smaller tree logs spaced equally on one side of the trailer with one end perpendicular to the oak butt log and the other end resting on the bed of the trailer. This made a loading ramp. We fastened each end of a ½ inch wire rope to the trailer and pulled the resulting loop under the center of the log and back toward the trailer. We hooked a chain into the center of the loop, hooked the chain to a tractor, and rolled that log right onto the trailer by driving the tractor away from the trailer. It worked like a charm. The log rolled right up the ramp. We secured it in place using chains and chain binders. We were ready to take it out of the Woods.

The day Dad picked to move the log out of the Woods was warm. Although it was still winter, the weather had warmed, and the frost was out of the ground. The soil in the Woods was sandy with the recent thaw. It was loose. But the log needed to be taken to the sawmill, and this was the day Dad picked, so...

We hooked one tractor to the trailer and the second tractor we hooked in front of the first using a chain. Given the condition of the ground, the weight of the load and the fact we were going to pull it through standing water, Dad felt we needed power, coupled with all the speed we could muster. We knew the standing water wasn't deep, about 6 inches at most, but it spread about 15 feet across. The ground underneath was wet and soft.

At Dad's signal, we started. Rob driving the lead tractor, Dad driving the one hooked to the trailer. Everything started off okay. We moved that load, then came the standing water. Rob's tractor got most of the way across, Dad's about halfway, but when the dual wheels of the trailer hit the standing water and sank a bit, everything stopped. The tractor wheels spun with no forward progress. We stuck both tractors and the dual wheel trailer.

Now what? We had all our power stuck at the same time in the same place. We had no way to get it out. Fortunately, the neighboring farm owned by Mr. Chuck Gonner had a John Deere 70 tractor. Dad walked to his farm and explained that he needed a pull. Mr. Gonner agreed to help us out. Rob recalls the feeling of relief seeing that big 70 pull in. We hooked it to our lead tractor with a chain long enough so that the 70 was on solid ground and it pulled the whole mess right out. Rob recalls thinking, *Why did we ever pick this day and why did we ever think we could move a load that heavy through what was a swamp?* Had the ground been frozen and the water solid ice, there wouldn't have been a problem, but it wasn't, and we sure put ourselves in a pickle.

That white oak tree made a great deal of framing lumber including the beam over the overhead door that allows access to the workshop. When we got the log to the sawmill, we measured it at 54 inches across the butt. Easily the largest log we ever harvested and one of the largest the sawyer had ever worked.

The sawyer, Lou Pershing, was a small man. When Dad was telling him about the size of this log, the sawyer commented, "I never saw a log I couldn't chin!" On the ride home, Rich recalls Rob asking what he meant to "chin a log"? Dad said he meant he could stand beside the log and put his chin on top of it. When we unloaded the log, he tried to 'chin' this log and was just barely able to do so.

Blasting

One building Dad built was a machine shed. It was located on the north side of the driveway leading to the house. The foundation footer was 30 feet wide by 70 feet long, which we dug by hand using picks and shovels. There was an interior footer which divided the building into a 30 foot by 30 foot workshop and a 30 foot by 40 foot storage area for machinery. The footer was poured concrete 36

ROBERT ALAN MCDONALD, KATHIE EILEEN MCDONALD COURTNEY, RICHARD EDWIN MCDONALD, MARY JO MCDONALD HELFRICH

inches deep. It had to be 36 inches because that's frost depth in that part of the country.

Dad, who had no block laying experience, laid all the blocks over a couple of years to a 12 foot height. There was also a second story covering the entire building. We performed construction on a time available basis—the other farm work came first. Construction projects and other maintenance projects were often done in the fall when the harvest was complete and the weather stable.

Rob recalls mixing mortar for Dad and carrying blocks. When finished, the diagonal measure indicated a variance of only one-quarter inch from a perfect square. Surprisingly good for a first timer.

The building required lumber for the floor joists and rafters. The majority came off the farm. In the winter, besides cutting wood for heating the house, we also cut timber for building. We would fell selected trees, cut them to length 8, 12, or 16 feet, load them on the dual wheel trailer, and haul them to the lumber mill where the material was cut to rough sawn lumber. We hauled the lumber back to the farm and ricked it to dry and cure. The tops we made into firewood.

An oak tree that Dad cut didn't fall properly. As it started to fall, the top fell a few feet then caught in an enormous sycamore. The oak twisted causing it to come off the stump driving the butt into the ground to a depth of about 4 feet. The oak came to rest at a 45 degree angle.

There was no moving that tree with any of the equipment we had or could locate. The sycamore tree that it was hanging in was too large to cut down, as there was no chain saw in the area with a bar long enough to go even half-way through it.

A fellow Dad knew came by with a tow vehicle he'd made. It had an A-frame winch. When Dad told him about the tree being hung in another one, he told Dad, "No problem. I'll hook onto the log with the winch and pull it right out of the ground." He'd built an A-frame winch onto the tow truck to lift cars and trucks. He hooked it up, but when he started the lift, instead of the tree moving, the winch bent to the ground. The tree didn't move at all. That poor guy left with a broken tow truck. And we still had a hung-up tree.

Dad decided the only way to get the tree down was by blasting. Dad asked Barney, Arch Croy, knowing that he worked for a mining company that used explosives, if he could get prima-cord from the mine. Arch said he could and, in a few days, came back with it. Rob got the job of climbing the tree, wrapping the prima-cord around two primary limbs that were stuck in the other tree. Rob set the blasting cap, climbed down to the ground, where Dad waited. One limb was 12 inches and the other 8 – 10 inches thick. Dad set off the charge. The resulting blast knocked bark off the limbs but otherwise did no damage. The tree remained where it was.

Seeing that the prima-cord wouldn't do the trick, Dad asked Barney if he could get dynamite. Barney said he would try. Days later he came back with 5 sticks of 60% nitro dynamite and some more prima-cord. Again, Rob got the job climbing the tree. With Dad directing things, Rob placed two sticks on one limb and three sticks on the other larger limb, wrapped both with prima-cord, set the blasting cap and came down to the ground. Dad set the charge off using the tractor battery. It worked. The resulting blast not only rattled the windows in our house, the neighbors' houses, but cut those two limbs like they'd been hit by a big axe. Dad knew exactly what he was doing. We got the tree down and nobody got hurt. When we went into the woods, we passed groups of folks that were fishing on our property. After the blast, they were nowhere to be found.

Right after the blast, we noticed small "leaves" falling from the sycamore. When these "leaves" hit the ground, they ran away. That's when we realized we had flying squirrels in the Woods.

Although most of the building was concrete block construction, which Dad laid, it was two stories, so we needed framing lumber, which we cut in our own Woods. Later when we decided to build a hog building, we cut that lumber, also.

Working in the Woods in the winter was enjoyable work. Doing all the tasks leading to a completed building resulted in a great deal of satisfaction. It was nice to step back after construction was

ROBERT ALAN MCDONALD, KATHIE EILEEN MCDONALD COURTNEY, RICHARD EDWIN MCDONALD, MARY JO MCDONALD HELFRICH

completed to see the result of all the demanding work. Some of these projects extended over multiple years. And we learned a bit about various trades. We would lay out a building, harvest timber, season the wood after it was sawn, lay block, perform rough carpentry, and even do plumbing and electrical rough-ins.

After Dad got the block laid, we framed the building using the lumber we had gathered over a couple of years. In addition, Dad found out about tongue-and-groove 2" lumber available at the railroad when refitting boxcars. We were able to get enough of it to floor the second story of the machine shed. We put up all the framing and installed the second floor.

None of us, including Dad, knew how to lay out the rafters. We wanted to make them up on the second floor then put them up all at one time. Dad called Russ Salberg, Grandma Nellie's brother-in-law, who ran the carpentry shop at the steel mill in Massillon. Russ knew the right formula and promptly prepared the layout for us. We made up the rafters and when we had that done, we raised them.

Some of the rafters were oak, but the majority were sycamore as we didn't have enough oak. We knew oak gets extremely hard when it dries. We found out that sycamore does, too. We were using 20 penny spikes to attach the rafters to the floor joist. We drove those spikes with 5-pound hammers. We didn't drill pilot holes, so we bent plenty of those spikes. Eventually, we got the rafters in place.

We used all the 1" lumber we had for sheathing, but it wasn't enough. Dad had to buy sheathing lumber to finish the roof, and he got an Amish crew to install it and install the shingles. We got the overhead door installed, but not the sliding doors and we didn't finish the east end second floor exterior wall. But the building was used without doors. Years later, Rich finished it. A picture of the finished building can be found in the pictures section in Chapter 23.

Bob Kuehner quit doing ornamental iron, so he never used the building. Because the workshop had a furnace, it was used for various things— even hog farrowing before the hog building was completed.

We had studied hog operations and had ideas as to what we wanted. By the time we got ready to build, Rob was in college; so for one of his projects in the College of Agriculture, he drew plans for the facility, using the information gathered previously.

Dad and Rich, who was still at home, did most of the construction work; The Woods was used for lumber and local sawmills were used as before. Eventually, the hog operation got built and put into operation. The building was primarily cement block. The finishing pens were metal roofed with the east side open. The roof was low to retain heat in the winter. The farrowing and growing pens were in a fully enclosed portion of the structure on the south side. Heat was supplied by LP gas burners.

Concrete Work

Mr. LaFord, who owned the farm behind Ed Miller's, was in the trucking business. He hauled Portland cement in tank trailers. Portland cement is used when making concrete.

Over time, the weight of cement and vibration from the road caused the welds on the interior compartments to break down, allowing the cement to penetrate the end compartments which are supposed to remain empty. Mr. LaFord needed to get the cement out of these end compartments for two reasons. One, it was heavy and decreased the amount of product being hauled. And two, it prevented the panel from being easily welded back in place.

Mr. LaFord's problem was getting the cement out of the compartment. Only a small person could get into the compartment through the manhole. Dad seized upon this opportunity. He had Rich, who was in his early teens, fit through the manhole, and was strong, but most importantly Dad needed Portland cement. Dad wanted to pave the barnyard, inside the barn, and the floors in the new hog operation. He and Mr. LaFord quickly came to an agreement: Dad could have the cement for taking it out of the small compartments.

When Mr. LaFord had a trailer needing service, he brought it to the Farm. Rich would get into the end compartments with a small

ROBERT ALAN MCDONALD, KATHIE EILEEN MCDONALD COURTNEY, RICHARD EDWIN MCDONALD, MARY JO MCDONALD HELFRICH

bucket which he would fill and pass to Dad. Dad would fill his buckets then carry them into the machine shed where he had a supply of 55 gallon drums which could be sealed with locking rims. Each compartment would net 20 to 30 gallons of Portland cement and there were two compartments in each trailer: a 55 gallon drum per trailer. Over time this operation netted a dozen 55 gallon drums of Portland cement.

Rich said Dad told him not to worry about cement lung, he was too young to get it. Rich says he came out of the trailers looking like a gray ghost.

Dad bought a cement mixer which mounted on the Massey-Ferguson 65 tractor. The capacity of the mixer was 1 bag of cement (94 pounds) to which sand and gravel plus water were added to yield ⅓ yard of concrete. Mine-run sand and gravel were obtained from Berry Hill on the Farm.

As a result of this activity, the barnyard, the floors inside the barn, the floor of the farrowing house, and two of the finishing pen floors were poured. The primary crew was Dad, Rich, and Dick Courtney, Kathie's husband. Rich recalls Dick doing a particularly excellent job building a concrete dam out of green concrete around the water trough in the barn. It was a challenging task, one that Dick had no experience doing, but that turned out very well.

Rich recalls the work being done piecemeal, a couple hours in the evening completing a space about 4 feet wide. For the work around the watering trough, Rich, the mixer operator, would dump a load for Dick and then dump a second load for Dad to work while Dick worked on the first.

Rob was the cement finisher on the floor of the farrowing house, as he was home at the time. He also helped with the finishing pen floors. After the reclaimed Portland cement was used up, Dad had to buy ready-mix concrete to complete the finishing pens.

Another concrete job was pouring the porch floor on the south end of the house. This job went along well until Rob and Rich started working on a case of beer. Dad didn't partake as he remarked,

THE MCDONALDS

"There really wasn't enough left for me!" Neither Rob nor Rich were even close to sober. Mom was alarmed and hid Rob's car keys. Hiding the keys wasn't necessary as both boys knew they had all the beer they wanted and had no intention of going anywhere. Mom, being a mother, was a bit upset, but Dad came to their rescue. He told Mom, "Let them go, they're just being brothers."

Farm fences constantly need repair or rebuilding. Every spring, before the cows could be put out on pasture the fences were checked. Sometimes repairs were sufficient and at other times major repairs involving new posts and wire or a complete rebuild of a section was required. We always had to have on hand fence posts and new wire. The source of posts was either used railroad ties or new locust posts cut off Arch Croy's farm.

Arch's farm had been strip mined. After the coal was removed, the mining company was required to sow grass seed and re-forest on the steep grades. Reforestation was primarily done by planting locust trees. Locust made excellent fence posts, often lasting ten to twenty years. They were hard, durable, and rot resistant. Periodically, when our fence post supply was depleted, we would take the chain saw and cut locust posts.

Harvesting fence posts was arduous work because we were constantly on steep banks, often so steep we couldn't use tractors to pull the logs. We would cut down the tree, trim the branches, and get the tree to the trailer for loading. We didn't cut them to fence post length, usually about eight feet, until they were at the trailer. We would haul the load back home and unload where the posts were exposed to weather. In a year, the bark would loosen allowing removal. After that, the posts were ready for use.

ROBERT ALAN MCDONALD, KATHIE EILEEN MCDONALD COURTNEY, RICHARD EDWIN MCDONALD, MARY JO MCDONALD HELFRICH

Chapter Twelve – Other Goings On

We were active. If we weren't working, we would be doing something else. Usually, it was something outside. Most of the time it was harmless fun. But it could get downright dangerous. We were blessed by good fortune and didn't get hurt too badly.

The season dictated the games played and activities. In spring and summer, we played baseball. First at home in the front yard. Of course, we didn't have enough people to play a full game, so we improvised. And we worked on our skills: playing catch, which grew into pitching drills for Rich and, of course, hitting. Later, we played in organized teams. Dad would reorganize the work if there was a baseball game, especially if Rich was pitching.

In the winter, we ice skated, and rode the sled down every hill we could find. Mary was the best skater. Mom and Dad didn't have the resources to get Mary in a training program, but she got instruction while at college. In the fall, we played football and practiced kicking, throwing, and catching.

Parachuting Impact

Rob became curious about parachuting. He had been reading on the topic and discovered that the landing impact was about the same as jumping from a 10-13 foot height. In the barn, the second story timbers spanned a 40 foot width. The timbers were approximately 14 feet from the barn floor. So, to experience the impact, Rob jumped off a timber to the barn floor. The barn floor was locust, a dense wood with little to no flexibility. About as hard as concrete. Rob hadn't considered that landing on the ground would have less impact than the barn floor. Fortunately, Rob didn't suffer an injury but decided, based on how badly he had been jarred, that one jump was enough!

Rich saw Rob jump and decided that it was a demonstration of toughness so he figured, if Rob could do it, he could too. Rich made his jump without letting anybody know what he intended. Rob says that had he known Rich was going to try it, he would have tried to

ROBERT ALAN MCDONALD, KATHIE EILEEN MCDONALD COURTNEY, RICHARD EDWIN MCDONALD, MARY JO MCDONALD HELFRICH

stop it, but he didn't know about it until years later. Luckily, Rich didn't incur a significant injury, and he also decided that once was enough. Rich recalls adding a bit of hay or straw to the landing area, which did no good at all.

Since the boys would go up and walk the timbers that divided the barn floors and hay mows, Kathie also tried it. She says she was scared but did it because her brothers goaded her into it. Rich and Rob never understood why she would listen to the two of them. Mom called us Yaps and dumb ones at that!

When she successfully mastered walking across the timbers, her brothers urged her to jump off but into the hay mow. She recalls doing it once just to prove she could do it. She doesn't recall how far the drop was into the hay but also decided that once was enough.

Another jumping game we played was flips off the top of the oat granary at the west end of the barn into the hay mow. It was fun.

We also enjoyed turning flips using Rob as the pivot man. Rob would lie on his back with his knees up. Rich and Kathie would run to Rob, put their hands on his knees and flip over with Rob, pushing them upright with his arms. This game could last quite a while.

Rob and Rich played mumbly-peg when they got Barlow pocketknives. These were two-bladed pocketknives; one longer than the other. To play the game, both blades were folded out with the longer fully open and the shorter blade half-way. The knife would be placed with the short blade touching the wood surface and flipped using a finger placed under the back of the knife.

The game is scored like baseball. Landing on the long blade alone was a home run, short blade a double, both blades touching a triple, short blade and back of the knife touching the surface a single. Landing any other way was an out. Kathie recalls trying to learn the game from Rich who played in the feed way using the wood floor.

We had badminton sets we enjoyed playing. We would set it up on the lawn between the house and Lawndell Road. We also took badminton to Atwood Lake and would play there while on vacation.

THE MCDONALDS

We used to go to the small swamp across the road from the house and gather cattails. We'd take them to the butcher-house and soak them in kerosene. Now and then we'd get the cattails out, light them, and run around the yard. Pretty soon, Mom would yell, "Put those out and throw them away!" We did. Then in a couple of days, we would gather some more, put them in coal oil, and do it again.

One of Rich's favorite activities involved stones; he liked to hit them with a broomstick or throw them. Rich says he does not know how many sticks he wore out. Dad once said that Rich depleted all the stones from the barn bank by hitting them over the hog lot onto the railroad. He was aiming for the cars on the siding. After running low on the barn bank, Rich began hitting the stones from a gravel pile Dad had delivered for concrete work that was being done. Rich developed a game where hitting a certain rail car was a single, another a double and so on.

One evening, just as we'd finished milking, we needed to take the cows to the night pasture. Rich was throwing stones from the barnyard at a target he'd picked out on the shed/corncrib right across the driveway. Rob recalls getting annoyed with Rich because he wouldn't come and help. Rich recalls it was his job to drive the cows from behind while Rob ran ahead and opened the gate into the night pasture. Rob yelled something like, "Come on!" in a demanding tone. Rich threw one last stone, and while watching it hit, the target began running. Rich was running in one direction and looking in the other. When he turned his head to see where he was going, he was running full tilt and came face-to-face with the post that stood right in the middle of the barnyard.

Rich went down hard! Rob says he'll never forget the sound of Rich's head hitting that post. Like the sound you hear when thumping a watermelon to determine ripeness – THUNK, only louder! Rob yelled for Dad, picked Rich up, and carried him to the gate and lifted him over to Dad. That was one time Dad spent money on a doctor. Mom called Doc Hill, in Beach City, and Dad drove Rich there. He'd split his head open about the middle of his forehead. Rich recalls Doc trimming the cut and putting in about five stitches. Mom was sure it was going to leave a nasty scar. Rich looked rough when he got home but he healed without noticeable scaring. Doc did an excellent job.

Getting Into the Haymow

The dumbest thing Rob did was to attempt to hoist himself into the haymow using a rope and a pulley. Mom and Dad went somewhere leaving Rob and Rich at home. Kathie was at Aunt Eleanor's. Rich was four of five, which meant Rob was eleven or twelve.

The boys went to the barn and Rob got a rope, which unfortunately had to be spliced together using a knot to make it long enough to go through the pulley and back to the floor.

He got the rope through the pulley then tried his invention. He got part way up, the rope stuck, Rob let go, and fell backwards landing on his upper back and hitting the back of his head hard. Rich says he recalls the sound when Rob's head hit the barn floor— a loud THUNK.

Rob recovered but was so dazed or dizzy he couldn't see properly. He told Rich that he couldn't see, but at first Rich wasn't buying it. Rob used to pull pranks on Rich and Rich decided he wasn't falling for it. But finally, Rich became convinced and led Rob to the house.

They went upstairs and Rob went to bed after telling Rich to stay upstairs. Rich remembers playing in what became Kathie's room until Mom and Dad came home. Rich remembers hollering hello to them out one of the bay windows. Dad asked Rich, "Where's Robert?" Rich responded, "He's sleeping." This was very unusual, as Rob didn't sleep during the day, and he was supposed to be watching Rich.

Rich recalls Dad calling Robert from the bottom of the stairs and getting no response. Dad came up and found Rob asleep. When Dad tried to wake Rob, he began convulsing. Dad picked Rob up and took him downstairs to the bathroom, where they put Rob in the bathtub filled with ice water. Rich thinks Mom may have called Doc Hill to ask what to do or that Dad's military training kicked in. After a while, it worked. The convulsions stopped. They took Rob to the doctor, who put Rob in the hospital. Fortunately, the concussion didn't do permanent damage, or so Rob says.

Horsemanship

We all rode horses. First, it was Bill. Then Kathie got Ginger. Bill and Ginger produced Jonny and finally Janey. When smaller, we found it easier to mount if we used the back porch. We could step right off the porch onto the horse's back. This was before we enclosed the back porch. For the girls, and when we were younger, our legs were short, so this really helped.

Rich recalls discussing after school activities with classmates. He was a bit envious when they made plans to get together after school to play football or baseball depending on the season. When they asked him what he was going to do, Rich told them he was going to get the pony out and watch cows. He was surprised how envious they were, telling him he sure was lucky to have a pony to ride.

Winter Sports

Winter in Ohio can get cold. But we looked forward to it for the outdoor sports: sled riding and especially ice skating.

Our favorite ice-skating spots were originally the pond across the road from the house, the pond in the night pasture, and the creek. The pond across from the house was a good spot when we first moved to the Farm. It wasn't deep, which meant it would freeze quickly and if the ice broke, you weren't in danger.

The pond in the night pasture was also good if there was water in it. Some years the pond dried up. When there was water, it was large, not hard to get to and it wasn't deep, so it froze quickly and wasn't dangerous. It had a nice sloping bank where we could build

ROBERT ALAN MCDONALD, KATHIE EILEEN MCDONALD COURTNEY, RICHARD EDWIN MCDONALD, MARY JO MCDONALD HELFRICH

a fire so we could stay warm when resting. A great pond for skating parties.

When Mary got old enough to skate, four years old and older, Kathie and Rich got the task of taking her with them when they went skating. The process usually went like this. Kathie and Rich would carry Mary's skates, and they would walk down to either the pond or creek. Once they got there, they would put Mary's skates on making sure they were tied securely. Then Mary would start skating. Kathie and Rich would start putting on their skates and start skating. About that time, Mary's feet would be cold so she would complain. There was nothing to do but help Mary take off her skates, after taking off their own, and carrying her to the house because her feet hurt so bad she couldn't walk. Mary says Kathie and Rich must have really hated her because of this, but neither ever mentioned it.

Despite the discomfort, Mary was a particularly good skater. So good that Kathie suggested that she take skating lessons when in college. She did take lessons and became even better. Since she started taking lessons late, she didn't reach her full potential. Once during Mary's college career, she was in a special performance put on by the college. Rich recalls going down to OU with his girlfriend, Jackie, and taking Mom so she could see Mary's part in the show. Mary had practiced diligently, but unknown to her, a small sliver of wood had gotten caught in the runner of one skate. That little sliver of wood threw Mary off, preventing her from showing Mom her full talent. She didn't find out about it until the performance was over.

One year we were skating on the night pasture pond and our cousin, Gretchen Lab, came down to skate. Gretchen was the oldest of our cousins, in college at the time. We were having a wonderful time when Gretchen took a hard fall. She got up but was in a great deal of pain. Her shoulder was out of joint. She asked us to help her up to the house where Mom and Dad were, which we did. When we got there, she told Dad how to pull her arm and put it back into place. Rob recalls the incident vividly, never having seen a person with a dislocation before. But Gretchen, although in pain, was very matter of fact and got it resolved without the need for medical assistance.

Skating on the creek was the best when the weather cooperated. The creek froze over every winter, but the quality of the ice wasn't always the same. We hoped for a cold snap, 15° F or lower and little to no wind for a couple of days. When we got that weather, the creek ice was hard, deep, and smooth as glass. You could really fly on it.

The Girl in the Haymow

Mary and her two good friends, her cousin, Emily (Em) Foster and Barbara Altland (Altland), were on the second floor of the barn. Em and Altland were the same age and in the same grade. Although Mary was two years younger, they were close friends. Altland's family lived in Harmon, a short distance from Em. Mary and Emily were athletic, used to horseback riding and farm work. Altland wasn't as athletic but was extremely bright and was excellent both as a student and in the band.

The haymow in the west end was full. The adjacent barn-floor, used as the straw mow, was five bales high, about 4 feet, on the north end below the ladder. The ladder, built into the barn frame, was used to climb into the haymow. The bottom rested on the barn floor, and the top was morticed into the 12 inch by 12 inch square at the top. Each side was 4minch by 4 inch oak with rungs, also oak, spaced 12 inches apart. The ladder was in good repair, no damage anywhere.

Mary and Em went up the ladder to throw out hay for feeding. Altland, who normally didn't climb into the haymow, decided to go up, too.

At the top, a person had to go around and over the 12"x12" beam— what we called the square — to get into the mow. Mary and Emily easily accomplished that task, having done it many times before. Altland somehow made it over the square and went into the mow. After getting into the mow, she was petrified and somehow managed to cling to the supports that tied into the square and supported the barn roof. She wrapped her arms and legs around the

ROBERT ALAN MCDONALD, KATHIE EILEEN MCDONALD COURTNEY, RICHARD EDWIN MCDONALD, MARY JO MCDONALD HELFRICH

timbers that held up the barn roof, clinging to those beams for dear life!

Mary and Emily tossed out hay bales and climbed down traversing the square in reverse. This was nothing new to them, but as Mary recalled, it was always hard getting around the square backwards. It would be easy to miss a rung or lose your grip. Mary was always a little leery of going over the square.

The thought of letting go of the support beams wasn't something Altland wanted to do. Mary and Em were down. Altland's arms and legs remained wrapped around the support timbers. Mary never got close to that support; she remembers being even more scared of that space than going over the square.

Altland tried to move but something in her brain said, "NO! "What are you, Nuts? I'll have to let go of this nice safe timber to get to the top of the ladder." There she remained, wrapped arms and legs around the support timber. There she stopped. The two in the straw mow tried encouraging her. "You can do it. Don't worry, your foot will find the rung. Don't be afraid. You won't fall." When that didn't work, they tried shaming her into it. "Don't be chicken. Anybody can do it." And other similar comments like that didn't work either.

There they were- one standing on the square and clinging to the timbers which supported the roof and the other two down on the bales in the straw mow not grasping the gravity of the situation. Somehow, they still thought shaming and heckling was going to get her down and out of the mow. This wasn't going to end well.

Dad heard the commotion and came into the barn. He saw what was going on. His first words were, "You two shut up! We've got to get her down from there." Mary believes this is the only time that Dad got after Emily. Mary and Em immediately became quiet. Dad climbed up the ladder to the square and began explaining how he was going to help Altland get down. He went into the mow and escorted her, getting her arms and legs unwrapped from around the timber, and over to the place where the square met the ladder.

THE MCDONALDS

Dad tried several approaches. First, he suggested he would climb down the ladder just far enough for Altland to stick her leg over the square and he would guide her foot to a rung. That way she would be in front of Dad and couldn't fall while they climbed down. Altland wouldn't do that, Dad didn't think he could carry her in his arms safely, so that was out. Dad stood on the ladder and Altland went over the square to perch on his shoulders.

Because she was so frightened, Altland put her hands over Dad's eyes. He couldn't see anything. Dad calmly said, "You're going to need to move your hands so I can see what I'm doing." That didn't work. Altland's hands remained over Dad's eyes. The least safe way that there was of getting her down, but it worked. Finally, the girl was out of the haymow and safely on the barn floor.

Pranks

We spent time in the woods and swamps on the farm. There were trees to climb, grape vines to swing on, wildflowers, and wildlife to learn about. We also found it was fun to prank our cousins and friends who lived in town.

Rob liked to get the city people out at night and get them to run or walk into one of the mud puddles. People who live in the city don't see well at night, but Rob knew where all the mud puddles were or could see them fine. He'd take off running and either jump over the shortest parts or run around and city kids would run right into them.

Down in the woods near the north line fence was a cable used by the underground gas line inspectors who walked the right-of-way at scheduled times during the year looking for leaks. This ended when they began using airplanes, but the cables remained. We crossed the creek all the time using the cables.

There were two cables, one above the other about 42 – 48 inches apart attached to trees on either side of the creek. To cross, you had to get up on the cable and hang on to the top while walking on the bottom.

ROBERT ALAN MCDONALD, KATHIE EILEEN MCDONALD COURTNEY, RICHARD EDWIN MCDONALD, MARY JO MCDONALD HELFRICH

It was easy to get up on the cable at the west end, so we'd show the city kids how to get on and begin walking across. They'd get on and start out over the creek. We'd get on behind them and start bouncing the cables. They'd get scared, fearful of falling in the creek, and start yelling. This is exactly what we wanted. We don't recall anyone falling in, but if they did, the risk wasn't great. The creek was only a couple of feet deep under the cable and the drop was less than 7 feet.

Rich knew of a bee tree: an old, dead, hollow tree bees used as a hive. Rich had several guys with him when they went into the Woods. Rich came upon the bee tree and pushed it over. Since he knew what was going to happen as soon as he pushed it, he took off as fast as he could go. Until the tree hit the ground, the others didn't know about the bees. They sure found out! Those bees stung every one of them. For the slow ones, it was worse.

Dad and Grandpa Dan wired the house for electricity. Somehow the light switch at the bottom of the stairs leading to the second floor had a short that only happened if the person using the switch was standing on the metal register in the floor. If the person stood on the first step, nothing happened. But they got a mild shock if they stood on the register, which was the natural place to stand due to the height of the light switch. We all knew this and always stood on the step when using the switch. But visitors didn't know this and to Kathie's particular delight, she enjoyed having a guest learn where to stand when working the light switch.

Frog Gigging

While there was water in the pond in the night pasture, frogs were plentiful. And, from the sound of them, they were big. Dad, Bob Kuehner, and Ray Geis decided a feast of frog legs would be a good thing. So, on the appointed evening we went frog gigging. We had lights to 'shine' the frogs so they would sit still till we could gig or whack them over the head and bag them. Then we took the catch to the house where the frogs were killed, and the legs harvested. We had a large dinner of frog legs and French fries cooked in peanut oil. Kathie remembers helping gig the frogs at other times by shining the light in the frog's eyes and holding the bag open when the boys got the frogs.

Shooting

Around age ten, Rob got a pellet gun. A couple years later, he got a .22 rifle. Of course, Dad explained firearm safety and the rules. A gun is loaded until you check and make sure it isn't. Never point a gun at anything you don't want to kill. You can kill all the starlings you can hit, along with all the pigeons, rats, and groundhogs. Do not shoot to hit the barn roof when hunting pigeons. Punishment for disobeying firearm rules was loss of the gun.

Along with the .22, Rob got a cleaning kit and was taught how to use it; even though Dad wasn't much on cleaning his guns, he was all for someone else cleaning them. Rob's gun was a bolt action, 7-shot repeater with iron sights. When Rich got old enough, he also got a .22 nearly identical to Rob's but his came with a telescopic sight.

Kathie and Rich also learned to shoot using the pellet gun and later the .22. One of the frequent visitors was Bobby Kuehner, who, a couple of years younger than Rob, also had a pellet gun. His was a Sheridan and Rob's was a Crossman. But both were .22 caliber and accurate. Starlings were not safe on Sundays.

It wasn't long before Rob and Bobby discovered rat killing. The floor slab in the old hog barn had cracked due to rat tunneling activity and dropped a few inches. At night, rats would come through the crack into the hog pen and eat spilled hog food. The boys discovered they could sight their pellet guns on the crack, turn off the light, wait a few seconds, turn on the light, and shoot a rat. They would take turns because the pellet guns were single shot and took time to load. With two people shooting, they could kill more rats.

Later, Rich joined the party and was the light operator. As he got older, he learned rat killing.

ROBERT ALAN MCDONALD, KATHIE EILEEN MCDONALD COURTNEY, RICHARD EDWIN MCDONALD, MARY JO MCDONALD HELFRICH

Kathie knew what the boys were doing. Realizing there were rats in the chicken coop, she used the pellet gun on them. But there was a problem. The pellet gun was only supposed to be pumped a maximum of 10 pumps. Ten pumps wouldn't always kill a rat. So, Kathie added a few. She didn't want to have to shoot twice. The extra pumps put the pellet gun out of commission, eventually. So, Kathie switched to the .22 rifle loaded with long rifle hollow points. She became a qualified rat killer.

Mom got a new chicken feeder. Kathie spotted a rat on the new feeder getting a meal, so being a qualified rat killer, Kathie shot the rat and killed it. Unfortunately, the bullet went through the rat and damaged the feeder. Mom wasn't too happy about the damage. But the feeder only lost a small amount of feed, so its use continued.

Baseball

Both Rob and Rich played Little League baseball. Rob played in Beach City and Rich played in Brewster. Rob's career was short; two years when he was eleven and twelve. Before Rob was eleven, Beach City didn't have a Little League team, but one was formed when he was in the fifth grade. With Dad's encouragement, Rob joined the team.

During the summers, Dad made time for baseball. Often right after dinner (the noon meal), we would take a break and play ball in the front yard. Dad would pitch, Mom would field, and Rob would hit. One of Dad's pitches, he pitched underhand at first because Rob was only five or six, hit Rob while he was batting right-handed. Rob didn't like getting hit with the ball, so he switched sides of the plate and became a left-handed batter. It turned out to be an advantage because most pitchers that he faced were right-handed, giving a lefty an advantage. When Rich came along, he watched Rob and since Rob hit lefty, Rich did too.

THE MCDONALDS

Dad envisioned both boys as pitchers. He taught us to throw "over the top." Getting our hand above our head, instead of to the side, when pitching. This technique resulted in a downhill trajectory of the ball when throwing from a mound. Later, when we learned to throw a curve, the ball would break violently down in the classic 12 to 6 movement when it approached the plate.

Rich's Little League career started when he was nine. Rich went to school in Brewster, so he played there with kids he knew.

Each year Brewster had tryouts, and the coaches would select players in a round robin format. Rich's first year was as a nine-year-old. He recalls that he and one other kid were left at the end of tryouts. Their baseball skills weren't too impressive. Dick Youngman, one of the coaches said, "I'll take them both."

Rich recalls he didn't have baseball hitting and fielding skills, but he could throw, he could run, and he was strong for his age. In that first year, he developed hitting and fielding skills and his throwing became pitching. That was the only time he got picked last!

Rich moved up the next year to the town team where the better players were. Tom Kirby was the coach. Tom knew the game, knew how to get the best out of his players, and developed winning strategies. The Brewster Little League team became a force in the area. The big rivalry was Navarre, who was coached by our mailman, Mr. Hammond. He and Dad would talk baseball during baseball season. Mr. Hammond would say, "I know who I'm going to see pitching against me when we play Brewster— Rich McDonald."

Player for player, Navarre was the better team, but they didn't have Tom Kirby managing and didn't have Rich pitching. They couldn't beat Brewster.

Dad used to schedule the farm work around Rich's baseball games, especially when he was pitching. On pitching day, the work would be a little lighter. We'd still work, but instead of 600+ bales

ROBERT ALAN MCDONALD, KATHIE EILEEN MCDONALD COURTNEY, RICHARD EDWIN MCDONALD, MARY JO MCDONALD HELFRICH

of hay, we'd only do 400. But as Rich would say, even after a full day's work, he could be fully rested if he could take a 15 – 30-minute break.

One day, when Rich wasn't scheduled to pitch, we did a full day making straw. Brewster was playing Richfield who wasn't as good as Navarre, but they had been improving. Tom Kirby was worried about them. When Rich and Dad got to the Richfield Park before game time, Tom told Dad he wanted Rich to pitch, and asked how hard had Rich worked that day? Dad told Tom we'd worked hard that day because he didn't think Rich would be pitching. Tom went to Rich and asked, "How do you feel? I'd like you to pitch." Rich said, "I'm fine. I can do it." That night, Rich threw a no-hitter.

Rich's baseball career continued into Pony League, then into High School including American Legion in Massillon and briefly to Ohio University. Rich attributes his baseball career to being stronger than the other players due to farm work, which during the winter included splitting elm wood for the furnace with an axe.

Rich's biggest fan was Dad. Well, after the season, usually in the winter, Rich recalls lengthy conversations with Dad about specific games. Dad's recall was such that he knew what pitch Rich had thrown to a specific batter in every game situation. Dad would comment on the reasoning used to decide which pitch would be thrown in various situations. Dad's recall amazed Rich. It was as if Dad was in Rich's head thinking right along with him. Their conversations help him better understand the various situations he would face in games.

Rich had a decent fast ball, but his out pitch was the overhand curve. The break on the ball was sharp and violent. Rob would catch and Rich would pitch during Rich's workouts. Rob would say, "I know they can't hit that curve 'cause I can't catch it, and I know it's coming." Rich would start the ball just below a batter's belt, right down the middle. When the batter saw it coming, he couldn't wait –

it looked so good! Just as it crossed the plate, the ball would break and by the time it reached the catcher it was in the dirt, about a two-foot drop. Rich recalls Coach Bob Wren at Ohio University taking notice when he threw it in practice for the first time. Wren told the catcher, "Have him throw that again!" Rich did with the same result. After that, Wren knew who Rich was.

Unfortunately, during the winter, Rich hit his elbow when ice skating. He may have suffered a bone chip and he "lost the feel" for the sharp breaking curve and was never able to get it back.

Six-man Football

When Rob was a freshman in high school, he went out for the football team. Beach City, being a small high school, played six-man football. They played in a league made up of other small country schools south of Beach City in Holmes, Wayne, and Tuscarawas counties.

The rules and even the field used for six-man football are different than eleven-man. It's tackle football with all the usual equipment. With only six players, some positions are eliminated. The offensive line is three players: a center and two ends. The backfield is made up of a quarterback and two halfbacks, one on either side of the quarterback. Every player is eligible to catch a pass. The field is 85 yards from goal line to goal line with a 10 yard end zone and is less than 50 yards wide. There are four downs to get a first down, but the distance is 15 yards. Drop kicking could be used for extra points if the team had anybody who could drop-kick.

The rules varied depending on game location. If the game was on Beach Cities' field, the quarterback could take the snap from the center and hand the ball to one of the halfbacks directly. But if the game was in one of the other counties, the ball had to be lateralled. Forward passes were permitted at all venues.

Rob doesn't recall Beach City having an outstanding season but did win a few games. Beach City played one more year of six-man football, but due to the school district consolidation, Rob was going

ROBERT ALAN MCDONALD, KATHIE EILEEN MCDONALD COURTNEY, RICHARD EDWIN MCDONALD, MARY JO MCDONALD HELFRICH

to Brewster where he played eleven-man football the next two seasons. In Rob's junior year, Beach City switched to eleven-man, played Brewster, and won.

In Rob's junior year, Brewster's football team compiled a record of 0 and 10. They were few in number and undersized. It was said they were small but made up for it by being slow.

The schools Brewster played were larger, in fact some were consolidated schools, which included Lake and Northwest, making them much larger. What happened was Brewster would hold its own in the first half or for three quarters but would tire at the end because all the players had to play both ways, including special teams. Rob recalls that he was 135 pounds and played right guard. The tackle next to him was 155 pounds. They were the big side of the line. The left side was 135 and 130 pounds. Rob's back-up was 110 pounds. What we learned is to never quit and we didn't.

The last game of the year was always Navarre. It was a grudge match. The best-known rivalry in Stark County was Massillon/McKinley, but Navarre/Brewster was just as intense, albeit on a smaller scale. That last game wasn't going Brewster's way, down 20 something to 6 or so. There was less than three minutes on the clock when the Brewster captain said, "Okay, on this play, we get 'em." On the snap, the fight started. The refs called the game at that point. It never resumed.

The next year, Navarre, Brewster and Beach City were merged into one school. Rob's class attended and graduated from the Navarre building. All summer the talk in all three towns was how the kids were going to get along, especially Navarre and Brewster. How many fights were there going to be? When school started, there were no fights; we got along very well and the football team, playing in the Federal League, put up an 8 and 2 season. A school record that stood for many years.

THE MCDONALDS

Entertainment

In Rob and Rich's bedroom was a wind-up Victrola record player. Where it came from, we're not sure, but with it was a collection of 78 RPM records. We'd wind up the record player and play the 78s.

The records we liked the best were: *The Ballad of Casey Jones, The Wreck of Old 97,* but our very favorite was *The Big Rock Candy Mountains* written and performed by Harry McClintock. We don't recall who performed the other two. Johnny Cash recorded them both, but that was years later. Probably because of the railroads running through the farm and the fact that Grandpa Dan worked for one of them, we gravitated toward railroad songs. Plus, those songs told stories.

The Big Rock Candy Mountain was the story of what hobo heaven would be like. We were familiar with 'Bos, as they were often called, as they traveled by rail whenever they could. We knew that Mom always fed them, and they sometimes slept in the barn.

Being a 'Bo was a hard life. These men – we never saw any women bumming – were out of work, had no money, might steal so we tried to keep valuable things out of sight, but because of the phrase: "For the grace of God, there go I," we did what we could to help them.

'Bos had a code system that they used to mark places where they got handouts. The story was that they wouldn't steal from people who fed or befriended them. Mom not only fed them but would also give them clothes, especially in winter.

Occasionally a 'Bo would offer to work to earn a meal or money, but we don't recall Dad putting any to work, but he might give them produce, potatoes, tomatoes, corn, and beans. They especially liked getting meat. They weren't particular - chicken, pork, or beef - they were happy to get. And, if they could get some smokes - cigarettes or tobacco - it would make their day.

An encampment was called a Hobo Jungle. It was there they gathered, spent the night around a fire for warmth, and cooked hobo stew – where everything was tossed in the pot and cooked together.

ROBERT ALAN MCDONALD, KATHIE EILEEN MCDONALD COURTNEY, RICHARD EDWIN MCDONALD, MARY JO MCDONALD HELFRICH

Harry McClintock, being aware of the hobo life, either wrote the lyrics for *The Big Rock Candy Mountains* or heard them from 'Bos and wrote them down. Burl Ives also recorded the song, but his version wasn't as complete. The lyrics we heard on the old 78 were:

One evening as the sun went down
and the jungle fire was burning,
Down the track came a hobo hiking
and he said, "Boys, I'm not turning."

"I'm headed for a land that's far away,
Besides the crystal fountains.
So come with me, we'll go and see
The Big Rock Candy Mountains."

In the Big Rock Candy Mountains,
there's a land that's fair and bright
where the handouts grow on bushes
and you sleep out every night.

Where the boxcars all are empty
and the sun shines every day
and the birds and the bees
and the cigarette trees,
the lemonade springs
where the bluebird sings
in the Big Rock Candy Mountains.

In the Big Rock Candy Mountains,
all the cops have wooden legs
and the bulldogs all have rubber teeth
and the hens lay soft-boiled eggs.

THE MCDONALDS

*The farmers' trees are full of fruit
and the barns are full of hay.
Oh, I'm bound to go
where there ain't no snow,
where the rain don't fall,
the winds don't blow
in the Big Rock Candy Mountains.*

*In the Big Rock Candy Mountains,
you never change your socks
and the little streams of alcohol
come trickling down the rocks.*

*The brakemen have to tip their hats
and the railway bulls are blind.
There's a lake of stew
and whiskey too.
You can paddle all around it
in a big canoe
in the Big Rock Candy Mountains.*

*In the Big Rock Candy Mountains,
the jails are made of tin
and you can walk right out again
as soon as you are in.*

*There ain't no short-handled shovels,
no axes, saws, nor picks.
I'm goin' to stay
where you sleep all day,
where they hung the jerk
that invented work
in the Big Rock Candy Mountains.*

*I'll see you all this coming fall
in the Big Rock Candy Mountains.*

ROBERT ALAN MCDONALD, KATHIE EILEEN MCDONALD COURTNEY, RICHARD EDWIN MCDONALD, MARY JO MCDONALD HELFRICH

Radio and Television – Grandma and Grandpa Jones had a floor model Zenith Radio. It received AM, FM, and Short-Wave signals. Rob recalls lying on the floor in front of the radio listening to the old radio programs. That radio was a gift to Grandpa Dan from his children. It was top of the line for its day. Of course, when Grandpa received it, he didn't want to take it. Mom always said it was so hard to buy anything for Grandpa Dan, he never wanted gifts, but after he had them for a while, they became his favorites. This seemed true of every gift, even the shirts he was given.

We had a radio in the house, and it wasn't too long before Dad found a way to have one in the barn. It was hung on one of the support posts in the center of the milking parlor. The electrical outlet it was plugged into was wired through the light switch. When we turned on the lights, we also turned on the radio.

The radio was tuned to WHBC in Canton. The station carried the Cleveland professional sports teams: the Indians baseball games and the Browns football games. During the week, the Breakfast Club was on in the mornings and on Saturday, we heard Big John and Sparky, a kid's program. In the evenings when there were no sports, we heard The Lone Ranger and Sergeant Preston of the Yukon. We listened to the radio as we did the chores and milked. All summer we listened to the Indians' games.

When we were working across the barn, it was hard to hear. So, we sometimes tried to put off animal feeding when there was a program of particular interest. Of course, we couldn't hear it at all when our work was on the second floor. This made us hustle when getting the hay and straw down.

Rob recalls seeing a television for the first time. It was at the Jeffers. The picture was so small they had to put a magnifying device in front to see the picture from across the room.

TVs became increasingly popular, eventually Mom and Dad decided to buy a TV, used of course. They found a used Philco with a 13 inch picture, which they bought, brought home, and placed in the dining room near the east window where it was easy to connect the antenna.

In those days, TV was only on a few hours a day. Programming started about 4:00 PM and signed off at midnight with the playing of the national anthem. Before the programming started and after sign-off, you got to watch the test pattern.

The best TV watching times were evenings and Saturday mornings. After finishing milking, and if our homework was done, we could watch TV for a brief time, an hour if we were lucky. It was the era of TV Westerns. Gunsmoke was on Saturday nights, and we always watched it.

Ed Miller, a neighbor who lived a short distance south on Justus Avenue, and who didn't own a TV, would watch TV with us. Ed always walked to the Farm most evenings. He would visit with us while we milked and then would come into the house and sit in the TV room, the west room on the first floor, and watch the Westerns. Ed was a bachelor, and his family was gone. He became like a member of the family.

The TV room furniture was sparse. Dad had a sturdy rocking chair, an overstuffed chair where Ed or another adult sat, and another chair for a third adult, most often Mom. Cushions salvaged from previous furniture were on the floor and were used by the children. Nothing fancy but functional.

Fun Things & Earning Money

The mother cats used the haymows as maternity wards. They placed the kittens in larger spaces between the hay bales, where they were safe. Kathie enjoyed playing with the kittens, but Dad had a prohibition on playing in the haymows—he didn't like having the hay bales broken. So, Kathie says she would wait until Dad wasn't around to find the kittens and play with them.

Rich and Kathie enjoyed killing wasps with bug spray. Mom would buy bug spray, which she would use to spray the screen doors, keeping away flies and other insects. These sprays would shoot several feet, making them ideal for wasp killing from a distance.

ROBERT ALAN MCDONALD, KATHIE EILEEN MCDONALD COURTNEY, RICHARD EDWIN MCDONALD, MARY JO MCDONALD HELFRICH

They would take the new spray cans, because they shot further, to the old corncrib/machine storage building, and blast wasp nests. Sometimes the can would be empty before they finished. This didn't please Mom too much because she couldn't spray the screens.

Rich and Kathie had jobs mowing Annie Grosklaus and Johnny Wilson's lawns. Both had two mowers so they could mow continuously. Kathie recalls making about $1.50 per lawn or $3.00 a week.

Briefly, Rob had the job of mowing the Welty Cemetery, reached by going west on Lawndell Road to the intersection with State Route 93. The job paid $10 for each mowing and took parts of two days as the mower was a 20 inch model, which was difficult to start. Thus, increasing the time it took. Rob only did the job a few times.

Rich Has a Date

One evening, when Rich was five or six, we were sitting around the table having just finished supper. For a reason known only to Dad, he asked Rich if his male organ got stiff. Rich responded that it did. Dad then asked if Rich knew what that was good for. All conversation stopped immediately because everybody, including Mom and Kathie, were still at the table. Rob vividly recalls the conversation because he remembers thinking, *Why would Dad ask such a question? And how is he going to get out of this?* Rich looked at Dad with a straight face and said, "No I don't, what is it for?" Pretty quick thinking, Dad calmly replied, "It's for flipping beans!" The comment cracked Rich up. Mom looked a bit relieved, also.

In the eighth grade, Rich began noticing girls. He noticed differences from boys, and those differences went beyond hair length. Being raised on a farm with horses, cattle, hogs, dogs, and cats, Rich had a fairly good idea of the attraction. Rich knew that if Dad found out about his interest in girls, he would get teased unmercifully. Dad would really embarrass the boys if either of them even looked at a girl.

One girl really interested Rich. So, he arranged to meet this special girl at the Brewster Movie Theater. As an eighth grader, Rich didn't have transportation and he certainly didn't want Dad to know anything about his interest. This meant he couldn't say anything to Mom either. So, a ride to Brewster in the car was out. Rich decided he would slip out the bedroom window, climb down to the ground, and walk to Brewster.

Rich planned carefully. He went upstairs early that night, but instead of going to bed he got into clean clothes and went out the window over the front porch and climbed down the arborvitae to the ground. He walked out to the road and headed west on Lawndell on foot. To be sure he could get back into the window after climbing back up the arborvitae, he placed a small wood block under the sash so he could get his fingers under it and raise it when he got back home.

He had a plan, but flaws began to appear. It was winter, cold, dark, and it had snowed. Rich decided he didn't want to be seen, because should one of the neighbors see him, it would be reported to Dad or Mom, so when a car came down the road, he hit the ditch until it passed. The ditch was full of snow. It could be damp as well as cold. Rich followed Lawndell all the way to the intersection with Route 93 and 62, a little over a mile. Then, after turning right, he followed 93 into Brewster, where the movie theater was located. That was well over another mile. And there was more traffic on 93 which meant more hiding in the ditch.

Thinking back, Rich concluded he would have been much better off had he cut across country at a 45 degree angle just after crossing the bridge on Lawndell. The route would have taken him across the north pasture, up the lane on the adjoining farm, across Route 62 just below Uncle Bud's house, across his fields until coming out on Route 93 just before the bridge over Sugar Creek. It would have taken a half to three-quarters of a mile off the trip, and he would have had little chance of being seen, for some reason he didn't want to trespass. Probably because of the way we were raised.

ROBERT ALAN MCDONALD, KATHIE EILEEN MCDONALD COURTNEY, RICHARD EDWIN MCDONALD, MARY JO MCDONALD HELFRICH

As it turned out, the trip took much longer than planned, what with taking the long-cut and hitting the ditch regularly. And his clothes were none too clean, a bit damp, and cold. When Rich got to the theater, the second feature was on, and this special girl had already gone home.

Rich had no choice but to repeat the trip home. This of course involved more trips into the ditch which resulted in getting colder and wetter. The next day, Rich tried to explain the situation to the girl. She let Rich know she didn't like being stood up. Rich tried to explain, but he got nowhere. And on top of it all, he had to walk back home and climb back through the window. As far as Rich knew, Dad and Mom didn't find out.

Family Traits

The McDonald family wasn't known as huggers and Mom and Dad didn't very often tell us in words that they loved us, but they let us know in other ways. We ate well, were always clean (except when working on the farm), we had rules to follow giving us structure, we had work to do which taught us responsibility, and we learned to respect our parents, relatives, neighbors, our teachers, and very importantly, we learned to respect other people and their property.

Rob and Rich, comparing notes, learned that neither of them could cut a corner short when walking on a sidewalk. Even when we could see that others took a diagonal route at a corner we stayed on the sidewalk, not trespassing on someone's yard. We don't remember ever being told that we had to do this, but we both instinctively knew that Dad wouldn't do it and wouldn't want us to, either. So, we didn't and still don't.

Chapter Thirteen - Vacation

Most years there would be a lull between the end of the small grain harvest after baling the straw and storing it in the barn and before making second cutting hay—about the end of July or the first part of August. Mom and Dad would set aside a day for vacation. Or, as they called it, a cookout at Atwood Lake State Park.

On that "t" day, we'd get up, milk the cows, take them to the pasture, feed the hogs, take the milk to the dairy, returning with whey and doing any other necessary chores. Mom would prepare the food for a picnic. After loading the food, our swimming clothes, and ourselves in the car, Dad would drive to Atwood. About 11 AM we would arrive. We'd get a charcoal fire going to cook the burgers and dogs—if anyone thought to bring the matches. Once, that didn't happen. All the men had stopped smoking. Grandma Nellie, who along with Grandpa Dan, came along that year, remarked that this was the most disorganized cookout she'd ever witnessed.

Once the fire was ready, we'd cook the food, eat, and go swimming after waiting 30 minutes so you didn't get belly cramps. After swimming, we'd relax a bit until about 4 or 5 PM, eat a snack, and load up and head for home, where we'd complete the evening milking and hog feeding. About 8:30 PM we'd be done. Altogether we'd get about a 6 to 7 hour "vacation".

The next day we knew the one thing we'd hear from Dad would be—no matter how quickly we got up or how fast and hard we went to work— "I guess you don't appreciate what's done for you! You had a day off yesterday and now you aren't getting things done." The implication being there would not be any more off days—ever! Rich said he mistakenly thought the trip to Atwood was a reward for the work we'd already done that summer. Dad corrected that notion.

Dad normally took Sunday off anyway, so we usually only worked six days. Of course, morning and evening chores didn't count as work, which were done on Sundays and Christmas, just like any other day.

ROBERT ALAN MCDONALD, KATHIE EILEEN MCDONALD COURTNEY, RICHARD EDWIN MCDONALD, MARY JO MCDONALD HELFRICH

Chapter Fourteen – Family Time

Holidays of Christmas, Thanksgiving, Easter, Independence Day, Memorial Day, Labor Day, and our birthdays were celebrated.

Christmas always meant a Christmas tree. Sometimes we could cut a tree on the farm. Usually, we get a tree from somewhere else, often from Johnny Wilson's tree farm in Baltic. Rich recalls we about always got a poor-looking tree, usually it was too big even for the space we had.

Mom liked the Christmas tree placed in the bay window, which was a wonderful place for a tree. It was easily seen from outside and its light traveled around downstairs. One rule for the Christmas tree was that it could be large, as the space was wide, and the ceilings were ten feet tall.

One year, we had an unruly tree that we wired to the woodwork to keep upright. We didn't do the best job because it fell. When it did, it took Mom's most delicate and precious ornaments with it to the ground. After that, we choose smaller, more manageable trees.

Mom and Kathie baked preparing for Christmas. They baked cookies and fudge both plain and with walnuts. Kathie became very proficient at fudge making. Rob and Rich really liked the fudge, especially the walnut fudge. They thought there was nothing better than getting fudge when they got back to the house after working in the barn.

Mom and Kathie started baking early in December and hid the fudge and cookies where they thought the boys wouldn't look, or at least they pretended to do so. But Rob and Rich were excellent fudge and cookie thieves. They knew the hiding places, which were on the top shelves of the kitchen cabinets and on the shelves in the closet off the dining room. The two thieves would ease into the house when Mom and Kathie were otherwise occupied. Usually, Rob would climb up on the cupboards and toss candy to Rich. By the time Christmas came, some of the boxes or tins would be completely empty. This sometimes vexed Mom, especially when she was intending to serve a guest only to find an empty box, but she and Kathie usually made some more. Dad certainly was aware of the

ROBERT ALAN MCDONALD, KATHIE EILEEN MCDONALD COURTNEY, RICHARD EDWIN MCDONALD, MARY JO MCDONALD HELFRICH

boy's thievery, but as long as he got a cut of the loot, he kept quiet about it.

Having a birthday meant you got to pick the cake you wanted, and the world's best cake baker would bake it — Mom! And then you also got ice cream, often homemade. Since it was your birthday, you didn't have to turn the crank but could if you really wanted to.

Mack fixing himself a hot dog off the grill, one of Bob Kuehner's creations

Independence Day became a favorite holiday for its historical significance and because we were usually done with the first cutting hay by then. Sometimes, however, we brought in the last of the first cutting on that day.

THE MCDONALDS

We always had a cookout: hamburgers and hot dogs, potato salad, potato chips, pickles, home-made ice-cream, cake and pies, soft drinks—an infrequent treat—and a watermelon in the milk house trough. When we got a little older, there was a case of beer in the milk house. We always had company on the 4th, and we shot off fireworks or used carbide to blow the lids off paint cans or five-gallon buckets. In the evening, we'd often go up to Massillon to the fireworks show at Tiger Stadium. We had an exciting time!

Relatives and Friends

Both Mom and Dad's families lived close. Mom's side, Grandma and Grandpa Jones and Aunt El, Uncle Pink Foster, along with their three girls—Sue, Sara, and Emily lived in Harmon—less than two miles away and Uncle Don Jones, Aunt Dorothy, and their three children— Dan, Marged, and John— lived in Navarre about five miles away. Dad's side, Aunt Tiny (Hester) and Uncle Dutch (Clarence) Lab and their five children—Gretchen, Tom, Jim, Joe, and Sam— lived in Canton about 15 miles away, Aunt Betty and her husband Uncle Bud (Roy) Wisselgren and their two boys—John and Donnie— were less than a mile as the crow flies and Aunt Dudy (Julia) and Uncle Eddie Bartko and their son and daughter–Graydon and Debbie— lived in Massillon about 8 miles away. For some time, Dad's mother, Grandma Julia, lived with us. Grandpa Sam, having sold the farm near Massillon, had moved to Missouri. Grandma Julia stayed behind by what we thought was a mutual agreement. We later learned the proceeds of the sale were divided between the two.

Nearly every Sunday, we had company. We never knew who it might be. Often it was friends, often members of Dad's army outfit. Other times it would be relatives on Dad's side, the ones that lived a little further away. But one thing was certain, Mom would feed them at least one meal and often two. It was a lot of work for Mom, but everyone loved what she prepared, especially her pickles and beets.

ROBERT ALAN MCDONALD, KATHIE EILEEN MCDONALD COURTNEY, RICHARD EDWIN MCDONALD, MARY JO MCDONALD HELFRICH

We made homemade ice cream regularly. We had a one-gallon freezer and a couple two-gallon freezers. In the summer, we would buy ice at the icehouse in Navarre or go to Canton.

In the winter, we often didn't need to go any further for ice than one of the watering troughs or the creek. The ice we got that way always seemed colder than when we bought it. The ice cream froze more rapidly.

To get ice out of the creek, we would take the double bitted axe and a burlap bag to the creek where we would cut a square out of the creek ice with the axe. One particularly frigid winter day, we had company and were going to make and serve ice cream. Rob and Rich went to gather ice. Rob didn't bother putting on his stocking cap. He didn't think they would be gone long. He misjudged how cold it was. Big mistake!

Rob cut a square chunk of ice and Rich tried fishing it out. When Rich did so, he accidentally pushed the square down into the hole, the current caught it, and the ice went downstream under the ice. Well, there was nothing to do but cut another square, so Rob did. This one got fished out successfully and put into the burlap bag.

Rob threw the bag over his shoulder, and he and Rich walked back to the house. When we got to the house, Rich noticed Rob's ears were white. This condition was pointed out to Mom. Immediately, Mom got wash rags and soaked them in lukewarm water and put them on Rob's ears, which were frozen. Mom's remedy worked and Rob's ears thawed out. The only damage was peeling skin.

To make the ice ready for use in the freezer, we would beat the ice with the flat side of the axe while it remained in the bag. We found that using a hammer or sledge would damage the bag and by using the flat side of the double bitted axe, we could get more use out of the bag.

Most Thanksgiving meals were at Grandma Jones'. And we had other get-togethers there as well. Weather permitting, we usually had a ball game. Uncle Don was the designated pitcher and umpire.

That way, he could cheat so that the team Sue was on couldn't win. Sue dearly loved winning, and Uncle Don's cheating drove her to distraction. It was great fun, and Sue didn't hold a grudge.

John Wisselgren and Rob, being close in age, would get together by walking to each other's farms by cutting through a neighbor's who owned a farm between the two properties. There was a convenient lane that made the trip easy.

The McDonald family would have cookouts at each other's homes and would get together regularly for other reasons such as holidays as well.

Bathing

When we first moved to the Farm, there was no running water or electricity in the house. It wasn't long before Dad and Grandpa Dan corrected these conditions. Rob does recall taking baths in the washtub in the kitchen. When finished, Mom would carry the tub containing the water out the back door and toss the water on the ground next to the house. The kitchen didn't get heat. Its primary heat source was the cookstove. Rob recalls taking a bath as being something you did quickly, especially in the winter.

Before installing the bathroom, provision had to be made for wastewater, so Dad dug a pit for the septic system on the west side of the house. Digging was easy and Dad was going so good he didn't realize he dug it too deep. He had to toss 2-feet of dirt back into the hole. The bathroom was built and for 30 years, there was only one bathroom.

Rob remembers the first bath he took in the new bathtub. He recalls filling the tub about halfway with water and having a fun time taking a bath. But Dad went out to the septic tanks which weren't covered yet, when he came back in, he told Rob that he used way too much water. In the future he needed to bathe with less.

With six people in the house, baths had to be planned. But sometimes planning wasn't enough. When we were going somewhere that involved the whole family, the girls went into the kitchen, on the north side, where the double wash tubs Mom used

ROBERT ALAN MCDONALD, KATHIE EILEEN MCDONALD COURTNEY, RICHARD EDWIN MCDONALD, MARY JO MCDONALD HELFRICH

for laundry and for washing the milking equipment were kept. The girls, Kathie, and Mary, and sometimes Rich got to take their baths in the wash tubs. Rob, being older, seems to have missed this adventure. This was particularly difficult in the winter. The lack of heat coupled with the draft coming under the back door which Mom tried to stop with newspapers folded and placed around the sides and bottom of the door made these bath times remembered as being particularly unpleasant.

Years later, a concrete floor was poured into the cellar. This enabled installation of an automatic washer and dryer – a blessing for Mom – and installation of a shower that the men used. When Rich did the major remodeling, he installed a beautiful bathroom in the west room on the second floor. (See photos showing the upstairs bat

THE MCDONALDS

Chapter Fifteen – Bo's Story

"Get 'er Bo!" Rich said. Instantly, the cow that had moved into grass at the roadside rejoined the rest of the herd moving up the road toward the barn. It was milking time. Rich knew Bo wouldn't hear the command. Bo passed almost three years ago. The big black-and-tan dog wasn't anywhere near the cows during the move, but Bo was boss dog and no animal on that farm crossed him. He was feared and respected. The mere mention of his name was enough, even after his passing.

Rich and Bo - buddies

He worked the cows like any well-trained herd dog. Bo moved up one side of the herd, across the back, then up the other side. He never got in front because that would stop them or get them going in the wrong direction. What was unusual was that Bo wasn't trained. For him, it was instinctive or behavior he learned on his own. If a cow strayed, he put her back with the rest of the herd.

Not only was Bo respected and feared by the other animals, but his reputation permeated the entire area. All the neighbors knew Bo, and he knew them. Bo was the protector of whoever was the smallest and that extended beyond members of our family.

ROBERT ALAN MCDONALD, KATHIE EILEEN MCDONALD COURTNEY, RICHARD EDWIN MCDONALD, MARY JO MCDONALD HELFRICH

Mary with the pups in Bo's litter. Six shown.

Bo was whelped on the McDonald farm. The offspring of a mixed breed bitch we called Mutti, that someone had dropped off and Drum, the male black and tan coonhound that Mack owned. Rich recalled Dad putting Mutti, who was in season, in the oat granary on the top floor of the barn and locking the door so she would spend the night alone. The next morning, upon opening the door, Mack was surprised when Drum walked out with Mutti. Drum had gotten up on top of the granary and entered through a small hole placed there, which we used when filling the granary.

Mutti looked like she may have been part boxer; she was muscular with a square head, but she wasn't exceptionally large. Her problem was that she liked eggs and would eat them when she had an opportunity. Not a good trait, especially since the chickens and eggs were Mom's income, thus she wasn't necessarily a welcome addition. After weaning the pups, the dogcatcher was called, and Mutti went elsewhere.

None of us can remember how many pups were in Bo's litter or what happened to all of them. Rich thinks there may have been about seven. Mary recalls Dad remarking that if there were any more, Mutti wouldn't have had enough teats to nurse them all, as she had just eight. Rob remembers there being two males that looked very much alike. One was Bo. Mary believes the runt went to Mr. Hammond, the mailman, who always said how smart that dog was.

Mary doesn't recall whether the pup was male or female. She recalls the decision to keep Bo out of all the pups. She thinks Rob, Kathie, and Rich wanted Bo. Mary wanted a female that had a white stripe on her nose. Mary believes Dad wanted Bo, so she got out voted. She remembers being told that she already had the dog she called Baby, so she should be happy. Kathie recalled that she also favored another pup but was okay with Bo.

Mary believes, and Kathie concurs. The others got good homes as we took them to the Stark County Fair where they were adopted.

Bo's daddy, the male black and tan coonhound's name was Drum. We called him Drumbo. When we were looking for a name, we just shortened Drumbo to Bo and there you have it—Bo. Short and easy to say and remember.

Bo grew to be a large dog. Tall like Drum and muscular like his mother. He looked like his daddy, shiny black with tan highlights on his eyebrows, muzzle, and paws. Bo's head was large, as were his neck and chest. In fact, he resembled a bear. Bo could stand on his hind legs, place his paws on Robert's shoulders, and look directly into Robert's eyes. We weighed him on a platform scale at 95 pounds. Bo was also fast and nimble.

For the first six months of Bo's life, he didn't listen to or obey any commands. Rob recalls being afraid Dad would get rid of him, although he was friendly, fun, and outgoing. *A dog that wouldn't listen to Dad didn't have a future,* Rob thought. He was sure wrong about that. Dad must have seen or sensed something in that dog because of all the pups in the litter, Bo was the one Dad kept. Bo was so contrary that Dad would call him, "Come here Bo," and Bo would turn the other way and amble off. But something happened when he was about six months old. All at once, Bo listened, began to obey, but most surprisingly began to figure things out for himself and then act on those things. He had a perfectly good brain. In fact, he was the smartest dog any of us ever knew.

ROBERT ALAN MCDONALD, KATHIE EILEEN MCDONALD COURTNEY, RICHARD EDWIN MCDONALD, MARY JO MCDONALD HELFRICH

Bo's Education

In those days, the hog operation wasn't anything fancy. In the winter, we would put the sows into one of the two box stalls in the barn for farrowing. If the box stalls were full, we placed them into whatever space was available. It wasn't unusual for a sow to farrow when it was freezing, so we would gather the newborn pigs, place them in baskets, and take them into the house where we would warm them on the registers. Once they were warm and dry, we'd take them back to their mothers to nurse. This worked well. Then we learned about infrared lamps. By using the infrared bulbs, we didn't have to bring the pigs into the house to warm up. In warmer weather, the sows farrowed outside sometimes or in the spaces used in winter.

Pigs are naturally good at finding food. So those born in the winter searched for food in and around the barn and those born in the summer found food in other ways, mostly outside.

We always had pigs running around the farm and in the summer, a herd of 10 to 30 pigs, which weighed up to 50 pounds, would be in the yard rooting for grubs. Once the pigs were large enough that the fence would hold them, we moved them into the hog barn which had finishing pens.

Looking for grubs or flower bulbs, the pigs could plow the yard to a depth of two to three inches in days. This set Mom off. She wanted to have a nice-looking yard. Mom was always chasing pigs out of her yard. Mom would go after them with her broom. The pigs would run into the pen with their mothers where Mom wouldn't chase them. Mom would go back to the house to do her chores, and the pigs would go back to rooting.

Bo saw this. He figured out that Mom didn't want the pigs in her yard. So, Mom's yard became Bo's yard, and he chased them out of it and into the hog pen. He taught the pigs that a nip on the side wasn't comfortable. When they saw that dog coming, they headed out on their own. All at once—no pigs in the yard. Nobody told Bo to do this or taught him; he simply saw what Mom wanted and did something about it. This endeared him to Mom.

Bo figured out that each animal had a place to be. Pigs and hogs were supposed to be in the hog barn, or lots. Cattle were in the barn, barnyard, or a pasture depending upon the season. Chickens were in the chicken coop or in the yard around the chicken coop. Yes, everything in its place. And Bo knew where everything went and anything that wasn't where it was supposed to be got his personal attention. They learned that Bo wouldn't bother them if they stayed where they belonged. If they didn't, a nip or a big black dog behind them got them where they needed to be.

Bo found how to be efficient in keeping his eye on things. The barn was two stories with three-barn floors each with a "stacker door" looking out. One stacker door had been removed leaving an opening to the overshoot, which was a metal roof protecting the first-floor doors. That overshoot was a perfect place for a dog to sit and survey the entire farmstead. Bo went out on the overshot, sat down, and looked to see that everything was in its place. If not, he dealt with it and returned to his vigil. Nobody taught Bo to do this, he figured it out himself. Mary recalls Bo being on duty on the overshoot at 10 AM every day. You could set your watch by him.

Bo wasn't tied or restricted. He knew the farm boundaries and stayed within them. He was a free spirit and trusted to do only what he should do, and he did.

One summer day, a herd of about 30 pigs got themselves onto the railroad. Bo spotted them, knew they were out of place, and returned them, after considerable effort, to the boar and sow lot. Managing 30 pigs by one dog was really something to see, but there was no quit in Bo. He got it done.

There was one exception to Bo's not bothering an animal that was where it was supposed to be. That was the boar hog, "George," as named by Mr. Wayne Shetler, a neighbor who, besides farming, was the local animal hauler. Mr. Shetler used George to service his sows. George liked the work. Mr. Shetler would bring his truck to the sow and boar lot, back in, and drop the tailgate. He would say: "Come on, George." And George would walk up the ramp into the truck. Mr. Shetler would take George to his farm, where George would get off, take care of business for the next few days, and then get back on the truck and come home, where he would walk off and go back to his home in the boar and sow lot. George was huge. When we sold him, he weighed 725 pounds. George wasn't fat; he was simply big.

Bo figured George needed to know who top-dog was, and from time to time, needed a reminder. So now and then, Bo would hop over the fence and into the sow and boar lot. Bo would get George out in the middle of the lot, ½ acre, and begin circling the hog so the boar would turn round and round watching the dog. Then Bo would dart in, grab one of the hog's hind feet in his mouth and flop the hog. Bo would do it two or three times and then hop back out of the lot over the fence. He'd leave behind old George snorting, who would have loved nothing better than to stick one of his 6" tusks into Bo. Rob saw Bo do this and said to him, "You better know what you're doing 'cause that old hog would like to open you up." After hopping the fence, Bo looked over at Rob and gave him a look that said, "He won't get me." And he never did.

Bo the Protector

Bo always protected the smallest. And it wasn't necessary for you to be one of the McDonald family. If you were small and had a problem, Bo was your protector. But Bo issued warnings if things went further than he thought they should.

Robert, being older, was bigger than Rich. Rich and Rob would be horsing around like boys do and if Rich felt like he needed help, he'd holler like he was being hurt, and Bo would grab Rob's pant leg. Rich and Rob did this so much that Rob's pant legs were shredded, and Bo wore off his lower teeth. Bo would give the pant leg a tug to let Rob know he was there and didn't like Rob picking on Rich. When Rob let go, and Rich quit hollering, Bo would let go also.

THE MCDONALDS

But if Rob didn't or if Rich hollered some more, Bo would grab a bit more pant leg and tug a bit harder. If that didn't get things stopped, Bo would grab Rob's leg meat, not hard, he wouldn't break the skin, but he was letting Rob know things were going to get serious. What happened after that is anybody's guess, because Rob never went further. Rob recalls being glad Rich didn't keep hollering, too.

Rob recalls, "One day I saw Bo going down the railroad tracks hundreds of yards away. I figured since Bo was out of the way, I'd give Rich a tussle and Rich wouldn't have his protector handy. I grabbed Rich and he hollered. The next thing I knew was something hit me up around my shoulders and knocked me down. Bo came back! Rob never heard a thing until Bo hit him. Rich won that one and Rob learned to choose his battles more carefully."

One day a neighbor, Arch Croy, and Arch's young son, Dale, were at the farm. Dale was 3 or 4. Dad picked Dale up and tossed him up in the air. Dale liked Dad and wasn't really scared, but like all youngsters, he hollered. Bo had Dad's pant leg and gave it a tug. Dad put Dale down and said, "It's okay, Bo!" Bo let go and that ended it. But Dale was smaller, so Bo was on his side.

Bo wasn't a house dog. He was supposed to sleep outside summer and winter, usually under the back porch. According to Mom, Bo didn't belong in the house, but we would sneak him in. We might hide him under cushions in the TV room; where Mom would come in a say, "I smell dog. Get that dog out of here."

Mom was a fastidious housekeeper. For a farm wife with four active children and a husband, there was always cleaning to do. Mary recalls Mom sweeping and mopping the kitchen floor every day after breakfast, and each week dusting the baseboards all over the house. Being that nothing would do but have a clean house, it was no surprise that Mom wouldn't want a dog bringing dirt into her house.

When we would get Bo into the house, we would take him upstairs to where our rooms were and whoever he was with, that's the room he would go to. Rob didn't understand how Bo always knew which room to go to but finally figured out that his nose told him.

Bo belonged to all of us, but his main man was Rich. Occasionally, Rich and sometimes Mary snuck him into the house through the living room and upstairs, where he spent an occasional night in Richard's bed. We tried to keep this from Mom, but she knew about it or found out shortly after. Kathie recalls asking Mom about this later and got a small smile in reply. Mom had it figured out.

We would tell him when sneaking him in, "Don't let Mom catch us." He would slither in, crouched low to the floor, to make all 95 lbs. of Bo as small as possible. He was quiet as a mouse. Once upstairs, he danced and skipped down the hall to Richard's bed as he knew he was in for the night. He slept frequently on his back stretched out next to Richard, like a human brother. Next morning, we snuck him out in the same manner.

Bo often looked into the TV room through the outside door which had a window. Later that room became Mom's bedroom. Mom always said he looked like a big bear out there peering in at us. That was his way of asking us to sneak him in.

Mary, being the youngest, would sometimes come home from school and no one would be home. Mom would be away shopping, and Dad would be out in a field or somewhere else. So, Mary would bring Bo in with her. She said she was never remotely afraid when Bo was with her. No wonder Bo was 95 pounds of muscle and teeth. It wouldn't have been pretty if someone had bothered Mary.

Bo Keeps Everything in its Place

While Bo rarely needed commands, he would do what we asked him to do, especially if it had to do with a farm animal being out of place.

THE MCDONALDS

Since Bo was so good at his job, keeping things where they needed to be, the fences and gates didn't always get the attention they needed. We could go away for the day, come back, and find a gate wide open or damaged and Bo keeping the livestock in. But one day, the gate to the boar and sow lot was open and one sow decided she was going for a walk in the cornfield next to the house. The corn was at full height—about 13 feet. The sow went right up the driveway past the house—about 50 - 60 yards and into the 4-acre corn field. Getting a hog out of a cornfield is tough. We're not sure a human can do it. In fact, we're not sure a human can do it with help.

Anyway, toward the cornfield the sow went with Dad after her. She was too fast and got into the cornfield before Dad could cut her off. Dad turned around and said, "Get 'er Bo." With that, Bo went in after the sow. In less than 10 seconds, we'd lost track of both. Dad, Rich, and Rob went back to whatever they were doing before the hog got out. In about 30 minutes, they completely forgot about Bo and the sow. Over 2 hours later, out of the cornfield came an exhausted sow and one determined Bo. That sow headed straight down the driveway and into the boar and sow lot. Once inside, lay down and stayed that way to rest up. That hog was exhausted. For Bo, it was just another day of him doing his job.

Mary recalls her favorite story: the mailman came, and Dad was feeding the sows, which at that time were kept in Jonny's lot right close to the mailbox. Dad left the gate open and sat down under the buckeye trees to read the paper. It was likely Dad sat on the bucket he used to feed the sows. He was always using buckets as stools. While happily reading the paper, all 16 sows waltzed right by him and proceeded into the field directly across from the mailbox, crossing the road.

Dad didn't notice a thing. Highly likely he was reading the sports section. Anyway, just as the last sow was entering the corn field Bo showed up barking and alerted Dad. Dad said, "Go get 'em Bo," and he did. All morning, he worked to get those sows out of that corn field. Mary reckoned Bo was rounding those sows up in one bunch for about three hours. We were eating lunch and heard Bo bark. Sure enough, he was putting all 16 sows in the lot. Dad went out quickly, shutting the gate. Bo was so tired he laid down in front of the gate and slept there all afternoon.

Another critter that liked to go for walks was the rooster. Somehow, he left the chicken coop area and went up behind the barn. That wasn't an extremely great distance – about 100 to 150 yards – but far for a chicken. But Bo found him and brought him back strutting like chickens do all the way back to the coop with a big black and tan dog tracking back and forth behind him. That rooster thought there were two dogs behind him. He was moving along smartly.

Bo the Hunter

There were groundhogs, and Rob liked to shoot them. But Bo was a groundhog hunter extraordinaire. Probably because his daddy was a coon dog and partly because Bo had his own way of doing things.

The first time Rob took Bo groundhog hunting, Rob was carrying his .22 rifle and walking out near the middle of the field. Bo was on his own hunting ahead like dogs are supposed to do. Bo would trot along like he hadn't a care in the world and suddenly he'd dart into the edge of the field. The next thing you'd see is Bo standing on the dirt mound that the groundhogs leave near the entrance to their hole. Bo had the holes memorized—a combination of memory and smell—and he'd dart to the hole and catch the groundhog out in the open. The groundhog wasn't quick enough to get back to his hole and Bo would have him. Bo would take the dead groundhog to the railroad right-of-way where the digging was easy and bury it for days. He'd later dig it up when he wanted a meal.

Well, Rob figured out that he would not get any shots with Bo ranging out in front, so Rob needed to change hunting tactics. Rob would have Bo walk out in the field with him until Rob got to a spot where he thought he'd spot a groundhog and get a shot. Rob would have Bo lie down and stay while Rob would lie down and watch. Bo would stay there if Rob insisted. But once Rob saw a target, he knew he had one shot because Bo would be on the dead run and might catch it, even if the shot missed. The only other way would be to leave Bo at home, but he didn't like that very much.

Bo loved being with any of us, but he particularly liked Rich. They had a special bond. One place they liked to go was down (south) on the railroad tracks, where just beyond the Farm border was a trestle that spanned Bean Creek. Bean Creek is shallow and clear and with creek dwelling things. Rich recalls coming back one day with Bo. They were playing and having a fun time. Bo seemed to be really into having fun, when suddenly he darted down the side of the grade and stuck his head into a groundhog hole. He came out with a groundhog. Rich said Bo knew where all the holes were and could time his attack so that he would catch the groundhog just a foot or so from its hole. Rich said occasionally Bo miss-timed it but usually got the groundhog.

Whatever we were doing, Bo would be either helping or with us. At haymaking time, which was a good part of each summer, Bo would ride the dual wheel trailer from the barn to the field where we would load it. He loved riding. When we got to the field Bo knew he couldn't help loading so he would hunt groundhog.

Bo not only liked aged groundhog, but he was partial to hog offal. When we butchered, we didn't use the lungs and sometimes the liver and heart. Hog lungs are heavy, but Bo would pick them up and take them to the railroad by going over the fence that was at least four feet high. How that dog was strong enough to go over that fence with a load of lungs seems incredible, but he did it every time. He'd age the hog offal the same way he aged groundhog, by burying it on the railroad. Bo was a fat and sassy dog after butchering time. In fact, he ate little dog food although he did like cracklings.

Bo Understands

Bo understood people's talk. At an early age, we found we could simply say things to Bo, and he would react appropriately. For example, we had implements that we used to haul things around the

ROBERT ALAN MCDONALD, KATHIE EILEEN MCDONALD COURTNEY, RICHARD EDWIN MCDONALD, MARY JO MCDONALD HELFRICH

farm. We had a hay wagon, a dual wheel trailer, a manure spreader that we pulled with the tractors, and we had a truck. We used the different implements depending upon what we intended to do.

If we were going to pick green corn to feed the hogs, we'd use the manure spreader. It was box shaped which lent itself to tossing corn into it without the corn falling out easily, and it was easy to unload when we fed the hogs. We used the hay wagon to haul hay and straw. But the most useful was the big dual wheel trailer. We used it for hay, straw, firewood from the Woods, and anything else we needed to move. Bo loved going for rides.

As we were heading out, we'd say, "Bo, get on the manure spreader, wagon, trailer or truck." Bo would go to the specific piece of equipment and hop on. He always got it right. Although that seemed surprising, Bo must have had a command of the language. There's simply no other explanation.

Rich recalls Bo being with him when he'd feed the cattle by taking the truck with a load of hay down the road to the curve, where he'd toss the hay into the pasture. Rich was only about 10 at the time and he had to look out through the steering wheel to see where he was going. Bo was sitting on the seat and his view was unobstructed. Rich says Bo navigated!

Sometimes Bo anticipated the use of a piece of equipment. One day Rich went out to get the Minnie (Minneapolis Moline tractor), parked with the drawbar poking into the equipment tongue but not attached. Rich fired up the Minnie and pulled away. Bo thought he was going to get a ride, so he jumped into the manure spreader even though Rich didn't tell him to. When Rich pulled away, the manure spreader didn't move. Bo was surprised and let Rich know with a strange look.

One day, Mom walked into the barn where Rob was and asked if he'd noticed an Amish man who stopped by. Rob recalled seeing a buggy before and said yes, he'd seen the buggy but hadn't spoken to the Amish man. Mom said the Amish man wanted to buy Bo. Bo's reputation had gotten him noticed. Mom said, "What do you think?

THE MCDONALDS

Should we sell Bo?" Rob, thinking Mom wasn't serious and knowing Bo was just steps away with his ears up, said, "Sure, we could sell Bo. I wonder what we'll get." When Rob said that, Bo's attitude changed. His head dropped; his tail dropped. He looked miserable. Rob was shocked. Bo understood everything said. Rob was sorry he'd said anything. Rob immediately said, "No, we'll never sell Bo!" Old Bo perked right up and came over to Mom and Rob with his head held high. There never was any talk of getting rid of Bo again.

As time went on, we found that we could tell Bo things and he'd not only do those things, but he could remember what needed to be done when certain events happened. He knew the neighbors and what they might need when they came to the farm. He took part in games with us and our friends. And he offered company and protection.

Bo was part of our daily work. He helped whenever he could. He sometimes could do things better or quicker than we could.

Dad decided to send a heifer to the sale barn in Kidron, Ohio, for sale. We called Wayne Shetler to haul the heifer. He backed his truck up to the barn door leading into the milking area where the loading was to take place.

Wayne's truck was a Ford F-600, red. It was a straight truck with 20 inch rims. It had a stake bed which stood about six feet high above the floor. A canvas tarp covered the top. The bed was about four feet from the ground. The back end consisted of a double tail gate. On one side, the left, it was hinged at the bottom and could be lowered to the ground, making a ramp so animals could walk up for loading. The other side was hinged on the right side so the gate could be opened and could swing 270 degrees and be secured alongside. The way the truck was configured, it could be loaded from ground level, or it could be backed up to a raised platform and loaded that way.

That day, Wayne dropped the tailgate, placed portable gates on each side of the resulting ramp, and secured them in place with rope. Dad, Rob, and Rich had the heifer in the milking area with a rope

ROBERT ALAN MCDONALD, KATHIE EILEEN MCDONALD COURTNEY, RICHARD EDWIN MCDONALD, MARY JO MCDONALD HELFRICH

around her neck. Everything was ready. All the heifer had to do was walk up the ramp and get on the truck.

We put a second rope on the heifer and handed it to Wayne, who was at the top of the ramp. As time went on, Wayne moved down the ramp and wrapped the rope he was using around one stake at the top so he could pull downhill on the rope. This placed Wayne in a precarious position as he ended up on the right side of the ramp about a third of the way down.

The plan was Wayne would pull, and we would push and encourage the heifer to go up the ramp.

Like most plans, this one had a flaw. The heifer decided in her cow brain she didn't want to go up the ramp. Not even one foot would she put on the ramp. Dad, Rob, and Rich pushed, twisted the heifer's tail, yelled, and said vulgar words, while Wayne pulled—no luck. The heifer wasn't getting on.

Bo was in the barn with Dad, Rob, and Rich. He tried to help, but Dad kept saying, "No! Bo, get back! Bo stop." In short, Dad wouldn't let Bo put that heifer on the truck. It was driving Bo crazy.

After Dad would tell him to stop, he'd sit, but he couldn't remain still. While sitting, he'd be moving trying to get into the action. Bo knew he could load the heifer if we just got out of his way.

Dad was worried about Wayne given the position he was in blocking part of the ramp. But Wayne had an advantageous position to pull the rope. We tried loading that heifer for at least a half hour. All three of us humans were tired, and we hadn't even gotten that heifer to put one foot on the ramp, let alone go up it. All the while, Bo paced back and forth, knowing full well he could get this job done if we'd just let him.

Finally, Bo had enough of our fooling around. He darted in, nipped the heifer's heels, and put her right up the ramp, almost running over Wayne, who ducked as the heifer went over his head. If Wayne had gotten hurt, it wouldn't have been funny, but he didn't, and it was. Wayne didn't know whether to be angry about nearly getting run over or happy that the animal was loaded. The look on his face was priceless.

After that, Bo was the prime mover when it came to loading. Wayne would get in position—out of the way, around the corner at the top of the ramp— and Bo would put the animal up the ramp or through the gate. All Wayne would say is, "Okay, Mack, have Bo put 'er on." And Dad would say, "Okay, Bo!" and the animal would go up the ramp on the truck. Simple. Bo taught us how to load.

Bo Decides What Animals Can Stay

The cats and dogs that were on the farm before Bo could stay, but any dogs that showed up were risking their lives. A couple foxhounds came through. They'd gotten separated from their owner/master and had gotten lost. Bo found them and lit into them with full force. It was two on one, but the fox hounds never had a chance. Bo was bigger, meaner, and he was fighting for his home. Bo whipped the foxhounds in short order. They left with their tails between their legs.

At first, cats were okay. Bo really didn't mind them. But a large tom cat came through the farm and Bo treed him. Dad saw Bo had the cat treed and called Bo off. Bo obeyed and started away from the tree. That's when the cat decided he could come down. Bo saw the cat hit the ground and Bo went after the cat. It was an even fight for about 5 seconds. The cat scratched and bit Bo on the nose. That's when the bones began crunching. Bo put an end to that cat. From then on, strange cats were on Bo's unwelcome list and even the ones already on the farm had to tread carefully.

One of the farm cats irritated Bo. He chased the cat into the front yard where the cat climbed an arborvitae tree. Bo was angry. He jumped up as high as he could and grabbed a tree limb in his mouth, ripped the limb off the tree, and brought it to the ground. Bo was tearing 2-inch limbs off to about 10 or 12 feet from the ground. Bo couldn't climb the tree, but he sure could jump. That cat saved itself by going high up in the tree and staying there until Bo calmed down or ran out of limbs.

ROBERT ALAN MCDONALD, KATHIE EILEEN MCDONALD COURTNEY, RICHARD EDWIN MCDONALD, MARY JO MCDONALD HELFRICH

The unfortunate thing about this character trait – hating cats – was that after a while, there were no more cats on the Farm. This led to a surplus population of mice and rats.

Bo Didn't Always Obey

Mr. Borders, a neighbor whose farm was the second one when going north on Justus Avenue, had loose hay in a mow that he couldn't use and offered it to Dad. Naturally, Dad agreed to take it off his hands for loading and hauling it away.

Dad and Rich hooked up a tractor to the hay wagon and started for the Borders farm. Bo started following. When the tractor and Rich went someplace, Bo figured he needed to go, too. Not wanting Bo to get hit by a car, Dad firmly told Bo, "GO HOME!" Bo watched where they were going, saw the tractor turn north on Justus Avenue, so Bo went north on the railroad which paralleled Justus Avenue. When Dad and Rich got to the Borders farm, there was Bo.

They got the hay loaded and were ready to head home. Rich was on top of the load intending to ride home there. Not wanting anything to happen to Bo, Dad decided to pick him up and toss this big dog up to Rich where they both could ride safely.

Unfortunately for Dad, Bo didn't understand being tossed up 6 to 8 feet on a wagon. Bo got excited and lost control of his bowels. Rich recalls Dad exclaiming, "Bo shit himself." Dad, being under the dog, got the worst of it. He had dog crap down his arm and all over his shirt and coat. Bo did get on top of the load and rode home in style. Dad had a less auspicious homecoming.

Bo's Passing

Rich recalls the morning that Bo wasn't around. It was Bo's habit to greet us every morning as soon as any of us came out of the house. He was always happy to see us. He seemed even happier on frosty winter mornings.

But one day, Bo wasn't there to greet Mack, who called and no Bo. Mack did not know where Bo was, but thinking that he would show up soon, Mack started the chores. Still no Bo. Later that day, Rich recalled a neighbor stopping by and telling him and Mack that the neighbor believed Bo was alongside the road just east of the Farm. Rich and Mack got the Massie with a carryall and went up the road to the east. They found Bo lying there.

The strange thing is that they couldn't find a mark on the dog and there was no blood. They think a car hit him, but this seemed strange because Bo was careful around motor vehicles because of the experience he had as a pup.

When Bo was young, he liked to lie under the car where it was cool, and he wasn't too particular about getting out of the way when the car started. Rich recalls one day when Dad got into the car and started it. He knew Bo was laying behind one of the rear wheels. Dad put the car in reverse and backed up just enough to pinch Bo. Rich said he hollered that the dog was back there, and Dad didn't pay any attention to Rich's shouts at all. Bo was making a racket, as he was hurting. After a brief time, Dad moved the car forward and Bo took off. Rich recalls Dad saying, "That should teach him about cars." It seemed too because Bo was always careful around them but not afraid as he really enjoyed going for rides.

Rich recalls burying Bo next to the machine shed. Rich says that was the hardest grave he ever dug and can still visualize that last patch of Bo's fur before covering him. Rob recalls getting a call from Dad while at Ohio University letting him know what happened to Bo. Just getting a call from Dad was unusual because he didn't believe in spending money on long-distance phone calls. But Dad was just as upset about losing Bo as we all were. In fact, Dad suspected that the driver of the vehicle that hit Bo may have been one of the guys at the coon hunters' club that had a clubhouse about a mile east of the Farm on that same road. Rich recalls being with Dad and going to the clubhouse where Dad confronted the entire group. Dad and Rich assured that no-one there had anything to do with Bo's death.

Bo's passing remains a mystery to this day.

ROBERT ALAN MCDONALD, KATHIE EILEEN MCDONALD COURTNEY, RICHARD EDWIN MCDONALD, MARY JO MCDONALD HELFRICH

Bo's Legacy

Because Bo wasn't around, we immediately needed to repair fences and gates that had been neglected. The barnyard was in poor shape. The cows got out in the middle of the night. We chased them around in the dark. It took hours before we could go back to bed. Dad decided repairs were necessary.

At about this same time, the railroad was eliminating the siding. The steel rails were salvaged but the ties were surplus. The ties were free if removed at no cost to the railroad. Dad jumped on that deal. We went to work picking up and hauling railroad ties. We stacked them up near the barnyard.

Dad had a friend who just bought a tractor mounted backhoe. Dad got him to dig a trench about 30 inches deep where the barnyard fence had been. We had removed the fence. The railroad ties were soldered in the trench. We now had a barnyard fence that was solid railroad ties. It was a great fence that lasted well over 20 years.

Chapter Sixteen - Bill

Bill, about age 14, ready to go

Grandpa Sam McDonald bought Rob a pony. Rob recalls it this way.

I Think I'll Call Him Bill

Shortly after moving to the Farm on Lawndell Road, a large stock truck pulled into the driveway and drove up toward the barn, stopping near the gate to the barnyard. Dad and Rob naturally went up to see what was going on. The truck driver got out of the driver's side door and Grandpa Sam got out of the other side.

Grandpa Sam asked Rob, "Do you see anything on the truck you like?" All Rob could see was cows and a hog or two, so he said, "No, I don't." To which Granddad replied, "What about that pony?" Until that point, Rob hadn't seen the pony. Rob recalls the pony being black, with four white feet and not too big. Later, Dad would say that the pony still had a curly tail, meaning he was around eight weeks old. Rob then said, "Yes, that pony is good." Granddad replied, "Well, he's yours." Rob recalls looking over at Dad, who was just as surprised as Rob was. Granddad never told Dad he was buying Rob a pony.

After unloading the pony, Granddad asked Rob, "What are you going to name him?" After a brief thought, Rob replied, "I think I'll call him Bill."

Rob recalls Dad trying to get him to come up with another name, but Rob, being pretty set in his ways even at four, stuck to Bill and that was his name. To this day, Rob doesn't know how or why he picked Bill. At the time, there were two workhorses on the farm, Dan and Bird. So, the name Bill didn't conflict with anything, but Rob admits he didn't have any other reason for the name except it's what popped into his head at that moment.

Bill began his life on the McDonald farm that day and spent all the rest of it there. But Bill, like all pets, had his share of work to do once he got old enough to do it.

Bill as a colt with Rob on his back. Notice his ears. Bill doesn't look happy.

First, he had to grow up. So, he was placed in a stall, fed hay and grain, watered, and, of course, exercised. He grew into a good-sized, very handsome pony. During this time, he was handled and by the time he was two, Rob, with Dad's direction, began breaking Bill to ride. That work was done in the barnyard.

While in the stall, cows could get behind Bill and would butt the young pony. Bill never forgot what the cows did to him. He never forgave them. He hated cows his entire life. Because of this, Bill couldn't be put into a pasture with cows. He would chase and bite them at every opportunity. While this limited his grazing opportunities, it was useful when Bill moved cattle around the farm. He was born to move cattle, sometimes more rapidly than anybody wanted him to. It wasn't long before Bill could be ridden outside the barnyard and anywhere on the farm. Dad found a pony saddle at a sale and with the saddle came a martingale—a tooled leather strap—which mounted across the chest with the ability to fasten a strap to the bridle which would keep the pony's head from being raised too high. However, Bill never needed the martingale for that purpose, so we seldom used the martingale, unless we wanted Bill to look his best. His bridle was one we had on the farm and Dad used what he described as a "broken" bit, more correctly known as a "Snaffle" bit, made of two pieces of steel interlocked in the center. This type of bit is quite easy on a horse's mouth but severely limits a rider's control of the animal.

Although he started out being less than pretty, Bill grew into a handsome, well-gaited pony. He remained a stallion his entire life and fathered beautiful offspring, including Mary's Jonny. Bill had sound feet and was never shod.

Rob recalls when he was about five or six, he had a cowboy hat, gloves with fringed gauntlets, vest, chaps, boots, and a two-gun holster set. Rob said he really thought he was something sitting on Bill when they both were fully outfitted.

ROBERT ALAN MCDONALD, KATHIE EILEEN MCDONALD COURTNEY, RICHARD EDWIN MCDONALD, MARY JO MCDONALD HELFRICH

Rob on Bill in full regalia

Dad said Bill was Hackney, a pony derived from an English breed of carriage horse famous for throwing their forefeet high when trotting or pacing. Bill was quite handsome when trotting—he could really step! Dad always wanted to get a harness for Bill and use him on a small cart or carriage, but that never happened.

Dad was right about Bill's breeding. He very closely matched the description of Hackney Ponies found in Wikipedia. (See References for a more complete description.)

Bill would be classified as a large pony, not big enough to be a horse, but certainly not small either. We never measured or weighed Bill, so a guess of about 12 hands tall (48 inches) and about 500 pounds in weight should be close.

THE MCDONALDS

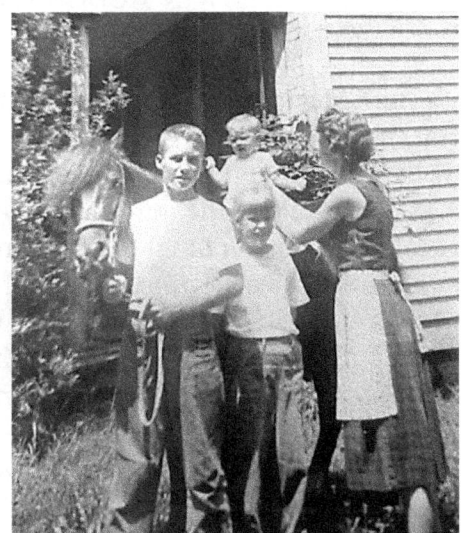

Mary on Bill just before turning 1-year-old. Mom holding her on with Rob and Kathie.

All the McDonald children learned to ride Bill. Even though Bill was a stallion, he was even-tempered and sensible. If one of the McDonald children was on his back, or someone that knew how to ride, Bill was a dashing, quick moving animal. But if that person were inexperienced, Bill would plod along like an old plug. Mary noted the same temperament in Jonny.

Bill with Kathie, Rob, and Rich on his back. Behind Bill is Uncle Charlie McCorkle, Dad, Mom, with Aunt Hattie McCorkle cut off.

ROBERT ALAN MCDONALD, KATHIE EILEEN MCDONALD COURTNEY, RICHARD EDWIN MCDONALD, MARY JO MCDONALD HELFRICH

Bill was high spirited and wasn't shy about pulling stunts. When he was just a colt, he was in the night pasture with Dan and Bird. Dad took Rob with him to round up the horses and take them to the barn. Rob recalls standing along the trail where Dad told him to stay out of the way while Dad got behind the horses and started them up the trail to the barn. Bill came charging up the trail at full gallop and, without breaking stride, kicked Rob right in the stomach. No warning, just boom at full tilt. Rob was hurt but not badly and was lucky not to be kicked in the head. Rob was somewhere between four and five.

Bill's stall was next to the bull's pen, which was in the northwest corner of the barn. A set of steps led into the feed-way from the second story. Rich had a straw hat that he loved. He wore that hat everywhere, even to bed at night. Rich came down the steps and walked directly across in front of Bill's stall. Rich was so young that the top of his hat was just above the top board on the manger in front of Bill's stall. Bill saw Rich coming and just as Rich passed, Bill reached out and bit the crown right out of Rich's hat and ate it. Rich, who was only about three, was mad. Mom got him another hat, a red painted straw, but Rich never liked it as well as the one Bill ate.

Working Cattle

In the late summer and fall, the pasture would get short and tough. Rather than begin feeding grain and hay early, Dad would have the dairy cattle put on either the third crop hay or the wheat stubble, which had alfalfa and clover growing for next year's hay. To increase farm productivity, fences did not separate the various fields. That way, each field could be plowed right up to the adjoining field—no fence lines to get in the way and no fence to mend.

At first, Bill and Rob got the cattle watching job. Later Kathie, then Rich, and finally Mary got to do it along with Bill. This feed increased both the quantity of milk and the butter fat, both valuable when selling milk. Watching cows wasn't particularly hard, but it could get boring and sometimes unexpected things happened. The unexpected usually happened after the cows had grazed to their fill; just before taking them into the barn for milking which was about the time the watcher was getting tired after a long day, also.

Cattle watching happened in the late afternoon or evening for only an hour or two. The primary duty was to keep the cattle in the field that Dad wanted grazed, off other fields, and together, so they didn't stray. Cattle have wonderful memories and if they had once gotten somewhere they wanted to go that we didn't want them to, they would remember this for years and if they saw an opportunity, they took advantage.

The watcher needed to remain alert and anticipate what they might do. Bill liked anything that allowed him access to the cows that afforded him an opportunity to bite and chase them. Both things he liked and sought opportunities to do were fine with him. Just moving the cows up the road from the pastures to the barn afforded Bill the opportunity to nip. All one had to do was move Bill to a cow that was moving too slow or that wasn't staying where she needed to be, and he would bite them. They learned to stay away from Bill.

Rob recalls watching cows in the eight-acre field just east across the railroad. He was riding Bill, and it was a quiet evening, and the cows were about full and ready to be taken to the barn. A train came up the track, moving north. Just before reaching the road and crossing the other rail track, the engineer blew the whistle. It startled Bill, who was off like a shot at full gallop. Rob stayed on him but soon realized he couldn't get Bill to stop because of that "snaffle bit"—all Rob could do was turn him. Around the field they went, Bill at full gallop, Rob pulling the reign as hard as he could to turn him. They went around the field about four times. As that was going on, the cattle decided they were full and were going to the barn, a path that would take them right in front of the railroad train.

Mom saw what was going on — she was hanging out clothes on the line to dry. She brought the clothes she had in her hands and ran across the railroad tracks, waving the clothes to stop the cows from crossing. Mom saved the day, and the cows didn't cross the tracks and get injured. Rob finally got Bill to stop. Bill took one big gulp

ROBERT ALAN MCDONALD, KATHIE EILEEN MCDONALD COURTNEY, RICHARD EDWIN MCDONALD, MARY JO MCDONALD HELFRICH

of air and acted as if nothing had happened. He dearly loved to run. At full gallop, his tail would be straight out behind him. He was fast.

One evening, Rob, riding Bill, was watching cows in the field across from the house. Between this field and the Gobbler Knob field was a swamp. It was fall and the swamp was dry. Near the center was an open area in which swamp grass grew. In those days, it was unusual to see deer. But three deer were grazing on the swamp grass. Rob saw the deer, but they either didn't see him or didn't pay any attention. Bill didn't see the deer at first. Rob moved Bill toward the deer to get a better look. This startled the deer, and they took off. Their movement startled Bill and he took off in the opposite direction. Rob was trying to control Bill while continuing to look at the deer. It turned out alright as Bill calmed down, but the deer were gone.

Often, Bill would be used several times a day. He would be saddled the entire day. On one such occasion, Bill broke loose — either the rein broke or came untied. Bill had his opportunity. The great cow chase was on! Bill gathered the cows from the pastures or wherever they were, and he gave chase. He put those cows through fences, over the roads, into fields where they weren't supposed to be, or just ran them ragged.

Rob recalls Dad being mad at him. Probably because Bill was Rob's horse; it was Rob's fault whatever happened. Dad and Rob were trying to corral Bill and Bill wasn't having any of it. He was having way too much fun. Finally, from behind the barn he came down the driveway headed right for the road chasing a cow. Bill's eyes were wide and his nostrils flaring. Rob had somehow gotten into the driveway in Bill's path. Bill was at full gallop headed right at Rob, reins flying. Rob remembers being more afraid of Dad than being run over by Bill, so he stayed right in front of Bill moving to his right as Bill swept past. Rob grabbed a reign and brought Bill to a halt. The rest of the day was spent putting the cows back where they belonged.

THE MCDONALDS

Rich recalls watching cows in the 10 acre field directly across the road from the house. The field bordered the swamp which, being fall, was dry. Rich had a tiring day and was taking a rest by laying straight back on Bill's rump. Things were quiet until a pair of hunters, who didn't have permission to be on the property and who neither Rich nor Bill knew were anywhere about, snapped a tree, which let go with a loud crack. Bill jumped right out from under Rich, who landed on his back on the ground. Bill went after the cows. He put them through fences. Kathie thinks one cow made it through about seven fences, others through three or more, others he scattered, and one or two he chased as far as Justus—nearly two miles away.

Dad was hot! Rich was scared! Rich knew he was going to get blamed for failing to control Bill, and Rich knew he wasn't entirely blameless. After they corralled Bill, Dad lit into Rich. Fortunately, after chewing Rich's butt for a while, he asked Rich what happened. Rich told him about the hunters breaking the log. Dad knew the hunters didn't have permission to be on the property, so he immediately looked for a new target for his wrath. Rich said all they saw of those hunters was the tailpipe on their car heading up Lawndell Road. Rich says he saw no need to tell Dad he was lying on his back when it all started—somehow it didn't seem all that important. Some things are best left unsaid.

Bill liked treats. Because he couldn't be put in a pasture with the cattle, he didn't get to graze very often, so he took advantage whenever he got a chance. Mary remembers riding Bill when she was young. He would take advantage of her lack of arm strength and graze. Mary told Dad she couldn't hold Bill's head up, so Dad tied the reins around the saddle horn. That didn't faze Bill in the least. He got down on his front knees and grazed.

Bill enjoyed eating thistle flowers. He'd nip the flower right off. We never could understand how he could eat that without getting thistle spines stuck in the inside of his mouth or tongue, but he never seemed to.

ROBERT ALAN MCDONALD, KATHIE EILEEN MCDONALD COURTNEY, RICHARD EDWIN MCDONALD, MARY JO MCDONALD HELFRICH

Bill liked tobacco, either the chewing type or the inside of a cigarette. It didn't matter to him if it was tobacco. He also liked wintergreen mints. He'd eat them as long as we'd feed them to him.

Stud Services

There was demand for Bill as a stud. He was a good-looking pony, with a good disposition and he threw similar offspring. Neighbors requested services and others who had merely heard of him did as well.

One afternoon when Rob was working in the barn, a man with a young child came to the barn and asked to see Bill. Rob didn't know the man and hadn't been told to expect anyone, but not to be rude, he took the stranger to the horse stable where Bill was. The stranger looked at Bill and began to find all kinds of fault. Bill was the wrong color, he was too tall or short, his confirmation wasn't right, and so on. Rob, being young, about 12 years-old, was a bit intimidated by an older person talking this way about Bill. Rob kept his mouth shut but was really getting angry.

Eventually the man left. Later, Rob told Dad about the incident, just telling Dad that a man stopped by looking for stud service, looked at Bill but Rob didn't think he was interested. Dad told Rob that he knew who the man was and that he had told him to go to the barn to see Bill. The man was interested in Bill but had been playing a joke on Rob. When he returned, he enjoyed telling Dad how mad Rob had gotten but didn't say anything. Later Dad told Rob that if anything like that happened again to tell the person to get out of our barn. Apparently, Dad didn't think it was too funny either.

Chapter Seventeen - Mary's Jonny

Jonny—Portrait by Mary Jo McDonald Helfrich

Tell Us Another Jonny Story

    Being a teacher, Mary had numerous occasions to relate stories of her growing up years. Inevitably, her students would ask, "Tell us another Jonny Story!"

Mary tells of her recollection of Jonny's birth: If my sister, Kathie, hadn't bought Ginger from Fred Thompson in about 1962 and my oldest brother Robert didn't receive a pony bought at the auction house by our Grandfather Sam McDonald, I would never have had Jonny. Bill was her sire and Dad always thought he was part Hackney. All I know is that he was beautiful and sired beautiful foals. Ginger was a mare, and she was half Morgan. I was about 6 when Ginger got bred. And how I prayed that entire year. There were definite rules set down by Dad about my ability to purchase this foal from Kathie. First, she had to be a filly, and Kathie was to charge me 100 dollars to purchase her. The other items on my prayer list were my "wish list." I wanted her to be black like Bill because I loved him so. And I wanted 4 white feet, also like Bill, and I so wanted her to have a blaze.

ROBERT ALAN MCDONALD, KATHIE EILEEN MCDONALD COURTNEY, RICHARD EDWIN MCDONALD, MARY JO MCDONALD HELFRICH

Kathie with Jonny as a colt

The morning of March 27, 1963, when I was 7, my dreams came true. Ginger was stabled at Arch Croy's that winter in his barn. The milking and barn chores were finished, and we were just sitting down for breakfast. As I recall, it was a warm morning for March. Arch knocked on the door, stuck his head in, and said, "There is a white-faced heifer down in my barn." We all looked at one another and then it dawned on all of us. We had a filly with a blaze. We all trouped outside, and breakfast was forgotten. All of us loaded onto the truck. Dad, Mom, and I were in the cab, as I would fit behind the floor gear shift. Kathie and Richard in the back. I remember arriving in that green truck.

When we arrived at the Croy barn, there was Ginger and at her side was a sorrel filly with four white feet, a blaze, and the longest legs I had ever seen... she was going to be mine! I didn't even care that she wasn't black because she was the prettiest little filly I had ever seen! I couldn't buy her for a year. I still have my savings passbook from selling veal calves. It says Horse 100 dollar withdrawal written in by my Uncle Don as he was an employee at Navarre Deposit Bank.

Jonny's blaze had a crook near her eyes. Dad said, "You must have done that crook when she was in Ginger's tummy. I remember you pushing on her tummy to move her over." I never looked at her blaze without thinking that I had caused that crook in her blaze.

THE MCDONALDS

Mom thought she looked like a white-tailed deer. She was so fine-boned, and her little tail was red on top and clear white underneath. She was already getting the beginning of a flaxen mane and sorrel tail.

Mary and Jonny

Mom is the one who named her. We came home and noted on the calendar this special event. Mom said, "The March flower is Jonquil. I think we should name her that and call her Jonny for short." That is just what happened, and I always thought her name fit her perfectly.

Two weeks later, the scene shifted to dark, cold, and dreary. Ginger had kept Jonny out in a dismal rainstorm all night instead of remaining in the barn to keep her filly warm and dry. I remember arriving at Croy's and seeing an extremely sick baby. Poor little thing had developed bacterial pneumonia. It was one moment in my life I didn't see Dad hesitate to spend money and get a vet. We went home and called immediately. So, my joy had turned to heartbreak because then I knew the seriousness of the situation. Everyone feared we would lose her. Daily penicillin shots did the trick. She not only lived but turned things around and she thrived.

Ginger was usually a good and patient mother, but one day as we drove up to Croy's barn, they were together in the small pasture. Jonny was kicking up her heels and playing. She connected with Ginger's muzzle as she was eating grass. That did it. With ears flat and teeth barred, Ginger went after her and bit her. Jonny learned a valuable lesson that day about being kind to her mother. Also, to mind her feet.

Dad said Jonny could walk on eggshells. She was graceful, and

ROBERT ALAN MCDONALD, KATHIE EILEEN MCDONALD COURTNEY, RICHARD EDWIN MCDONALD, MARY JO MCDONALD HELFRICH

deerlike as she placed her feet. She moved like a dream and, though not as smooth as Bill, a gaited horse. Dad called her usual gait usual single footing. All I know was she had a running walk that was like sitting in a rocking chair and she always took a big lead with her left leg. Occasionally, like her sire, she would rack. Riding Jonny was smooth as silk.

Breaking

Having a good, fair, or poor horse depends on how the horse was broken—a misnomer but commonly used by horsemen–or trained. A good horse isn't broken in the sense that it is damaged but forms a bond with its humans. This is how Mary recalls Jonny's breaking.

Like most events in our lives, breaking Jonny was a family event. It happened in the barnyard. The old barnyard fence was wood plank attached to wood posts. The barnyard was the length of the barn—90 feet long and 40 feet wide. In the center of the barnyard, one of the posts, used to form the straw stack, remained. The floor was dirt. For horse training, the barnyard was ideal.

Because of her training, Jonny had no fear of the equipment or riders. She always loved to be ridden.

Dad was in charge. First, she had to become accustomed to the saddle blanket. Days were spent on just the blanket. She was rubbed everywhere with it so that it was a thing of comfort, making her feel good. Then it was put on and off her back. Next it was leading her with the blanket on and sometimes it slipped off, which was scary to her at first. Back on it would go after more rubbing until she was as familiar with that blanket as she could be.

The saddle was next. Dad put it on his arm, and he let her smell every part. While he was carrying it, he walked all around her, talking to her. He sat it upon her back and took it off immediately. This too was done multiple times, till this process was not scary either.

The saddle was cinched loose, and Jonny was on a lunge line.

Gradually it was tightened, and she was lunged until she was comfortable with it on her back. Finally came the day for mounting. Robert had the lunge line, and he stood so he could rotate her around the center post, a precaution which would allow Rob to snub Jonny if necessary. Kathie and Richard were the audience. Dad placed Mary on her back and walked beside Jonny so he could take Mary off quickly in case anything went wrong. Nothing did.

To teach her to neck rein, her reins were crossed. Thus, pulling on the right-side rein caused pressure on the left side of Jonny's neck. She learned to turn away from the pressure. Thus, pressure on the left side of her neck caused her to turn right and vice versa. Circles were completed to the right and then to the left on that long lunge line. The circles were small at first and gradually became larger and larger. Mary recalls the door on the walkway was typically open and once the circles got so large, Mary had to lean way to the side to avoid the door. The last measure was riding in the barnyard without the lunge line, and her reins were finally uncrossed. No longer in circles, but anywhere Mary wished to go within the confines of the barnyard. Jonny was only a little more than a year old when she was broken. Mary was so light, less than 60 lbs. so it was easy for Jonny. No strain was on her back. Mary was eight years old.

Mary and Jonny had developed a lifelong bond through breaking. Jonny came to Mary's whistle and to no one else. She always whinnied in response to the whistle, and then she came. Mary fondly remembers that Jonny would nuzzle her, starting at her ankle and not stopping until her nose was in Mary's hair. Richard would mimic Mary's whistle, but Jonny would lay her ears back and wouldn't come to him.

Fording Sugar Creek

This event occurred right after the 1969 flood. There was damage everywhere you looked and then this happened. Rob's memory of this event is Mary atop Jonny on the far bank, seeing Jonny gathering herself to jump. Before the jump, Rob remembers thinking, *Surely she's not going to allow that horse to jump* ... but

ROBERT ALAN MCDONALD, KATHIE EILEEN MCDONALD COURTNEY, RICHARD EDWIN MCDONALD, MARY JO MCDONALD HELFRICH

jump she did. And second, when the horse went under, *Oh my God we're going to lose Mary and Jonny*. Rob felt completely helpless; it happened so quickly he didn't have time to yell or do anything else to stop it.

Mary recounts the story: The gate across the bridge was always so tight, I could never open it independently. That is why I crossed the crossing that day. I could get the gate at the corner open and closed. I knew the creek was up, but what I didn't realize was how much the crossing had washed out in the '69 flood. Sugar Creek was more than halfway up the clay bank, which we used to climb out of the creek after fording. I remember hesitating before crossing, but thinking the crossing was as it had been before the flood, I crossed, and it seemed fine. I had no idea Jonny was completely swimming. We clambered up the clay bank, which was super slick, rode the Woods, and returned to tackle the crossing again.

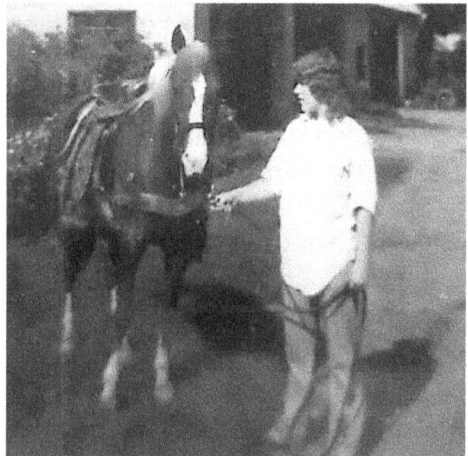

Mary and Jonny

When we came back, I remember being afraid Jonny would slip down that steep clay bank. When she hit solid ground, I could feel her gathering to jump. As I was afraid of her falling on me, I let her jump; she did. She hated the mud at the bottom of the bank. Jonny never wanted her feet dirty. (Rich recalls Bill having this same aversion. He didn't like muddy feet either. Mary remembers Bill even sidestepping around mud puddles.)

The next thing I knew, I was in water up to my neck. No horse was visible under me. She was completely submerged and when she came up, she blew water out of her nose and started swimming strongly back upstream to the other side of the crossing. Her tail was floating behind us like a rudder. She really had to swim to gain the other bank. When we got to the gravel bank on the other side, she stopped and shook water, just like the dogs after a bath. Then she turned her head and gave me the meanest look I ever saw on her face. She was so mad at me for getting her into that predicament. We were both waterlogged.

I rode to Kathie's to dry both her and me off. Kathie and Dick had moved to the farm where she lives currently. I recall Jonny stopping frequently to stare back at me as if to say, "Yes, I haven't forgotten what you allowed to happen. How could you do something so dumb?" It was dumb. She was right. When we got to Kathie's, her ears, which usually pointed forward, were laid back against her head. They had remained like that the whole mile to Kathie's. She was that mad. We were dry by now, so Kathie asked, "What is she so mad about?" I gave a long explanation, telling Kathie the whole story.

Jonny Turns Out the Lights

This winter, the horses were housed in the horse stable at the west end of the barn. Bill was across the barn with the fattening cattle. Ginger and Janey—Jonny's full sister— were loose in the area next to the bull pen. Jonny was in the small box-stall located on the wall of the barn that was under the overshoot. The horse stable was where the work horses, used on the farm before modern machinery, were stabled.

Jonny was directly in front of the light switch and behind a wooden box, permanently built-in, that was divided into two sections. The first section was directly in front of her stall. We used it to store old bailing twine which we removed when feeding hay. The second smaller portion of the box had a wooden grain chute leading directly to the upstairs oats' granary. This saved steps. Otherwise, we would be going upstairs to the granary to get oats at feeding time. A thick wooden slat was used to start and stop the flow of oats down the chute. The wooden box had a lid. In front of the

ROBERT ALAN MCDONALD, KATHIE EILEEN MCDONALD COURTNEY, RICHARD EDWIN MCDONALD, MARY JO MCDONALD HELFRICH

horse stable was the feed-way, which extended completely across the barn. At the north end there were narrow steps leading to the second floor. The walkway floor was tongue and groove pine lumber, polished from so much hay, straw, and sweepings.

Each night we threw bales of hay down into the feed-way. From there, hay was fed to the horses on one side and cattle on the other. But there were too many cows to just feed in the mangers, so each night I fed bales outside under the overshoot.

The light switch, which controlled both the bulb under the overshoot and in the feed-way, was right in front of Jonny's stall. Jonny was bored and confined in the box stall. Sometimes she would pull string out of the string box and to do that, she had to first open the long lid. I am not sure how she reached it, but she did. Next, she discovered how to operate the light switch. She took the end of her nose and curled it upwards, so it acted just like a finger and turned those lights off and on. One could look to the barn at two AM and see the lights going off and on. It was entertainment for her, and it relieved her boredom.

Her favorite activity was turning off the lights when I was taking out the hay to feed under the overshoot. Hungry cows surrounded me. Suddenly it was completely black. I had to push and shove cows out of the way after dropping the hay bale, making my way back to the switch. Once the lights were back on, I could see the delight on Jonny's face. She got me right where she wanted me, and she was "smiling."

At least four times a night, she would repeat this process until I was so mad at her that I would threaten and yell at her. She promptly would turn to the back of the box stall, lay her ears flat in anger, and stay there the rest of the night. That was fine with me because then I could feed the rest of the bales with lights on. By then, cow manure covered the hay bale that was still in front of the door. Guess who still had to pick it up and get it to where the cows could eat? I was so angry I would threaten her and really yell at her. This spoiled all her fun.

The bulbs were big and expensive. Jonny turned them off and on so frequently that we were burning out bulbs on a regular basis. Dad finally unscrewed the light inside the barn so she could only burn out the one outside under the overshoot.

Ginger, not to be outdone, learned how to open the grain chute to get herself grain. Dad nailed the box lid shut. It didn't take her too long to tear the boards off to open the box where the grain fell. Finally, Dad nailed the chute shut to end her foraging.

After this winter, the horses were never housed in that part of the barn again. They were moved to a big back room in the chicken coop. Dad had enough of them.

The Woodpile

Mary recalls being somewhere between nine and eleven when this occurred. Jonny would have been quite young at that time, two or three.

Dad being Dad got railroad car tongue and groove flooring from old, dismantled rail cars. The boys got the lucky job of removing all the nails and screws to "clean" the boards for use as the second story flooring in the machine shed we were building: another of Dad's savings measures. After cleaning but before installation, the flooring was stacked in front of the machine shed in neat piles 4 to 6 feet high.

Jonny had a short, shanked bit. Because her mouth was tender, she learned to place one side of the bit between her teeth. She was very adept at using her lower jaw to grab the shank and place it between her teeth. With the bit in her teeth, the only thing one could do was turn her. That's what happened this day.

Dad was working in front of the machine shed when I lost control of Jonny. We approached the wood piles from the west at full gallop. I was afraid she would run out on the road, so to stop her I aimed her towards one of the flooring stacks. Dad saw everything and I'm sure it scared him to death.

I thought she would stop by planting her front feet. Usually this took two hops, and we would stop. Instead, the next thing I knew, we were on top of the woodpile with boards being expelled from the top by her feet as she was trying to stop up there and keep her balance at the same time. We got stopped and, miraculously, I was still on her back. I was watching those boards being ejected off the pile. I recall her just standing up there with me on her back and not even afraid.

    Dad lit into me. I don't think he was ever as mad at me as he was on that day. I can't imagine Dad watching helplessly as this transpired. After stopping, I had to jump her down off that wood pile and it was at least 5 foot tall. That was as scary as getting up there. I was grounded from the horse for two weeks and I wasn't to gallop the rest of the summer. I recall getting a different bit after this, but by then, Jonny could get any bit between her teeth just so she could gallop. Nothing she liked to do better than run like the wind. With the new bit, there was a longer shank, and I could remove it from between her teeth. No more running away with me.

Chapter Eighteen - Ginger

Kathie was so glad to buy a horse of her own. She rode frequently around the farm and on Lawndell Road. Riding in the fields was not allowed due to causing holes when the ground was soft. Occasionally she rode to see Grandma Jones in Harmon, and later to see the Courtneys, who lived 4 miles east.

One time, she and her roommate from nursing school were riding on the road. Kathie was on Mary's horse, Jonny, and the roommate was on Ginger. They were going along chatting when suddenly the mailbox beside the road swung around the pole it was on. This startled Jonny. She took one big sidestep and took off. She sure could run. When Kathie finally got her stopped and the roommate caught up, the roommate asked, "How did you stay on her?"

ROBERT ALAN MCDONALD, KATHIE EILEEN MCDONALD COURTNEY, RICHARD EDWIN MCDONALD, MARY JO MCDONALD HELFRICH

Kathie holding Jonny and Rich holding Ginger

Horse Sense

Ginger was a very smart horse and knew how to wait patiently for help. The fence along the four acre field beside the house was woven wire. Mary noticed Ginger standing in the same spot beside the fence one morning. About ten in the morning, Mary, about eleven years old at the time, decided to investigate. She walked out to about 20 feet from the fence. Ginger was standing normally, so Mary started to turn and walk back to the house. Ginger gently shook her foot, which had somehow gone through the woven wire opening. She was stuck. Mary's hands were not strong, and the wire opening was very misshapen from Ginger putting her foot through it. She wouldn't let Mary leave unless she was free. She was tired of standing there. It took 30 minutes or more for Mary to dislodge that foot. The whole time, Ginger was quiet and cooperative. She never panicked.

Mary and her first cousin, Emily Foster, Aunt Eleanor's daughter, used to ride together, typically every Sunday after church. Mary and Emily were inseparable. Besides our Farm, they rode on the Secrest farm. Although we referred to the property as the Secrest farm, it was owned by Mr. Dillon, who purchased it shortly before. Dad rented the property for additional cropland. Because we were farming it, Mary and Emily had permission to go there and frequently did. Mr. Dillon planned to turn the property into a golf course so there were bridges built over Bean Creek, a spring-fed stream that emptied into Sugar Creek. The Secrest farm was south of ours, so Sugar Creek passed through this property after leaving our farm.

Mr. Dillon logged out the big woods on the property two springs in a row. There were trails which led to the different fields and the girls rode hard over these trails. They never walked anywhere; they galloped. Mary and Emily rode Kathie's Ginger and Mary's Jonny. The trails ran to Ohio Route 93 on the West. As it was cool, the girls rode in there. It was easy to get lost because the trails crossed and re-crossed each other. That's what happened to a ten-year-old Mary and twelve-year-old Emily.

The girls had gone the farthest they had ever gone on the logging paths. Darkness was falling. Intending to come home, they kept coming to a dead tree. They recognized the tree but always took the wrong turn at this intersection. Each time, Ginger pulled to the right. She was the lead horse and Jonny always followed her mother. But the girls ignored Ginger and turned left, which, of course, was the wrong way. Finally, it was dusk, and the girls came to that dead tree again. By now, they were terrified of staying in those big Woods all night. Mary finally had the idea that they should give Ginger her "head;" let her go where she wanted. She did, and Ginger took off at a dead run, with Jonny right behind. The girls were out of those Woods in less than 3 minutes after spending hours being lost. Ginger wanted rid of those two imbecilic girls and wanted to get her supper. She knew what she was doing all along if the girls had only listened to her.

ROBERT ALAN MCDONALD, KATHIE EILEEN MCDONALD COURTNEY, RICHARD EDWIN MCDONALD, MARY JO MCDONALD HELFRICH

We Would Ride Anything

We didn't just ride horses; we tried riding other animals as well. Usually that didn't work out too well as those other animals didn't care much about being ridden. But there was one notable exception, a red and white Holstein dairy cow we called Sadie 2. She was number 2 because her mother was Sadie. Rob was running out of names, so he started over.

Sadie 2 was handled when she was younger. She got used to it and we began to put Mary on her back and Sadie 2 didn't object, so we kept doing it. In the spring, summer, and fall evenings, we would go down the road across the bridge and get the dairy cows out of either the north or south pasture, then bring them up the road to the barn for milking. We would walk down to get them and walk behind them on the way back.

We took pity on Mary being little, so we'd put her on Sadie 2's back and Mary would ride the cow all the way up the road. There was no rope or anything else to control the cow. Often, people would be driving up the road and would have to wait behind the herd. They would remark, "Look at the kid riding the cow!" It was a novel sight. Few cows will tolerate being ridden. But when we reached the yard, we had to get Mary off the cow because Sadie 2 would go under the apple tree that had low branches to get her back scratched and that would knock Mary off. Most of the time we got Mary off in time, but sometimes, Mary had to deal with low apple tree branches. Occasionally, she got knocked off. But being resilient, Mary learned to duck.

Since Sadie 2 allowed Mary to ride, Kathie and Rich would get on if Mary wasn't along. When the two of them watched cows in the fall, they would ride her then, too.

Not only did Mary, Kathie, and Rich ride Sadie 2, but so did at least two of our girl cousins, Sara and Emily Foster. They remember Sadie 2 by name.

THE MCDONALDS

Chapter Nineteen – Animals We Knew

Spike and Cork

When living on the Booth farm in Harmon, we had two dogs, both male. The black one with a small white spot on his face was Spike and the white and black one was Cork. Spike was the largest, taller and rangy. Cork has a passing resemblance to Border Collies, but was predominately white rather than black, but he didn't seem to have a Border Collie's herding instinct.

The dogs moved from the Booth farm with us when we moved. Neither dog was particularly well trained. They didn't work cattle or anything else very well. Cork was somewhat of a sneak. He liked to get behind things. Every farm had a dog. We had these two. They were with us until they got old and passed on.

One spring morning, Rob was walking on the road back toward the house after taking the cows to the pasture. As he was passing the lower part of the field across from the house, Rob saw a skunk ambling across the field. Spring is mating season and skunks are active. Being early spring, the field had been plowed but not yet planted. Cork was out in the same field, and he too saw the skunk. Cork came racing toward the skunk. The skunk saw Cork coming and did what skunks do; turn his back on his attacker so he can use his most potent weapon: his skunk spray. When Cork saw the skunk turn, he thought, *This is my chance,* and went right at the back end of the skunk. The skunk did what skunks do – he sprayed. Cork was right behind him barking. His mouth was open, and the skunk spray went straight in.

If the taste of skunk is anything like the smell, it must be awful! Cork was rolling around, eating dirt, shaking his head, and doing anything else he could to get that awful taste and smell out of his mouth. It didn't work. He stunk for days.

ROBERT ALAN MCDONALD, KATHIE EILEEN MCDONALD COURTNEY, RICHARD EDWIN MCDONALD, MARY JO MCDONALD HELFRICH

Momma Cat

Cats lived in the barn. They didn't have an easy life. They ate what they could catch. When we milked, they got a little fresh milk, and they chewed on the filters we used to strain the milk as it was put into the milk cans.

Momma Cat was with us for quite a while. She raised kitten litters several times each year. She could do this because she was a great hunter, feeding herself and her kittens. She was fearless, even catching and killing rats. Dad commented that he saw Momma Cat —we called her that because she had no other name— kill a rat that was nearly as big as she was. He said she was rolling around on the ground with the rat until she killed it. Most cats won't take on a rat. Rats are tough and hard to kill, plus they're big.

Momma Cat was gray and not too large. She was friendly to humans, liked getting petted, but didn't hang around us very long at a time. She was always hunting.

One day Rob was in the milking parlor doing some work. He saw Momma Cat sitting on the ground on the opposite side. She was very still but didn't seem to be watching anything. Suddenly, Momma Cat leapt up landing on the top of the stanchions, about 5 feet off the ground; from there she leapt another five or six feet to the ceiling – the bottom of the haymow. Down she came repeating the process in reverse. When she landed back on the ground, she had a mouse in her mouth. The entire process couldn't have taken more than a couple of seconds. She was so quick, the mouse didn't have a chance to save itself.

Ray Geis, Dad's coon hunting buddy, had a rabbit dog, part Beagle, of which he was proud. Ray bragged that the dog hated cats and would attack them whenever possible. Ray, Dad, the dog, and Rob were outside east of the barn. Ray's dog was running around smelling everything it could. The dog headed for the open door leading to the milking parlor. Dad said, "Ray, you better keep that dog out of there because there's a cat in there and she doesn't like dogs." Ray replied, "If that cat gets in his way, he'll kill it." Dad responded, "Suit yourself."

Sure enough, the dog went through the door into the milking parlor. In less than a minute, the dog found the cat. The dog began howling and came boiling out the door running as fast as it could go with Momma Cat right after him. Dad looked at Ray as if to say, "I told you so!" Ray had no response.

Momma Cat didn't follow the dog far. She got him out of her area quickly, so she was done with him. We checked the dog and found cat claw injuries all around his eyes and muzzle. The dog never again went into the barn.

High Pockets

One of the spring chores that must be accomplished is cleaning out the barn after a long winter – hauling manure. In addition to getting the barn cleaned and the fields fertilized, this chore often resulted in hearing Dad's stories. One may think that hauling manure was something to be avoided because of the smell, but cow and horse manure isn't that pungent. Hog manure was a bit smellier, but the worst was chicken, which is extremely high in ammonia, primarily nitrogen. Fortunately, we only cleaned the chicken coop once or twice a year.

Cleaning out the barn is a late winter, early spring chore – March and early April. By this time, the cattle and horses have been in the barn all winter and the waste plus bedding has built up and has been tramped down by the animals. By this time of year, the weather was warmer, but the frost hadn't left the ground so the ground wouldn't rut easily. Working conditions were better – not so cold. Manure would be spread on the corn ground because corn needs more nutrients. Plowing, which happens in April and May, will incorporate the manure into the soil where it will decompose releasing nutrients.

We were cleaning out the loafing pen, the center section of the barn located between the milking parlor and feed way. Most of the cow manure was in the loafing pen and in the barnyard. Getting it

ROBERT ALAN MCDONALD, KATHIE EILEEN MCDONALD COURTNEY, RICHARD EDWIN MCDONALD, MARY JO MCDONALD HELFRICH

out was all hand labor with manure forks. The manure with bedding mixed in built up in layers, then tramped down making loading it into the manure spreader arduous work. Later, Dad got a tractor mounted loader for the Minnie, which reduced the manual labor.

We had been working on the loafing pen for a day or two and had the north side cleared down to the floor. We backed the spreader in with the beaters against the manger to allow us to work on the other side. Nothing could get behind the manure spreader and there wasn't anything on the north side of the barn that any of the cows would want anyway.

We had one cow we called High-Pockets. She was extremely long legged even for a Holstein. High-Pockets was a born jumper. She thought she was a deer. Fences, gates, and other obstacles meant little to her. She just jumped over them.

We had the barnyard doors open for light and ventilation. In came High-Pockets and another cow. The other cow may have butted High-Pockets, but it didn't take much to trigger a jump. High-Pockets was standing looking across the back of the manure spreader when she either got butted or saw something she wanted. Exactly what that was we never figured out as there was no hay or chop in sight. But she decided to jump over the beaters into a space she wouldn't fit into anyway. We saw her eyeing the jump but before we could stop her, she jumped.

She came down belly first right on the beaters. One shorter peg punctured her belly, not terribly deep, but she was stuck on the beater and hurt to boot. The look in her eye said, "Why did I do that?"

There we were with a 1200-pound cow stretched out full length on the back of the manure spreader. Now the question was, how do we get her off and keep from getting her hurt worse or even killing her? The three of us couldn't lift her, and we knew we couldn't move the manure spreader without doing even more damage.

Finally, we decided to rig the block and tackle, lift her off the beaters and move the manure spreader out from under her. We did this and once we got off the beaters and, in the air, we put hay or straw bales under her feet before lowering her. We got her back on solid ground and then doctored her wounds. She recovered, but Dad had enough of her antics, so she made a one-way trip to the sale barn at Kidron.

Why she did what she did we never understood but it certainly reduced our productivity that day.

Animal Surgery

Men and boys only attended breeding sessions with cattle, horses, and hogs, animal killing when butchering, castrating young boars and bulls, and other surgical procedures. Why the girls weren't included wasn't discussed. We assumed it was too gross for their delicate sensibilities. Men and boys aren't delicate or don't have sensibilities.

Boars to Barrows- Shortly after moving to the Farm, Dad began raising hogs. The brood stock he bought from Arthur Eberly, Uncle Don's father-in-law— purebred Chester Whites. Shortly after having the first litters, it became necessary to turn the young boars into barrows. In other words, they had to be castrated. Dad and neighbor Nick Schonlen shared this problem as Nick began raising hogs about the same time. They came to an agreement: Dad would help Nick and Nick would help Dad. Each would do the knife work on their own animals. Castrating a hog above 30 pounds is a two-man job. This arrangement worked for years until Nick moved. After this, Rob got the job of catching and holding the boars down while Dad performed surgery. As Rich got older, he was included.

The equipment used was basic – a single bladed razor blade and sheep dip as an antiseptic. Sheep dip was strong. Dad's arm would turn pink, and hair would fall off after using it. The operating theater was the south-west pen in the hog barn. It had the best light. Later Dad added salt as an additional antiseptic. Of course, the hog barn would be cleaned and disinfected with hydrated lime before surgery began.

ROBERT ALAN MCDONALD, KATHIE EILEEN MCDONALD COURTNEY, RICHARD EDWIN MCDONALD, MARY JO MCDONALD HELFRICH

The procedure was simple. The hogs were sorted by sex. Gilts were released. Boars were kept together in one pen. Rob would grab an animal's front and hind legs on one side of its body, pick the animal up, lay it down on its side, sit on its shoulder near the head so it couldn't move, and pull the right leg toward the head exposing the scrotum. Dad would disinfect the area with sheep dip, open the scrotum with the razor blade, remove the testicles one at a time and cut the tubes, then flush the wound with additional disinfectant. After that, the hog would be released and allowed out of the pen. The next boar would be caught, and the procedure repeated until there were no more boars. These sessions could involve 20 or more animals.

Because the work was hard and unpleasant, we often waited until there were a sizable number of boars that needed trimmed. Some of those young boars would get big. Often the boars would weigh as much or more than Rob or Rich, over 130 pounds. These large animals were hard to manage and would often try to bite the person trying to man-handle them. One particularly large boar who may have been missed during a previous session was over 200 pounds. Both Rob and Rich implored Dad to let him be, even though we would have to sell him cheaply or as a herd boar. Dad said no. That hog never got up after the operation.

Rich recalls Dad having trouble with animals getting an infection after the surgery. That's when Dad introduced salt. It must have burned because the hogs certainly reacted, rubbing their butts on the ground and squealing, but they didn't get infected.

Later when the hog operation was modernized with a full-time farrowing house, the boars were trimmed when they were smaller, before moving into growing pens. A holding device was used so castration was a one-person job.

Rupture Repair- For a brief time, it was necessary to turn the east end of the barn yard into a hog growing pen. A sizable number were housed there. The weather was cold. For warmth, hogs pile up in such conditions. That's exactly what they did.

Unfortunately, for the animals on the bottom, the weight caused the area around the anus to rupture and the large intestine to protrude. Rich recalls Dad calling the vet to determine if the animals could be saved. The Vet diagnosed the problem and sutured the anus shut after first pushing the intestine back into place. Dad asked the vet how the animal would be able to defecate. The Vet replied, "When the animal has to go, it will." The Vet was correct because that's what happened. The hogs thus treated healed.

This problem presented itself repeatedly. Rich recalls helping Dad perform the surgery. After observing the Vet, Dad felt there was no need to pay for such service, so Dad did the suturing after first tying the animal's hind legs and hoisting it on the barnyard fence.

Bulls to Steers- The task of turning bulls into steers was performed using a device which crimped the tubes leading to the animal's testicles. The bull was roped, snubbed to a post, and the crimping device applied. After a few seconds, the device was removed, and the animal released.

ROBERT ALAN MCDONALD, KATHIE EILEEN MCDONALD COURTNEY, RICHARD EDWIN MCDONALD, MARY JO MCDONALD HELFRICH

Chapter Twenty – Butchering

We butchered most meat consumed on the Farm. This included chickens, hogs, and cattle. It didn't take much time to butcher chickens or beef. But hog butchering was more complicated, involving long days. The butcher-house was used to process both chickens and hogs.

The butcher house, which could also be described as a summer kitchen, was purpose-built. But we didn't use it for beef. We butchered beef using the middle barn floor on the second floor of the barn. We only butchered cattle and hogs in cool months.

There were tools only used for butchering, including knives, especially one K-Bar that Dad used exclusively, skinning knives, standard butcher knives, and a meat saw. There was a copper dipper that would hold about a quart, a small dipper, a perforated skimmer made of brass about the same size as the small dipper, and a four-prong meat fork.

The bell scrapers were used to remove hair from hogs. Hooks, smaller ones used to hang hogs, and larger ones used to hang beef. A sycamore cutting board about 16 inches wide and 10 feet long was in the butcher-house kept on metal horses, which resulted in the work surface being about 42 inches high. The smooth side of the cutting board was only facing up when it was used; otherwise, the smooth side was facing down to prevent damage and contamination. Tripods used to hang hogs, and a single tree used to hang beef. A sausage press is used, as the name implies, to press sausage into casings and to press lard. A sausage grinder used for grinding meat was equipped with a pulley allowing attachment of a small electric motor. The sausage press and grinder were from Dad's parents.

Where all the tools came from isn't clear. Ed Miller and other neighbors who used the butcher house provided some of them. Dad bought some at farm sales. We kept all the tools in the butcher house.

ROBERT ALAN MCDONALD, KATHIE EILEEN MCDONALD COURTNEY, RICHARD EDWIN MCDONALD, MARY JO MCDONALD HELFRICH

Chickens

Older laying hens that had outlived their primary productivity were the ones that were usually butchered. The laying hens were being replaced by the next generation that Mom raised in the brooder house. The chickens being butchered were placed in a small pen, selected one by one. Kathie recalls having one chicken getting away and then having to chase her.

Dad usually chopped off the head and hung onto the headless bird until it stopped flopping around. That prevented it from getting too far away and beating itself up. Once, Dad tied twine around the legs and removed the head when they were suspended from the clothesline. It worked well.

We scalded the headless chickens in water heated in the butcherhouse. Scalding was necessary for easier feather removal. Rob recalls the smell of a chicken after scalding as being unpleasant. The entrails were removed, the birds halved, washed thoroughly, wrapped, and placed in the freezer.

Depending upon the number processed, it could take several hours.

Cattle

Usually, one head of beef would be butchered at a time, occasionally two. The selected animal would have a rope around its neck, led up the barn bank on the north side until it was nearly to the barn floor, where it would be shot and bled out. It wouldn't be taken into the barn, so the blood would soak into the ground instead of pooling on the barn floor.

We would drag the dead animal onto the barn floor where we would skin it, remove the entrails, and hang it from a rafter by using a block and tackle or chain hoist. We would hoist the animal as skinning progressed, making the process easier. Once skinned, we would let it hang to cool completely, then halve and quarter it.

Finally, we took the meat to a butcher shop with a walk-in cooler, where it would hang for about a week, then be cut into roasts, steaks, and the hamburger ground. Hanging beef so that it ages is critical for tenderizing the meat. We didn't have a walk-in cooler, nor did we have the equipment necessary to cut beef. Fortunately, there were shops in the area that provided this service for a fee.

To prepare for beef butchering, we would clean the barn floor by sweeping. Rob typically got to place the block and tackle on a pulley affixed to a rafter. He would climb up on the square (a timber that spanned the entire barn width—40 feet), climb out on it, reach out and hang by one arm from an adjoining rafter and thread a rope through the pulley about 15 feet above the barn floor. The rope would raise the block and tackle.

After butchering, we cleaned the barn floor, which typically had little debris. The hide we would fold and place in a burlap bag and sell it. The entire process would take about half a day.

Hogs

The time required for hog butchering was a full day for up to three hogs. (The most hogs killed in one day that Rob can recall was six, but that was a community affair with neighbors' hogs included.) Fewer hogs didn't mean a shorter day. A full day was about 12 -16 hours. Also, twice during that day, the cows were milked, and the hogs fed. Hog butchering took more time because it involved more tasks.

Rob recalls one day when three hogs were scheduled as being the coldest day of the year. That morning the thermometer read about -15 degrees. We decided to butcher that day, so we went ahead regardless of the cold. As the day progressed, it warmed up, getting up to zero. The cold worked out in our favor. The meat cooled quickly with no chance or spoiling. It sure was nice getting into the butcher-house with that furnace putting out heat.

Preparation for butchering started the day before, especially if the butcher-house hadn't been used since the prior year. It was cleaned, swept, and scrubbed down with water and soap. Wood was

ROBERT ALAN MCDONALD, KATHIE EILEEN MCDONALD COURTNEY, RICHARD EDWIN MCDONALD, MARY JO MCDONALD HELFRICH

gathered for the furnace. We placed the scalding trough outside with access into the butcher-house via two large swinging doors. We placed a wood top over blocks so that the top rested about two feet above the ground, right next to the scaling trough.

Kettles, one cast iron in the front furnace opening and the copper kettle on the back furnace opening, were filled with fresh water. We inspected all the equipment to be sure it was functional. The equipment included tripods for hanging the hogs after killing and scalding, hog hooks for use with the tripods, scrapers for hair removal after scalding, the sausage press, the sausage grinder, and the cutting bench. The equipment wasn't scrubbed until butchering started, as it needed to be clean with no rust formed on any part of it. We stored kettles and the sausage press with lard left on them to prevent rust.

The day began about 5:30 AM. The cows were milked. Then the fire, an important job, started. Only wood is used, and care had to be taken, so the fire didn't get too hot or later in the day didn't go out. Initially, a hot fire is necessary so that the scalding water is ready quickly, but later, a slower fire is needed so that the lard or meat being cooked didn't burn. Managing the fire was a job that Rich really liked and was particularly good at.

Final preparation for hog killing began. The .22 rifle loaded, the sticking knife was prepared for use, and the means of transporting the dead hog to the butcher-house area ready. When the scalding water was about to boil, we went into the hog barn, selected a hog, moved the animal into the walkway, shot the animal and drained the blood by severing the artery in the animal's throat. A shot to the head dropped the animal but the heart continued to beat which allowed the blood to be evacuated. We took care that the animal wasn't unduly excited, killed quickly, and humanely.

Next the animal was taken to the scalding trough and placed on the top. The trough filled with boiling water using five-gallon buckets with enough water to cover the animal. Chains were used to lower the animal into the scalding trough where two of us working together with the chains turned the animal to assure a complete even scald. The animal was lifted out of the trough using the chains and placed on the top. Then we set to work with the scrapers removing all hair from the animal until its skin was completely clean and hair free. We usually shaved the areas around the head with sharp knives to remove all the hair.

The hog resting on the tabletop was picked up and moved to a spot outside where we placed tripods. We prepared the animal for hanging by slitting the skin and inserting a hook into the tendon near each rear foot. The hook attached to the tripod, and the hog raised by anchoring two tripod legs and pushing the other upward until the hog was suspended.

Then Dad would remove the entrails. He didn't trust us to do this, as he wanted to be sure there were no knife slips with the contents of the gut being spilled on the meat. After gutting, the hog was completely and thoroughly rinsed with cold, fresh water. The head was removed, and the hog cut in half through the backbone. The hog continued cooling in the fresh air. This day, cooling was quick with no danger that any of the meat would spoil. In fact, the meat was nearly frozen.

In the meantime, water was added to the kettles, the fire stoked for a second scalding. When the water was ready, a second hog was selected, and the process repeated. Later, it was repeated a third time.

After the third (or last) hog was killed, one of us would feed the rest of the hogs.

Breakfast was a run into the house and grab something and come right back. Lunch wasn't much better, but we took more time and more than one person at a time could go in and eat. If things were going well, everybody would go at once, but lunch (dinner, as we called it) didn't last long, 15 to 20 minutes.

Then it was back to processing the hogs. One by one, the hog halves were carried into the butcher-house and processed. We removed the skin with the fat on from the cuts of meat. We cut the fat into cubes and placed it into one of the iron kettles. The hams and bacons were cut out. The shoulder roasts we were going to keep were cut and placed for later wrapping. All other cuts were separated and were ground into sausage. The less than desirable cuts, head meat, heart, and liver were placed in the small iron kettle—this became krepple. Some folks made this into head cheese or scrapple.

All day, the copper kettle had hot water used for final equipment cleaning. The first butchering of the season required the most cleaning as the lard that remained on the kettles solidified and gathered dust and dirt when sitting. The lard coating prevented rust. All of this had to be removed often using a sandstone and elbow-grease along with hot water and soap. Both Rob and Rich frequently got this job. It wasn't finished until Dad pronounced it clean.

After all the hogs were processed, the lard kettle was placed on the front furnace opening and cooked to render the lard. Rob often got the task of making sure the lard was properly rendered – cooked so that it would not spoil but not burnt, making it useless. A metal stirrer which had a hoe shaped end sticking straight out of the metal handle was used. When the cracklings rattled just so, the lard was done.

It took two men to remove the iron kettle of hot lard from the furnace using rough sawn oak plank over 2x2 inches and 6 feet long. The kettle was placed near the sausage press, which was also used to press the lard. It was easy to ladle it into the press using a copper dipper, then pressed. The resulting cracklings formed a cake at the bottom. Periodically, the cracklings were removed so that more pressing could be done. With three hogs, there would have been about six or more cakes. The cracklings were hard and were added to dogs' food as a supplement. They enjoyed chewing cracklings, and the extra fat gave them very thick, glossy coats. We stored rendered lard in metal cans with lids. Each can held about two gallons.

The small iron kettle containing the krepple meat was placed on the front furnace opening and cooked until Dad judged it done. At that point, we removed the kettle from the furnace and spread the contents on the cutting board. Each piece of meat was checked, and all bones removed. After this, the meat ground using the sausage grinder, then put back into the small kettle, which was put back on the furnace after adding cornmeal, flour, salt, and pepper. The krepple cooked until Dad judged it done. The kettle was removed from the furnace, and the contents ladled out into loaf pans where it cooled and congealed. Later we froze it. Krepple was primarily a breakfast dish, served sliced and fried.

Rich says it always amazed him watching Dad season the krepple just-so. As the mixture was cooking on the furnace, Dad would taste test it regularly. He would remove the meat and add just a bit of salt and pepper to get it exactly right. He would keep this up about as long as it cooked. Rich recalls thinking, *I'll never have the talent to season it exactly right. Boy, Dad really is smart.* Now Rich realizes Dad was hungry and was getting himself a snack. He would offer it to us, but we rarely ate very much of it. We saved up for Mom's supper.

The sausage cuts were ground using the sausage grinder. Processing sausage changed over the years. At first, all the sausage was stuffed, by use of the sausage press, the meat forced into natural gut casings, which are cleaned hog intestines. At first, Mom got the job of preparing the casings. Mom hated that job. She may have gotten help from Minnie Lantzer. But that didn't last too long after Mom or Dad found out casings can be purchased ready for use.

Before preservation by freezing, sausage was canned using either quart or half-gallon jars. After freezing became available, stuffed sausage was packaged for freezing. Still later, we found stuffing unnecessary, so it was just wrapped in one-pound packages. Finally, we determined it wasn't necessary to season the meat before freezing – it kept better without salt – it was freezer wrapped in one-pound packages.

Supper after butchering consisted of Mom's homemade corn meal pancakes, fresh sausage, and apple sauce. After that, we'd milk. Usually, one of us would break away and feed the cattle and hogs before supper. After milking, we'd finish anything left over in the butcher-house. Sometime between nine and eleven o-clock, we'd come in, clean up, and go to bed.

ROBERT ALAN MCDONALD, KATHIE EILEEN MCDONALD COURTNEY, RICHARD EDWIN MCDONALD, MARY JO MCDONALD HELFRICH

Rich recalls having his friend, Mike Kirby, with him on butchering day. As usual, supper that day was Mom's corn-meal pancakes and fresh sausage. Rich recalls Mike eating about six sausage patties. Mike's father asked Dad why he let Mike eat so much sausage. Dad told him, "I thought he was hungry." When asked, Mike still remarks, "That was good eating!"

Occasionally, we would butcher a hog and turn the whole thing into whole-hog sausage. Everything except the bacons, because the amount of meat found in bacon didn't justify turning it into sausage. All we had to do was let the word out that we had whole-hog sausage. Before the day was out, it was all sold. Our sausage recipe limited the amount of fat to just the amount that was needed for cooking. The flavor when the hams are added is unforgettable, which is why it sold out the way it did.

Since we had the only butcher-house in the area, neighbors and relatives also used it. We helped them butcher, too. That butcher-house was also a fine place to make maple syrup in the spring, and in the fall, make apple butter and have a sweet corn roast cookout.

Apple butter making was a community project. Arden and Lois Grossklaus had a good apple orchard, so they usually supplied the apples—several varieties. We would go to their house to make snitz—apples cut in small chunks that would cook quickly and evenly. Arden would take apples to a press for cider. Then the snitz and cider would be taken to the butcher-house where it would be cooked in the large copper kettle. After cooking, it would be canned in quart or pint jars. There were two apple butter stirrers kept in the butcher-house.

Chapter Twenty-One – Weather Events

The Muskingum Watershed Conservancy District included the farm. As described in the Purchase and Easement Appraisal Data—Rural dated December 12, 1935, damages for Easement were $2,617 paid to Stahl, Jessie N. and McWhinney, C. Ethel. This order of condemnation was for the United States of America. The Farm is located upstream of the northernmost flood control dam placed on Sugar Creek, the Beach City Dam.

When a heavy rain occurred that would endanger towns and villages downstream (south), the dam operators could legally and without payment of further damages close the floodgates and back water onto our farm and others around us, thus protecting persons and property downstream. Water release was at the dam operators' discretion. Property owners received a onetime payment for all future damages at conservancy creation. There were no additional payments, no matter how often flooding occurred. Of course, Mom and Dad were aware of the easement when purchasing the Farm.

Without risk of flood loss, only about half the total acreage could be cultivated. Some land used for crops was within the floodplain. Floods occurred nearly every year, but most occurred with only minor damage and early in the spring that weren't critical to Farm operations.

We experienced major floods: February 1958, July 1969, and September 1979. Each resulted in substantial damage. Only the two floods of '58 and '69 did the high-water mark reach that shown on the survey map done in conjunction with the easement.

Two other significant weather events were The Great Blizzard of '78 during which the cattle were stranded in the pasture without grass or hay, and the flood of '79.

ROBERT ALAN MCDONALD, KATHIE EILEEN MCDONALD COURTNEY, RICHARD EDWIN MCDONALD, MARY JO MCDONALD HELFRICH

Easement Map

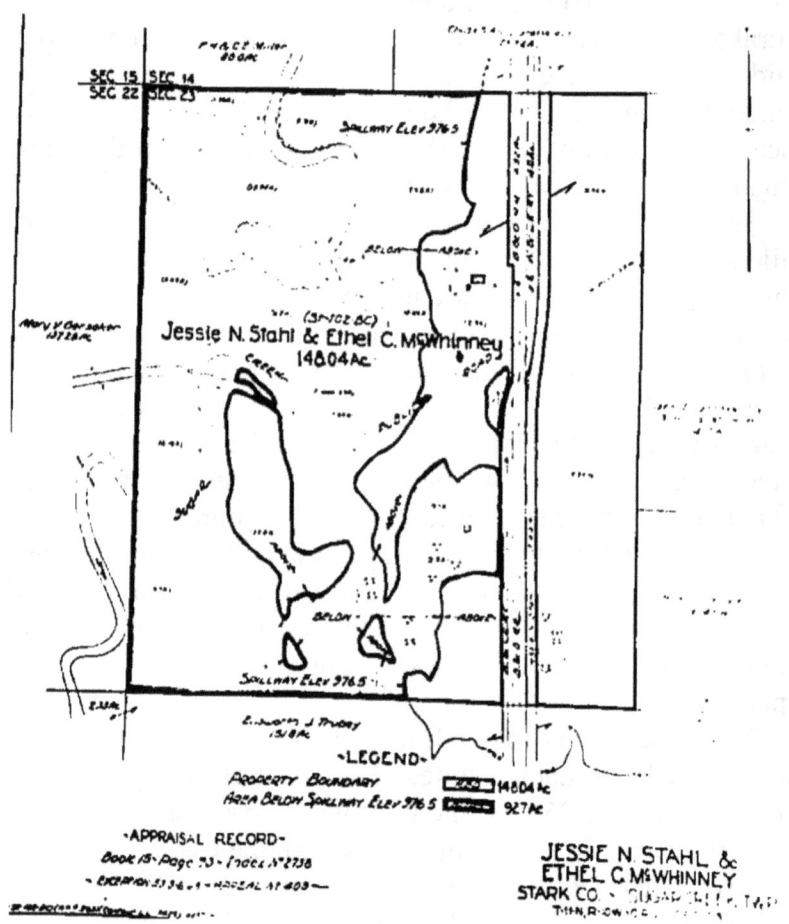

This map shows the Farm as the original quarter section number 23. The total acreage is provided as the portions both above and below the spillway elevation.

THE MCDONALDS

1958

The February 1958 flood occurred in the winter. Crops weren't damaged, but it resulted in the destruction of all the fences around the pastures. Until the fences were rebuilt, the cows couldn't be pastured. Besides the cost of the fencing, all the spring planting was delayed, resulting in lower crop yields that year.

The ground was completely frozen when the rain came. It couldn't soak into the ground and a major flood resulted. The dam was closed, and the water backed up. While backed up, freezing weather returned, and the water froze. It receded after the floodgates were opened. As the water went down, the ice crushed all the fences and gates.

We couldn't take our milk to the dairy because of the flood. Brewster was completely cut off for days. We fed the milk to the hogs, but we made home-made ice cream: one to five gallons of it a day. We had two 2 gallon freezers and one 1 gallon. We had ice. All we had to do was go into the field next to the house and pick it up, as the water had come that high. We made vanilla, chocolate, and strawberry ice cream. Mom put frozen strawberries in the mix, making strawberry ice cream. It was the best strawberry ice cream any of us ever had either before or since.

Dad used a post-hole drill (notice the word drill, not digger) which the Gonner farm owned. The drill mounted on the side of a tractor, which was used to move the device along but supplied no power to the drill. To prepare a post-hole, the tractor was driven to the spot, the auger with the point lowered to the ground and the post-hole drilled using a hand-crank. Since both ours and the Gonner farm line fences needed replacing, both used the drill. Harry Pepper, who was the tenant farmer of the Gonner farm, and Dad shared the hand drilling.

Dad drilled hundreds of post holes by hand that spring. Once the hole was prepared, a post was placed, and it was set by replacing the soil which was tamped so the post was solid. Then the fence was strung, tightened, and stapled in place. Many of the posts were used

ROBERT ALAN MCDONALD, KATHIE EILEEN MCDONALD COURTNEY, RICHARD EDWIN MCDONALD, MARY JO MCDONALD HELFRICH

railroad ties obtained from the railroad. Others were locust posts, many of which were cut from Arch Croy's farm.

Other post holes were hand dug for fences that weren't line fences. Grandpa Dan helped Dad with digging and fence building.

When finally finished, the farm had all new fences, which lasted for years. This made our work in subsequent years getting ready to turn the cattle out much easier. But that first year was extremely hard. Later, Dad bought a power-take-off post-hole digger, but before that, we dug post holes by hand.

July 4th, 1969

The 1969 flood nearly put the farm out of business. Mom and Dad suffered from it for years; they may never have gotten completely over it. (See description of the *1969 derecho* in References.)

Since the Farm was under easement, there was no governmental help, and charities didn't offer help, not that Mom and Dad would have accepted it. The help we got we got from neighbors, but they were affected, too. Mostly their help was giving us needed pasturage or hay to make. Fortunately, the first cutting hay was in the barn before the flood, but not the small grains, straw, and corn. Over half of the crops were lost.

In 1969, Rob was serving in the Army, stationed in Oakland, California. Rob graduated college in 1967 with a Bachelor of Science degree in agriculture/business. He planned to go into farming. Knowing Rob was going to get out in June, Dad and Rob sought an early-out, a program the Army offered so that a person could get into a work situation in time to plant crops. Rob's enlistment was up in June, so he applied for and got an early-out in April well within the three-month maximum.

Dad rented some nearby farmland, purchased additional seed and fertilizer, and when Rob got home, they got to work tilling, planting, and doing the other work that included milking about 15 head of Holsteins—Dad was converting to beef and had a herd of beef totaling 50 head on pasture and the hog operation which had been expanded by construction of the large hog farrowing, growing and finishing building. Planting consisted of corn which would be fed to both the cattle and hogs in addition to hay, oats, and barley. The plan was to maximize use of the existing equipment with an eye to buying either new or used equipment necessary for expanded operations during the following years.

By July 4th, the first cutting hay had been harvested; the corn was looking great at about chest high instead of being knee high by the fourth and deep green. The small grains, oats, and barley were about ready to combine. Things were really looking good. This should be the best year the Farm ever had and should spring us into the future.

The evening of the fourth, it rained. It rained all night. Total rainfall was about 12 inches. The next morning, the sun came out, but it was too late. The flood was coming.

Rob recalls getting a call from our Uncle Bud (Roy) Wisselgren, who needed help to get his cattle to his barn out of his woodland pasture that bordered Sugar Creek. Rob went over there by way of Justus Avenue, across Angleway to Route 62, then west to Wisselgren's.

The cattle had to be moved west on 62 because it wasn't possible to use the Farm lane that led from the pasture to the barn. The cattle weren't used to 62 and instead of turning right into the driveway leading to the barn, they turned left and went into the neighbor's yard, of which they made a mess. After getting them into the barn, Rob took off for home retracing his tracks going east on 62. He had to drive through flood water which, by this time, covered the road and bridges that crossed Sugar Creek. But he made it home.

He was fortunate to get there and back as he had to cross Sugar Creek both going and coming back, driving through water on the return trip.

While Rob was gone, Dad and Mary took the Massey 65 tractor down Lawndell to get Bill who was in the part of the south pasture that was on the east side of Sugar Creek. Dad was driving. Mary was

ROBERT ALAN MCDONALD, KATHIE EILEEN MCDONALD COURTNEY, RICHARD EDWIN MCDONALD, MARY JO MCDONALD HELFRICH

hanging on while riding on the drawbar. Dad stopped and let Mary off at the pasture gate to get Bill and start back up the road to the east getting Bill to high ground. Then Dad drove across the bridge. It was Dad's intention to use the tractor to go into the north pasture and round up the beef cattle who had already moved to the highest ground at the northwest corner of the farm.

Before Dad could open the gate into the north pasture, he saw a wall of water coming across the fields from the northwest. He later described the wall of water as two to four feet high. By this time, Mary had Bill out on the road headed east. Because Bill didn't have a halter on, she was leading him by his mane and chin. Dad turned the tractor around and headed east. He had the tractor in high gear and charged across the bridge.

Dad quickly caught up to Mary and he yelled, "Ride!" Mary jumped on the pony and rode bareback with no bridle up the road. There was water covering the bridge roadbed. Once they got to the curve, they put Bill in the pasture as the ground was high on the north side and he would be safe. Dad and Mary continued on to the house.

Mary recalls that this was the only time she ever saw Dad shook up. He had seen that wall of water coming across the fields and knew that there was a possibility that he might not make back across the bridge and that Mary and Bill were in danger also.

By the time Rob got back home, the creek was rising fast. He, Rich, and Dad went down the road to get the beef cattle out of the north pasture, this time on foot. Rob started across the bridge, which was already about two feet underwater. Rob recalls Dad telling him to come back after he was about halfway across the bridge. It was an excellent decision because a short time later, the water had risen covering the entire bridge superstructure.

The dairy cows were in the barn since they had just been milked, but the beef—all 50 head—were cut off in the north pasture. They were on high ground completely surrounded by water. Had they remained in place they would have been safe, but they entered the torrent and instinctively began swimming toward the pasture gate near the bridge.

By this time, the water was so high both the gate and the bridge were entirely underwater. The cattle were swept downstream by the raging current and they floated right over the bridge without touching it. Most reached high ground, the large field that bordered the east side of the creek. However, about 16 of them, the younger stock, were swept into the far south pasture which was overgrown with maple trees. These animals ended up in the treetops. It was fortunate that they got into the treetops because they may have eventually drifted much further downstream and could have drowned.

One neighbor, the Baylor's, who owned the local swimming and recreation area about a mile away had a small boat with an outboard motor. Using the boat, Jack Baylor picked up our cousin, John Wisselgren, and here they came. Rob got into the boat and the three of them fished cattle out of treetops for about five or six hours.

We saw one of the beef cows floating about where the west line fence should be located. We couldn't see the line fence because it was underwater. Jack moved the boat near the cow, who didn't move. We thought she could be caught in the fence, so Rob went over the side of the boat, under the water, to check the cow's feet. Fortunately, she wasn't tangled in the fence; just using it to stand on so she could rest. We put a rope around her neck and towed her to safety right over the top of the bridge, which we couldn't see and fortunately didn't hit. The water was that high.

ROBERT ALAN MCDONALD, KATHIE EILEEN MCDONALD COURTNEY, RICHARD EDWIN MCDONALD, MARY JO MCDONALD HELFRICH

*The bridge over Sugar Creek on Lawndell Road
by Mary Jo McDonald Helfrich*

We continued the same method until we got all the animals to safety. Jack would nose the boat up to one of the animals, John or Rob would put a rope around its neck, and then we'd tow the animal to the nearest point of land, an island created by a hilltop that was above the water. The older/larger animals floated easily as their stomachs functioned as a bladder; they floated on their sides. The younger stock had a more difficult time. We were constantly worried as their thrashing around would cause their heads to submerge. They could drown. We had to keep them calm while we towed them; something they weren't used to.

Dad and Rich, who had an injured leg and had limited mobility, were standing on the hill overlooking the creek and pastures where they could see everything being done to get the cattle to high ground. Dad was justifiably frustrated and concerned.

We saved all 16 this way. The cattle rested on the hill-top island until we gathered all of them. The last steer was so cold after being in the water for about five hours, he refused to stand up when he got to the island. We left him in that position, laying in the shallow water with the sun beating on him, for 15 to 20 minutes, then he got up.

After that, the 16 on the island were put back into the water and driven across a small channel, putting them on high ground with the others. Then we drove the entire herd to the barn through a field of oats destroying a good portion of it.

Carloads of people had come down Lawndell Road to rubberneck. Kathie came home from work and lit into them, trying to get them to move, but they didn't want to listen to her. Dad came up ahead of the herd and he lit into them. Then they listened and moved out of the way.

Bill remained in the pasture all day until Rob could go back and get him that evening. And when he did, the water was so high that the gate wasn't usable, so Rob had to cut the fence to get Bill out.

It took days for the water to recede. The dam operators slowly released water, preventing downstream flooding. When the water finally went down, every plant underwater was dead and so were carp.

Over half the corn that was chest high five days before was flat on the ground — dead. The smell was awful. There was no pasture left. The milk cows all dried up. There was no milk to sell. Dad had to sell the milk cows at a loss as there wasn't enough to feed them and the beef cattle. This hurt the small grain yield, so the number of finished hogs had to be scaled back. It was a terrible year for the Farm and for Dad.

Mary recalls Dad standing on the hill during the time cattle were being fished out of the trees saying, "It's gone, everything is gone!" His life's work went downstream in less than a day. She also recalls being sent to the house with messages for Mom. Dad was trying to keep Mom informed. The trip to the house was anything but easy. There was water everywhere, and if she deviated from the best route, she would find herself in water or mud to her knees.

At that point, Rob knew he had to find something else to do. It affected Kathie and Rich badly, also, but Mary, who was just starting high school, may have been affected the worst. Mom and Dad held on to the Farm, but it took a high toll.

ROBERT ALAN MCDONALD, KATHIE EILEEN MCDONALD COURTNEY, RICHARD EDWIN MCDONALD, MARY JO MCDONALD HELFRICH

Before this flood, families of bluebirds nested in the willow trees that lined the creek bank surrounding the north pasture meadow area. They nested in hollows formed when branches broke off the willow trees. These birds were a treat to see every time we walked through this area. After the flood, the bluebirds were gone. The water rose high enough to flood the nests in the tree hollows.

Before this event, there were two coveys of quail, bob whites, on the Farm. One on the north side of the road and the other on the south. Afterwards both were gone.

The Blizzard of 1978

When the blizzard occurred, there were 10 to 16 head, young stock, in the north pasture in the meadow formed between the creek branches. Prior to the blizzard, the weather was wet and warm. The weather changed suddenly, becoming much colder. Rain became heavy snow. The standing water began to freeze as the temperature dropped, and snow fell on the ice building up leaving water underneath. (See description of The Great Blizzard of '78 in References.)

The snow/ice combination on the surface wouldn't support the weight of the cattle, leaving them in ankle deep water. They instinctively wanted to go west to the gate at the road, but that path led them through lower land making the water deeper and even more difficult to cross.

Mack and Marian were trying to move the cattle with no success when Rich arrived. Dad was wet and cold by this time, so Rich asked Mom to take Dad to the house to warm up, which Mom did. Rich spent the next several hours moving the cattle through the Woods north and west to reach higher ground. Rich had on a pair of rubber boots that weren't tall enough to keep him completely dry. The cattle resisted going in the direction Rich wanted them to go because it took them away from the gate.

THE MCDONALDS

After four or five hours, Rich finally got the cattle to high ground and to the gate on the road. Ralph Meade happened by and helped get the cattle on the road and up to the barn.

By this time, Rich was tired, cold, and wet. He and Ralph Meade went into the house to rest and warm up. Ralph Meade had a bottle of blackberry brandy. Rich says that brandy was just the ticket. It really warmed him up. He gained great appreciation for the medicinal qualities of blackberry brandy.

1979

In September of 1979, another major flood occurred. Fortunately, all the crops except the corn had been harvested, so the damage was limited.

The cattle were in the north pasture. As happened in 1969, they were cut off by rapidly rising water. This time the flood wasn't as severe, and the cattle weren't forced to swim to safety. They took refuge on the high ground in the northwest corner of the Farm. But there wasn't sufficient grass there to feed them.

Rich borrowed his father-in-law, Mr. Horner's, boat and hauled hay to the cattle for several days. The boat was a Jon-boat, 12 feet long and 4 feet wide, powered by a 9.9 horsepower outboard motor. Fully loaded capacity was 10 bales of hay.

Multiple trips had to be made because the water was held for days. Most trips Rich made solo, but one day Dad decided he needed to go along.

Dad recently purchased a new pair of boots, which he was going to wear on this trip. Rich recalls loading the boat with just 6 bales so that there would be room for Dad in the bow. Dad put on his new boots, which took about 15 minutes while Rich waited.

Finally, Dad got in the bow. Both Dad and Rich were wearing life jackets. Dad carefully arranged himself placing his boots well above the boat bottom, keeping them clean and dry. Rich was driving the boat but had trouble with the throttle. It stuck or had a hesitation when accelerating that caused a forward surge. Rich tried to be smooth and steady, but it surged forward. The resulting wave came over the square bow filling the boat to Dad's waist. Dad sat there holding his boots up keeping them high and dry. Dad exclaimed, "Richard, we're taking on water!" Rich got a look at Dad sitting in the boat in waist deep water with his boots up and saw a look of fear in those steely blue eyes he had never seen before.

The boat continued to take on water. The hay bales floated off. Rich had visions of losing the entire boat, having to pay for the loss, and having to get Dad to shore somehow. Rich got out of the boat and found he was in water up to his chest. But he was able to keep the boat from sinking. Rich got it back near the shore enabling Dad to get out and stand in knee high water.

Rich gathered up the floating hay and pushed it toward shore while Dad stood there not doing anything. Rich noticed they were missing an oar and asked, "Where's the oar?" Dad responded by pointing and saying, "It's out there. You forgot it." Rich got the oar, put the hay on the shore, and emptied the water out of the boat.

Rich made the trip, but solo. Dad never attempted the trip again.

After the water receded, the cattle were moved to the barn where they remained for the rest of the fall and winter.

ROBERT ALAN MCDONALD, KATHIE EILEEN MCDONALD COURTNEY, RICHARD EDWIN MCDONALD, MARY JO MCDONALD HELFRICH

Chapter Twenty-Two -- A New Beginning

1969 was a tumultuous year. It forced changes that were unexpected. It forever changed our lives.

In January 1969, Rob was looking forward to completing his enlistment in the U.S. Army scheduled for June and coming back to Ohio and being able to begin a career. Since his college degree was in Agriculture-Business, he expected to farm.

Kathie was completing nursing school and would take the State Boards to be recognized as a Registered Nurse. She was dating Richard (Dick) Courtney, who was in college studying business, specifically accounting and finance. Kathie would get a job in her chosen profession.

Richard was in his senior year of high school and was planning to go to college in the fall at Ohio University. He was looking forward to getting a degree, but just as importantly, to playing college baseball.

Mary completed the eighth grade and would enter high school in the fall. She had her entire high school and then college experience before her.

Mom and Dad were looking forward to an important year. All their children could be home before the year was out. They were working to ensure all their and their children's plans could move forward.

By April, we arranged farm expansion. We rented additional crop land. Rob had received an "early out" and would be home a couple of months before his end of enlistment date so he could begin his farming career.

When Rob got home, he had about $300 in cash, some civilian clothes, and his military uniforms, including fatigues, which would be useful for farm work. For transportation, he bought a car: a 1957 Desoto from Russ Salberg, a great uncle by marriage to Grandma Nellie's sister Annie.

Kathie completed nursing school, passed the state boards, and had a job. Rich was accepted to Ohio University and entered college

ROBERT ALAN MCDONALD, KATHIE EILEEN MCDONALD COURTNEY, RICHARD EDWIN MCDONALD, MARY JO MCDONALD HELFRICH

in the fall. Mary was riding Jonny, getting ready for high school, which began in the fall.

Just when things were going well, the July 4th flood happened and half or more of the crops were gone. The plan to expand the Farm was crushed. Money that was tight before became almost non-existent.

What happened next was what always happens next. Life goes on. We regrouped. We had been planning to re-fence the boar and sow lot and already had the materials on hand. So, we built a new fence. The ground was so water soaked we couldn't set the fence posts firmly. We built the fence, but it was never right. That fence was symbolic. It remains the worst fence we ever built.

Mom got a job working in the Treasurer's Office at Fairless High School. That income really helped. Mom kept working there until she retired. The retirement income also helped. Dad continued farming, but never again attempted to scale up. He primarily shifted to beef cattle.

In August, the BF Goodrich Company hired Rob as a traveling field auditor. He was gone for the next year. It was the beginning of an unexpected career. Having a college education in business opened the door. Rob married Charlotte, who had a son Jonathan by a previous marriage. Together they have two children, Lisa and Ben.

Kathie continued working and in December, she and Dick were married. Later, Dick finished his education with a master's and worked in accounting and finance for his career. Kathie was the Day Supervisor at the nursing home in Harmon. She oversaw the entire building having responsibility for the entire staff unless their department head was present. Together, they bought a farm a short distance south on Justus Avenue, which they expanded over the years. Kathie and Dick have four children: Stuart, Cadi, Laura, and Keith.

Richard went to college. Got a degree in business at Ohio University and returned to the area and began work as a carpenter, doing what he liked and was exceptionally good at. Eventually, he opened his own construction business. He married Jackie and raised two children: Aric and Cari.

Mary finished high school and went to college at Ohio University, where she studied education and speech and hearing therapy. She eventually sought employment as a speech and hearing therapist in North Dakota where she met and married Stan Helfrich. Mary and Stan have two boys: Jesse and Matthew.

Now you ask, "What's the rest of the story?" That, children, is up to you. When we started putting this together, we thought we'd write a few stories and that would be it. We found out the story doesn't end. New characters are added, old characters leave, but the story continues. Good luck! We know you will be fine, as Grandpa Dan Jones would say, "You come from good stock."

Out in the fields with God
By **British Anonymous**,
sometimes attributed to Elizabeth Barrett Browning

The little cares that fretted me,
I lost them yesterday
among the fields, above the sea,
among the winds at play,
among the lowing of the herds,
the rustling of the trees,
among the singing of the birds,
the humming of the bees.

The foolish fears of what might happen,
I cast them all away
among the clover-scented grass,
among the new-mown hay,
among the husking of the corn,
where drowsy poppies nod,
where ill thoughts die and good are born—
out in the fields with God.

ROBERT ALAN MCDONALD, KATHIE EILEEN MCDONALD COURTNEY, RICHARD EDWIN MCDONALD, MARY JO MCDONALD HELFRICH

Chapter Twenty-Three – Family Information

Farmstead Aerial View from the East

Farmstead Aerial View from the West

ROBERT ALAN MCDONALD, KATHIE EILEEN MCDONALD COURTNEY, RICHARD EDWIN MCDONALD, MARY JO MCDONALD HELFRICH

House viewed from the south, milk house behind automobile on the right

Farmstead viewed from the southwest, house, butcher-house, and barn with top of silo showing

THE MCDONALDS

From left to right – Milk House, House, Butcher-house (Summer Kitchen) viewed from the north

Barn from west

ROBERT ALAN MCDONALD, KATHIE EILEEN MCDONALD COURTNEY, RICHARD EDWIN MCDONALD, MARY JO MCDONALD HELFRICH

Barn and silo viewed from the east

THE MCDONALDS

Machine Shed

Barn from the Southeast

Farrowing House viewed from the East

Hog Finishing Pens viewed from the East

THE MCDONALDS

Upper Photo Dining Room with Aunt Eleanor and Kathie facing Charlotte McDonald, Laura Courtney, and Dick Courtney. Lower Photo (left to right) Aunt Eleanor, Laura Courtney, and Mom

ROBERT ALAN MCDONALD, KATHIE EILEEN MCDONALD COURTNEY, RICHARD EDWIN MCDONALD, MARY JO MCDONALD HELFRICH

Upstairs Bath after Remodeling

East Room with Bay Window, South Room with floor length windows

ROBERT ALAN MCDONALD, KATHIE EILEEN MCDONALD COURTNEY, RICHARD EDWIN MCDONALD, MARY JO MCDONALD HELFRICH

North and South Bedrooms note double doors in North Bedroom; one door to stairs the other to the hall

THE MCDONALDS

*Marian in front, back row left to right Richard, Mary, Kathie, Robert
Taken after Mack's passing January 1985*

ROBERT ALAN MCDONALD, KATHIE EILEEN MCDONALD COURTNEY, RICHARD EDWIN MCDONALD, MARY JO MCDONALD HELFRICH

Marian's Eulogy by Dr. Darrell C. Filler

Marian Pauline (Jones) McDonald
B. April 27, 1919 (85 years tomorrow)
D. April 23, 2004

Husband: Alpha C. "Mac" McDonald -Married December 24, 1942 -Died Jan. 27, 1985
Sister: Eleanor Foster
Brother: Donald (deceased)
Children: Robert (Charlotte), Kathie (Dick), Richard (Lori), and Mary (Stanley)
Grandchildren: Lisa, Ben (Jennifer), Stuart (Rachel), Cadi (Ralph), Laura, Keith, Aric, Cari (David), Jesse, and Matthew
Great Grandchildren: Aiden, Dean, David, and Courtney
Sisters-in-law: Dorothy Jones, Betty Wisselgren, and Julia Bartco
Nieces, nephews, great nieces, and great nephews and Aunt Norma Doerflinger

Marian was born and grew up in Harmon, the eldest child of Daniel and Nellie Jones. She lived all of her life in this area. She joined the Justice UB Church as a youngster and transferred her membership to St. Paul UCC on April 25, 1943 (61 years ago yesterday). She graduated from Navarre High School in 1937 where she was a member of the commercial club and went to business school for one year. After rearing her children, she worked in the office at the New Philadelphia Conservancy District for a year. Then she worked in the office of the Wheeling/ Lake Erie Railroad in Brewster for three years. Finally, she worked for the Fairless School Board in payroll for sixteen years. Her work in the world outside of her home is only part of the story of her life, for she dearly loved her family and worked diligently to care for them.

When I asked her what she felt was her greatest accomplishment in life she said without a moments hesitation, "raising my family. Each of my children is an accomplished professional. I'm proud of that." She gave credit to Catherine and Ted Edwards for introducing her to her husband, Alpha, or "Mac," as he was known. Among the remembrances of their mother, Marian's children recalled how hard she worked on the farm. She raised vegetables in her garden and then canned them to feed her family the rest of the year. And not only vegetables, but she also canned apples and cherries from the trees on the farm. She counted cooking and baking among her hobbies. She especially liked to bake pies and cakes. He daughter, Kathie, told me they would go through a cake a day when the family was growing. Her daughters also recall their mother's joy in raising flowers. Only in recent years did she reduce the size of her flowerbed. Zinnias, marigolds, and a variety of brightly colored flowers always welcomed visitors and family alike. In addition, Marian delighted in the blossoms of the flowering trees, such as the weeping cherry, dogwoods, and fruit trees. And transplanted pin oaks from others parts of the farm replaced the big old trees closer to the house.

took great pride in refurbishing the house and especially in Richard's carpentry work. I recall well my first visit last November to her home. She had her caregiver walk me through the upstairs to see the bedrooms. I thought I was in the Whitehouse in Washington, DC as I was shown the Red room and the Blue room. Marian had just cause to be proud of her home.

Marian enjoyed entertaining. When family or friends came, they were always fed. If they did not stay for one meal, then it was two and there was enough for everyone. Her own children, grandchildren, nieces, nephews, great nieces and great nephews can tell stories of playing in the hay in the barn. Marian's place was a fun place to be.

Marian had a great sense of humor and everyone enjoyed playing tricks on her. From a rubber lizard placed in the washing machine to running through the fields with cattail torches soaked in kerosene, Marian had her hands full!

Her "twin" sister Eleanor remembers being a little girl and their mother dressed both Marian and Eleanor in green gingham dresses. A man at Tuscazor Park in New Philadelphia would not be convinced even when their father said, "I know they are not twins. I'm their father."

Thoughts of a trip to Scotland, England, and Wales and an Alaskan cruise bring fond memories to those who were on these adventures with Marian. A teacup with a Red Rose teabag is in the casket with Marian, a gift from her sister.

Her health began to fail last July when she suffered with pneumonia and then came the diagnosis of cancer. After months of treatments, her body simply gave out. Through the past 10 months her family has been at her side and bedside. It has been my pleasure as her Interim Pastor for the past 6 months to be invited numerous times to come to be with Marian at her home and share Holy Communion with her, with her family and those who provided her care. Each time, we knew how meaningful it was for her to share this precious sacrament of the church. Thursday evening I was privileged to hold her hand and offer prayer inviting God to receive her spirit into God's heaven and mercifully, God did just a few hours later after hearing the voices of her children on the phone or in person. Marian loved her family and they loved her!

How blessed we are to have been a part of her life and for her to have touched ours.

ROBERT ALAN MCDONALD, KATHIE EILEEN MCDONALD COURTNEY, RICHARD EDWIN MCDONALD, MARY JO MCDONALD HELFRICH

Mack's High School football award

Varsity Letter

THE MCDONALDS

1928 Akron Garfield High School Football Team
AC (Mack) McDonald is believed to be in the front row fifth from the left

ROBERT ALAN MCDONALD, KATHIE EILEEN MCDONALD COURTNEY, RICHARD EDWIN MCDONALD, MARY JO MCDONALD HELFRICH

Songs and Poems

Mistress Pussy

Mistress Pussy, sleek and fat, with her kittens four,
went to sleep upon the mat by the kitchen door.

Mistress Pussy heard a noise, up she jumped to see,
kittens maybe that's a mouse, let us go and see.

Creepy, creepy, creepy on, silently they stole.
But that little mouse had gone back into his hole.

Home went hungry Mistress Puss with her kittens four
found their supper on the mat by the kitchen door.

Sung to us by Grandpa Mac. Retold by Aunt Mary.

Mousetrap

Once a trap was baited with a dainty piece of cheese.
It tickled little mousey so it almost made him sneeze.

Old rat said there is danger, be careful where you go.
Nonsense said the mousey I don't think you know.

So he crept in softly no one was in sight.
First he took a nibble, then he took a bit.

Snap! went the trap together, quick as a wink,
Catching mousey fast there because he didn't think.

Told by Grandma Jones. Retold by Aunt Mary.

Taffy

Taffy was a Welshman. Taffy was a thief.
Taffy came to my house and stole a piece of beef.

I went to Taffy's house, Taffy wasn't in.
Taffy came to my house and stole a silver pin.

I went to Taffy's house, Taffy wasn't home.
Taffy came to my house and stole a marrow bone.

I went to Taffy's house, Taffy was in bed.
I took the little marrow bone and beat him on the head.

Retold by Aunt Mary.

THE MCDONALDS

Old Thompson

Old Thompson had an old gray mule,
drove him around in a cart.
He loved that mule and
the mule loved him with all his muley heart.

When the rooster crowed,
Old Thompson knowed
the dawn was about to break,
so he raked and scraped and scraped and raked and
he scraped him down with a rake.

And the mule would say,
Hee Haw, Hee Haw,
Hee Haw, Hee Haw, Hee Haw.
When he scraped him down with a rake!

Retold by Robert

A song that Dad sang to us occasionally when in an especially cheery mood.
Located on the internet:
THOMPSON'S OLD GRAY MULE: THE PICKARD FAMILY: Free Download, Borrow, and Streaming: Internet Archive

ROBERT ALAN MCDONALD, KATHIE EILEEN MCDONALD COURTNEY, RICHARD EDWIN MCDONALD, MARY JO MCDONALD HELFRICH

Family Photographs

Julia Van Natta Rider
Julia Naomi Melton McDonald's
Grandmother our Great-Great
Grandmother

THE MCDONALDS

Family Picture 1911 Seaside, Oregon
Samuel S., Jessie Marie, and Julia Naomi Melton McDonald

ROBERT ALAN MCDONALD, KATHIE EILEEN MCDONALD COURTNEY, RICHARD EDWIN MCDONALD, MARY JO MCDONALD HELFRICH

Earnest Melton's grocery store in 1941
Believed to be in Lamar, Colorado

THE MCDONALDS
Jones Family Ancestors

Left to right: Meg Jones, back standing unknown, right Eleanor Jones. Likely this was taken during one of Great Grandmother Eleanor's trips to Wales. During the time Robert lived in the United Kingdom, 1988-89, the relatives remembered Eleanor's visit(s)

ROBERT ALAN MCDONALD, KATHIE EILEEN MCDONALD COURTNEY, RICHARD EDWIN MCDONALD, MARY JO MCDONALD HELFRICH

Meg Jones sister to Eleanor

THE MCDONALDS

Our maternal Great-Great Grandfather Jones

ROBERT ALAN MCDONALD, KATHIE EILEEN MCDONALD COURTNEY, RICHARD EDWIN MCDONALD, MARY JO MCDONALD HELFRICH

Our maternal Great-Great Grandfather Roland Jones Meredith

THE MCDONALDS

Five generations caught in 1896. Clockwise, from left: Telitha (Meredith) English; her nephew, John W. Smith; his daughter, Addie May (Smith) Fisher; her son, Clyde V. Fisher, brother of Zula (Fisher) Ley; and Martha Jones Meredith.

ROBERT ALAN MCDONALD, KATHIE EILEEN MCDONALD COURTNEY, RICHARD EDWIN MCDONALD, MARY JO MCDONALD HELFRICH

Booth Family Photo believed to have been taken at the Meredith farm, Day Avenue, Harmon, Ohio
From left to right: Mother – Flora Augusta Meredith Booth, Annie Booth, Nellie Francis Booth (our grandmother), Dorothy Booth, Eva Booth, Father - J. Franklin Booth

THE MCDONALDS

Booth Family Photo believed to have been taken at the Meredith farm, Day Avenue, Harmon, Ohio in 1908
From left to right: Eva Booth, Mother – Flora Agusta Meredith Booth, Annie Booth, Nellie Francis Booth (our grandmother), Father J. Franklin Booth, Dorothy Booth. The other children: John Booth, Beatrice Booth, and Norma Booth, weren't born when this was taken.

ROBERT ALAN MCDONALD, KATHIE EILEEN MCDONALD COURTNEY, RICHARD EDWIN MCDONALD, MARY JO MCDONALD HELFRICH

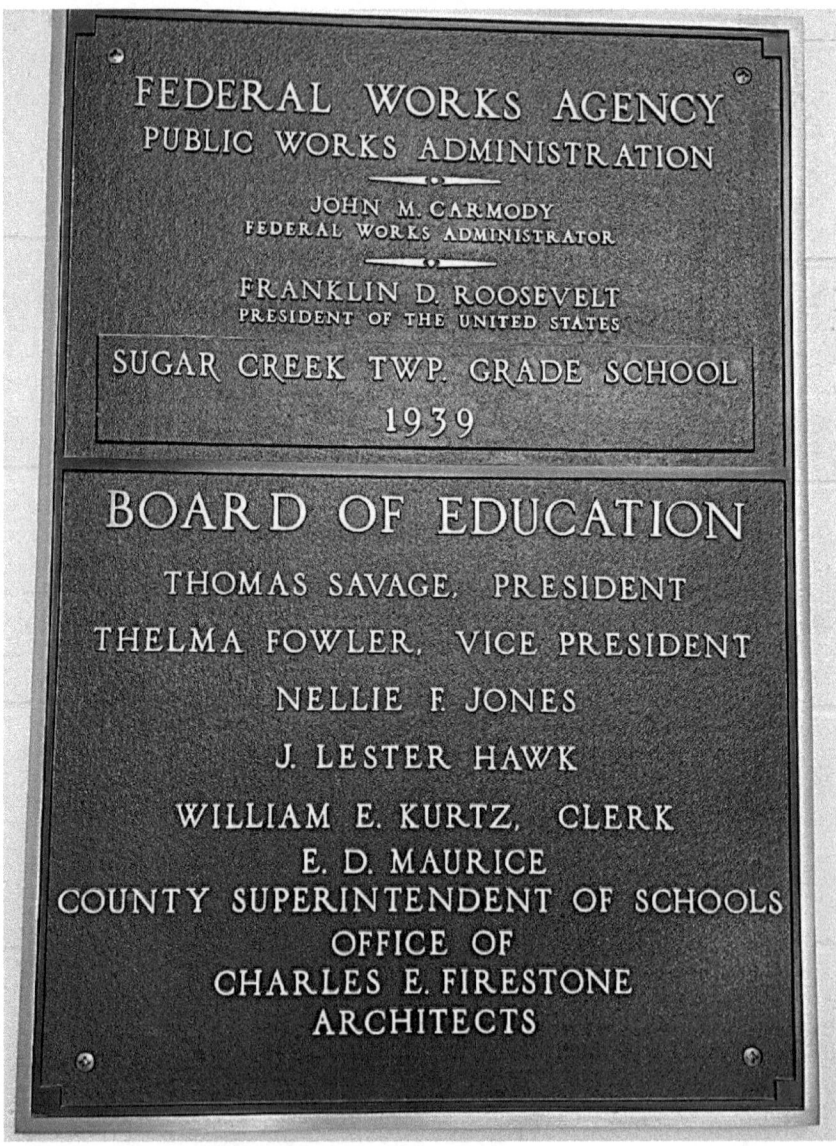

Navarre School Dedication constructed while our Grandmother Nellie F. Jones was a school board member

THE MCDONALDS

Chapter Twenty-Four – Family Artistry

Our maternal Grandmother's depiction of the Farm forms the cover of this volume, but her body of work was much broader. Many of her paintings were framed and are displayed in the homes of her grandchildren and great grandchildren. At Rich's suggestion, we asked that photographs of Grandma Nellie's work be provided so that we could include them. Each photo includes the name of the family member in whose home the painting is displayed. Many thanks to all those who have provided the photographs.

Included are works by members of the McDonald family: Mary Jo McDonald Helfrich, one of the authors, and granddaughters Cari McDonald Dunn and Cadi Courtney Buck. Grandma Nellie's talent was passed along.

ROBERT ALAN MCDONALD, KATHIE EILEEN MCDONALD COURTNEY, RICHARD EDWIN MCDONALD, MARY JO MCDONALD HELFRICH

Nellie Jones' Artwork

The Farm - serves as the cover of the book - Robert McDonald

Farmstead in Winter – Richard McDonald

Flowers – Mary Helfrich

ROBERT ALAN MCDONALD, KATHIE EILEEN MCDONALD COURTNEY, RICHARD EDWIN MCDONALD, MARY JO MCDONALD HELFRICH

Lighthouse on a Lake – Robert McDonald

Corn Harvest – Kathie Courtney

THE MCDONALDS

Log Cabin in Justus, Ohio – Birthplace of Varner Forster (Uncle Pink) – Sue Cieslak

Lake in the Smokies – Mary Helfrich

ROBERT ALAN MCDONALD, KATHIE EILEEN MCDONALD COURTNEY, RICHARD EDWIN MCDONALD, MARY JO MCDONALD HELFRICH

Old Mill Reflection in Pond – Dan Jones

Sunset over a Pond – Sue Cieslak

THE MCDONALDS

Jones Home in Harmon from the East – Richard McDonald

Seaside with Sailboat – Kathie Courtney

ROBERT ALAN MCDONALD, KATHIE EILEEN MCDONALD COURTNEY, RICHARD EDWIN MCDONALD, MARY JO MCDONALD HELFRICH

Jones Home in Harmon from the Main Road – Mary Helfrich

Farmhouse in Summer – Mary Helfrich

THE MCDONALDS

Farmhouse & Barn near Creek – Richard McDonald

Village Scene – Mary Helfrich

ROBERT ALAN MCDONALD, KATHIE EILEEN MCDONALD COURTNEY, RICHARD EDWIN MCDONALD, MARY JO MCDONALD HELFRICH

Hillside Farm – Robert McDonald

Ohio Winter – Mary Helfrich

THE MCDONALDS

Small Town Street – Richard McDonald

Farmstead by Stream – Kathie Courtney

ROBERT ALAN MCDONALD, KATHIE EILEEN MCDONALD COURTNEY, RICHARD EDWIN MCDONALD, MARY JO MCDONALD HELFRICH

Late Fall Lake Scene – Mary Helfrich

Farm Scene (unfinished) – Sue Cieslak

THE MCDONALDS

Rochester Square, Navarre, Ohio – Laura Courtney

ROBERT ALAN MCDONALD, KATHIE EILEEN MCDONALD COURTNEY, RICHARD EDWIN MCDONALD, MARY JO MCDONALD HELFRICH

Other Family Members' Art

The Sycamore by the Creek by Mary Jo McDonald Helfrich (Grandma Nellie would be proud.)

THE MCDONALDS

The Farmhouse by Cadi Courtney (Buck)

Reproduction of Biographical Record Stark County Ohio by Cari McDonald Dunn 1995

ROBERT ALAN MCDONALD, KATHIE EILEEN MCDONALD COURTNEY, RICHARD EDWIN MCDONALD, MARY JO MCDONALD HELFRICH

Chapter Twenty-Five – Family Recipes

During her life, Mom gathered recipes for all kinds of dishes. Some didn't have a recipe at all. Sometimes she used what she had and other times she improvised. But the important things like canning, preserving, and treats, she had recipes. To preserve Mom's work and to acknowledge her culinary skills, we've included many of them here. If we knew where she got the recipe, we included that information.

Canning & Preserving

Sauerkraut

Ingredients:
1. For each 5 lbs. of cabbage use 3 ½ Tbsp. Pickling salt

Directions:
1. Shred clean but unwashed cabbage (cabbage shredder works best, but other methods will work)
2. Mix cabbage and salt by hand
3. Place in crock, filling to about 5 inches from the top
4. Cover with a clean cloth, top with plate, and use a 1-quart jar filled with water as a weight on the plate
5. Scald cloth often during fermentation
6. Hold at 65 °, until fermentation is complete
7. Place in quart jars to 1 inch from top, add juice to fill (for extra juice use 2 Tbs. Salt in 1 qt. water)
8. Water bath at boil for 15 minutes to seal

Dill Pickles

Directions:
1. Cucumbers 3-4 inches in length or smaller, larger cukes may be quartered
2. For each quart jar:

- a. 4 heads dill
- b. 1 tsp. ground horseradish (optional)
- c. 1 tsp. mustard seed
- d. 3-4 toes of garlic
3. Brine:
   - a. 5 cups water
   - b. ½ cup vinegar
   - c. 1/3 cup salt

Directions:
1. Scrub cukes well in cold water, rinse well, cut off both ends and prick with fork
2. Fill each quart jar with dill, horseradish (if used), mustard see, and garlic
3. Place cukes in each jar
4. Mix brine ingredients in a suitable size pot and boil; while hot, pour into each jar leaving head space
5. Seal quart jars using zinc lids and rubber gaskets for shelf storage or seal using ball lids with ring for refrigerator storage
6. Water bath is not recommended for sealing as pickles can get mushy.

Pickled Beets

Ingredients:
1. 4 dozen small red beets
2. 2 cups vinegar
3. 4 cups water
4. 3 cups sugar
5. 1 lemon, sliced thin

6. 2 sticks cinnamon
7. 1 tsp. whole cloves
8. 1 tsp. whole allspice

Directions:
1. Leave one inch of stems on beets. Wash and scrub well. Boil till tender. Run under cold water. Remove skins.
2. Place beets in pint jars
3. Mix the other ingredients in a suitable pan and bring to simmer for 15 minutes
4. Pour over the red beets
5. Affix lids
6. Either invert jars to seal or cold pack

Spicy Sweet Pickled beets (Marian McDonald) – Laura Courtney
4 dozen small beets.
Simmer 15 minutes: 2 C vinegar, 4 C water, 3 C sugar, 1 lemon sliced thin, 2 sticks cinnamon, 1 tsp whole cloves, 1 tsp whole allspice. Pour over beets in jar. Seal.

Pickle Relish - Grandma Booth – Laura Courtney
Grind and mix and let stand 3 hours and drain: 1 gallon cucumbers, 1 green pepper, 1 red pepper, 1 C salt, 4 C onion.
Make a syrup of 5 C sugar, 5 C vinegar, 1 tsp cloves, 1 tsp celery seed, 2 Tbsp. mustard seed.
Heat vinegar. Add pickles and let come to boil and can in sterile jars.

Sweet Pickle Sticks – makes 3 pints

Ingredients:
1. 9 medium cucumbers about 4 ½ inches long
2. 6 cups boiling water
3. 2 ⅓ cups cider vinegar
4. 2 ¼ cups sugar
5. 2 Tbsp. Salt
6. 1 Tbsp. Celery seed

7. 1 tsp. turmeric
8. ¾ tsp. mustard seed

Directions:

1. Select fresh, firm cucumbers
2. Wash and cut into sticks. Pour boiling water over and let stand overnight
3. Next day drain, pack solidly into clean jars
4. Combine remaining ingredients and boil 5 minutes
5. Pour boiling hot liquid over cucumbers in jars
6. Place cap on jars screwing band tight
7. Process in boiling water-bath 5 minutes

Crisp Pickle Slices

Ingredients:

1. 4 quarts sliced, unpeeled, medium cucumbers (slice thin, round)
2. 4 medium round onions, sliced 6 cups
3. 2 green peppers (sliced 1 2/3 cups)
4. 3 clove garlic
5. ⅓ cup pickling salt
6. Cracked ice
7. 5 cup sugar
8. 3 cup cider vinegar
9. 2 Tbsp. Mustard seed
10. 1 ½ tsp. turmeric
11. 1 ½ tsp. celery seed

Directions:

1. Combine cucumbers, onions, green peppers, garlic, & salt. Cover with crushed ice. Mix well and let stand 3 hours
2. Drain well, remove garlic
3. Combine rest of ingredients

4. Pour over cucumber mixture
5. Bring to boil
6. Pack cucumbers & liquid into hot jars, leaving ½ inch headspace
7. Affix lids
8. Process in boiling water bath (half pints or pints) 5 minutes. Makes 8 pints.

Sweet Corn Relish

Ingredients:

1. 10 cups frozen or canned whole kernel corn
2. 7 cups shredded cabbage
3. 2 cups chopped onions
4. ¾ cup chopped green pepper
5. ¾ cup sweet red pepper
6. 2 Tbsp. Dry mustard
7. 1 ½ tsp. flour
8. ½ tsp turmeric
9. 1 quart cider vinegar
10. 2 cups sugar
11. 2 Tbsp. Salt

Directions:

1. Combine corn, cabbage, onion, green, & red peppers in a large kettle
2. Mix together mustard, flour & turmeric
3. Add ¼ cup vinegar to mustard mixture
4. Remaining vinegar, sugar & salt to corn, mixing well
5. Bring vegetable to a boil, reduce heat and simmer uncovered 15 minutes
6. Ladle into jars
7. Affix lids
8. Process in boiling water bath 15 minutes

ROBERT ALAN MCDONALD, KATHIE EILEEN MCDONALD COURTNEY, RICHARD EDWIN MCDONALD, MARY JO MCDONALD HELFRICH

Deserts

Ice Cream

1 ¼ cups sugar
2 eggs
2 cups cream
4 " milk
1 tbsp Knox Gelatine
½ tsp salt
1 tsp vanilla

Soak gelatine in 1 cup milk for ten minutes. Add another cup milk & heat. Stir occasionally to keep from scorching. Mix sugar & well beaten eggs & pour scalding mixture over them. Return all to saucepan & allow to scald until slightly thickened.
Remove from fire & add 2 cups cold milk & the cream.
This is for 2 qt. ice cream. But I find one & a half times this amount is about right for a gallon freezer. Double this amount makes the freezer too full after it is frozen. When I make that amount I just use 2 cups cream & add another cup of milk instead of a third cup cream. I think it is rich enough.
The recipe says to whip the cream but I have better results when I don't. There are usually little chunks of butter in the icecream when I whip the cream.

Rich's Mom's Ice Cream

1 ¼ Cups Sugar
2 Eggs
2 Cups Cream
4 Cups Whole Milk
1 Tbsp. Knox Gelatin
½ tsp. salt (** **Karen does not add the salt**)
1 tsp. vanilla

THE MCDONALDS

Soak gelatin in 1 cup milk for two minutes. Add another cup of milk & scald. Stir occasionally to keep from scorching. Mix sugar & well beaten eggs and pour scalding mixture over them. Add salt. Return all to pan & allow to scald until slightly thickened. Remove from fire & add 2 cups cold milk and add the cream. Stir in the vanilla.

Makes approx. 2 quarts of ice cream.

Note: For the 6 qt. ice cream maker we double the recipe:

2 ½ Cups Sugar
4 Eggs
4 Cups Cream
8 Cups Whole Milk
2 Tbsp. Knox Gelatin
2 tsp. vanilla

Crumb Cake

Ingredients:

1. 2 cups brown sugar
2. 2 ½ cups flour
3. ½ cup lard
4. 1 cup sour milk (put vinegar in)
5. 1 tsp. soda
6. 1 tsp. cinnamon
7. 2 tsp nutmeg
8. 1 egg
9. 1 tsp. baking powder

Directions:

1. Mix flour, sugar & shortening form pie dough
2. Reserve crumbs for top of cake also spices
3. Baking instructions are not recorded on the card. Based on Rob's memory, Mom used a clear glass pie pan greased or buttered. Suggest 350 ° for 20 – 30 minutes.

ROBERT ALAN MCDONALD, KATHIE EILEEN MCDONALD COURTNEY, RICHARD EDWIN MCDONALD, MARY JO MCDONALD HELFRICH

Welsh Cookies – Laura Courtney
Mix like pie dough: 2 & ½ C flour, ¼ tsp salt, 1 C Crisco.
Add 1 & ½ tsp baking powder, ½ tsp nutmeg, 1 C currants, 1 C sugar, 1 tsp vanilla, 2 eggs, ¼ cup milk.
Stir with spoon. Roll ¼ inch thick. Bake on hot griddle (300 degrees) until brown on both sides. While warm, dip in white sugar. Best to chill before baking.

(Note - in recipe scrap book that I received from Sue/Emily/Sara, there was this Welsh cookie recipe, and it said Dotty Storm's Welsh Cookies)

Monster Cookies – Laura Courtney
Beat till smooth: 1 stick oleo, 1 C sugar, 1 C brown sugar, 3 eggs, 12 oz jar peanut butter, 2 tsp vanilla.
Mix in 4 ½ cup oats, ½ cup chocolate chips, ¾ C M & Ms,
Bake 10-12 minutes at 350 degrees. Do NOT overbake.

Zucchini bread (Marian) – Laura Courtney
In large bowl, beat 3 eggs until lemon colored; then beat in 1 cup salad oil and 2 C sugar.
Add: 2 C grated unpeeled zucchini and 3 tsp vanilla.
Sift together and add: 3 C flour, 1 tsp salt, 1 tsp soda, ¼ tsp baking powder, 3 tsp cinnamon.
Add 1 C chopped nuts.
Mix well and pour into 2 oiled bread pans. Bake 1 hour at 350°F.
Cool 10 minutes then loosen edges and turn onto rack to cool (1 cup grated zucchini and 1 cup crushed pineapple is good too)

Banana cake - Grandma Booth – Laura Courtney
Cream together ½ C shortening, 1 ½ cup sugar
2 eggs - beat well.
Sift together: 2 C flour, ½ tsp baking powder, ¾ tsp soda, ½ tsp salt.

THE MCDONALDS

Mix in ½ cup sour milk, 1 C mashed bananas, 1 tsp vanilla. Serve with whipped cream.

(Note - no directions on how long to bake or temperature)

Cornstarch pudding – Marian – Laura Courtney
2 T butter, ¼ C cornstarch, ¾ C sugar, ½ tsp salt, 2 C milk, 1 tsp vanilla, and 2 egg yolks beaten (reserve the egg whites)
Melt butter and then blend butter, sugar, cornstarch, and salt. Gradually add milk and egg yolks into a heavy pan. Bring to boil. Add vanilla.
Whip whites until stiff. Fold egg whites into pan contents. Serve warm.
(Recipe has a note that states "Richards's favorite growing up.")

Aunt Mame's yellow cake – Laura Courtney (Grandpa Dan's favorite)
Cream ½ C butter and 2 C sugar
Add 3 eggs and 1 C milk
Stir in 3 C flour
Beat well
3 tsp baking powder
Vanilla

Rich Shortcake   Nellie Jones – Laura Courtney
¼ C sugar, 2 C flour, ½ C milk, 1 tsp salt, ½ C butter, 4 tsp baking powder, 1 egg
Bake 300 degrees for 30 minutes

Maple Cookies

Ingredients:
1. ½ cup oleo (could use margarine, but butter would be best)
2. 1 cup brown sugar
3. 1 egg

4. ⅓ cup sour cream
5. 1 tsp. maple flavoring
6. 2 cups flour
7. ¾ tsp baking soda
8. ¾ tsp salt
9. 1 cup nuts – last

Directions:

1. Cream the first two ingredients
2. Add the remaining ingredients and mix thoroughly
3. Baking instructions aren't on the card, suggest using a cookie sheet and a 350 ⁰ oven for 10 – 12 minutes. Can use maple shape to cut out the cookies.

Icing

1. ¼ tsp. maple flavoring
2. 3 Tbsp. milk
3. ¼ cup oleo (margarine or butter)
4. 2 cups powdered sugar
5. Mix thoroughly and spread on cooled cookies

Carrot Cake

Ingredients:

1. 2 cup sugar
2. 1 ⅓ cup oil
3. 4 eggs
4. 1tsp. vanilla
5. 2 tsp baking soda
6. 1 tsp. salt
7. 2 tsp. cinnamon
8. 1 cup walnuts
9. 2 ½ cup flour
10. One 15 oz. can crushed pineapples
11. Four (4 oz.) jars baby food carrots

Directions:
1. Cream sugar, oil, and eggs then add the remaining ingredients,
2. Mix well,
3. Bake @ 350° approximately 45 minutes.

Cream Cheese Icing

Ingredients:
1. 1 stick butter,
2. 1 tsp. vanilla,
3. 3 oz. cream cheese
4. 2 cups powdered sugar.

Directions:
1. Mix and spread on cooled cake,
2. Store in refrigerator.

Apple Crisp

Ingredients:
1. One dozen apples
2. 1 cup brown sugar
3. ½ cup sugar
4. 1 cup whole wheat flour
5. 1 Tbsp. cinnamon
6. 1 tsp. nutmeg
7. ⅔ cup butter or margarine

Directions:
1. Mix and place ingredients in a baking dish
2. Bake in a preheated oven @ 375° for 30 minutes.

Pie

Ingredients:

ROBERT ALAN MCDONALD, KATHIE EILEEN MCDONALD COURTNEY, RICHARD EDWIN MCDONALD, MARY JO MCDONALD HELFRICH

Bottom layer:

1. 2 cups of graham cracker crumbs
2. 3 Tbsp. sugar
3. ¼ lb. butter, oleo, or margarine

Middle Layer

1. 1 pkg. dream whip
2. ½ cup powdered sugar
3. 8 oz. cream cheese

Top Layer – any kind of "Thank you" brand pie filling.

Directions:

1. Place in pie pan and bake according to directions on the "Thank You" Brand pie filling.

Jolly Breakfast Ring

Ingredients:

1. 4 Tbsp. Margarine (butter)
2. 2 Tbsp. Brown sugar
3. 12 cherries
4. ¼ cup chopped nuts
5. ½ cup sugar
6. 1 tsp. cinnamon
7. 3 Tbsp. Chopped nuts
8. 2 cups Bisquick
9. ⅔ cup milk

Directions:

1. Melt margarine
2. In a 9-inch ring put 2 Tbsp.. margarine, brown sugar and cherries, sprinkle with brown sugar
3. In second bowl mix ingredients 5, 6, 7
4. In third bowl place Bisquick and stir in the ⅔ cup milk beat 15 strokes – will be sticky

5. Shape dough in 12 handfuls
6. Roll in butter & cinnamon mixture – second bowl
7. Place balls in mold and bake in preheated oven @ 400° for 25 – 30 minutes.

Peanut Butter Fudge

Ingredients:
1. 1 cup sugar
2. 1 cup brown sugar
3. ⅔ cup evaporated milk
4. ¼ cup butter
5. ½ cup peanut butter
6. 1 seven oz. jar marshmallow cream
7. 2 tsp. vanilla

Directions:
1. Combine sugar, milk & butter in saucepan
2. Bring to boil, stirring often
3. Cook to soft ball stage (234° - 236° on thermometer), stirring often
4. Add peanut butter, marshmallow cream & vanilla, stir to blend thoroughly
5. Pour into 8-inch square pan
6. Let set to firm, then cut in squares

Fruit Salad – Grandpa Dan's Favorite

Ingredients:
1. 1-quart strawberries – if frozen do not thaw before mixing
2. 2 cans chunk pineapple
3. 2 bananas sliced
4. 2 cans mandarin oranges

ROBERT ALAN MCDONALD, KATHIE EILEEN MCDONALD COURTNEY, RICHARD EDWIN MCDONALD, MARY JO MCDONALD HELFRICH

5. 2 eating apples – tart is best – peel, quarter, remove core and cut into chunks

Directions:
1. Mix all ingredients in a large bowl, chill in refrigerator
2. Serve either alone or with cookies or cake

Rhubarb Cream Pie

Ingredients:
1. 3 cup rhubarb
2. 2 crust pastry
3. 2 eggs
4. ¾ cup sugar
5. 3 Tbsp. Flour
6. 2 Tbsp. Butter
7. Dash nutmeg

Directions:
1. Cut rhubarb and put in unbaked shell
2. Beat eggs, add sugar, flour, butter & nutmeg
3. Pour over rhubarb
4. Top with pastry
5. Bake (oven temp and baking time not given – suggest 350⁰ for 20 – 30 minutes.

Hot Milk Sponge Cake

Ingredients:
1. 2 eggs
2. ½ cup milk
3. 2 tsp. butter
4. 1 cup sugar
5. 1 cup flour

6. 1 tsp. baking powder
7. 1 tsp. vanilla
8. ½ tsp. salt

Directions:
1. Put milk & butter in pan, melt – keep warm
2. Beat eggs about 3 minutes until fluffy
3. Add sugar very slowly – about 5 minutes
4. Add flour, salt, baking powder, mix well
5. Add milk mixture slowly
6. Add vanilla
7. Bake in greased 9x9 inch pan @ 350° for about 30 minutes or less.

Oatmeal Cake

Ingredients:
1. ½ cup water – bring to boil and add 1 cup oatmeal, let stand until needed
2. 1 cup brown sugar
3. 1 ½ cup flour
4. 1 tsp. soda
5. 2 eggs
6. 1 cup white sugar
7. ½ cup oil
8. 1 tsp. vanilla

Directions:
1. Mix ingredients adding the oatmeal mixture last,
2. Bake @ 350° for 30 – 35 minutes,
3. While baking, make icing

Icing

1 cup brown sugar, ½ cup cream, 1 stick butter – ¼ cup

Pour over hot cake.

ROBERT ALAN MCDONALD, KATHIE EILEEN MCDONALD COURTNEY, RICHARD EDWIN MCDONALD, MARY JO MCDONALD HELFRICH

Pineapple Nut Cake

Ingredients: Mix together:

1. 2 cups flour
2. 1 ½ cup sugar
3. 2 eggs
4. 2 tsp. baking soda
5. 1 tsp. vanilla
6. 1 can (20 oz.) crushed pineapple include juice
7. Last – add 1 cup chopped walnuts

Directions:

1. Pour into lightly greased oblong baking dish
2. Bake @ 350º about 40 minutes

Icing

1. 8 oz. Phila. Cream Cheese
2. 1 stick (1/4 cup) butter
3. 1 tsp. vanilla
4. 1 ½ cup confectioner's sugar
5. Mix thoroughly
6. Spread over cool cake

Jam Cake

Ingredients:

1. 1 cup jam
2. 1 cup shortening
3. 1 cup milk
4. 3 cups flour
5. Pink salt
6. Nuts to taste
7. 2 cups sugar
8. 4 eggs
9. 1 heaping tsp. baking powder
10. 2 Tbsp. Cocoa

11. 1 cup raisins
12. 1 tsp. all-spice

Directions:
1. No baking directions on card. ?350º for 30 minutes?

Chicken Log

Ingredients:
2. 2 (8 oz.) cream cheese
3. 1 Tbsp. Steak sauce
4. ½ tsp. curry powder
5. 1 ½ cups minced cooked chicken
6. ½ cup minced celery
7. ¼ cup chopped parsley
8. ¼ cup chopped almonds

Directions:
9. Mix all ingredients.
10. Serve on crackers

Pizza Dough

Ingredients:
1. 1 cup warm water
2. 1 tsp. salt
3. 1 egg
4. 3 Tbsp. olive oil
5. 1 package dry yeast
6. ¼ cup sugar
7. 2 ½ or 3 cups flour

Directions:
4. Put yeast in water, add salt, sugar, and oil mix
5. Add 1 or 1 ½ cups flour
6. Put egg in mixture and stir

ROBERT ALAN MCDONALD, KATHIE EILEEN MCDONALD COURTNEY, RICHARD EDWIN MCDONALD, MARY JO MCDONALD HELFRICH

7. Add the rest of flour until firm, test by sticking with finger, if it bounces, it is correct.
8. Let rise until it doubles in size

Pizza Sauce

Ingredients:

1. Two 8 oz. cans tomato sauce & a little water
2. Spices – onion, oregano, basil, margarine, celery salt, garlic powder or salt sugar, peppers
3. Cheese – provolone, parmesan, mozzarella.

Directions:

1. Put all ingredients in pan and simmer for ½ hour.
2. Put on dough.
3. Add cheese.
4. Bake @ 425º for 25 minutes.

THE MCDONALDS

REFERENCE INFORMATION

The following biographical document of Mr. John McWhinney, Jr. was taken from *Biographical Record Stark County Ohio, published by Chapman Bros. Chicago 1892.* It is included because of our respect and gratitude for the McWhinney's.

394   PORTRAIT AND BIOGRAPHICAL RECORD.

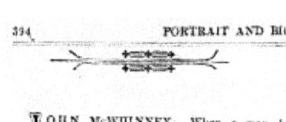

JOHN McWHINNEY. When a man is known to have experienced many trials, and to have labored hard to make his way in the world, it is a source of gratification to his friends to know that he has succeeded in reaching a height that enables him to take life very easy. This is the case with the gentleman above named, whose ability to make money has been abundantly illustrated, and whose career should encourage others to renewed energy, as it is not luck, but pluck, that has brought him a competency. He fought bravely during the late war as a soldier in the Army of the Cumberland, and is now numbered among the prominent tillers of the soil in Sugar Creek Township.

Our subject is a native of this county, his birth having occurred June 13, 1835. His parents were John and Nancy McWhinney, the former a native of the North of Ireland, while the latter was born in Pennsylvania. John McWhinney, Sr., emigrated when a young man to the United States, and in 1829 came to this county and made a settlement on the farm where our subject now lives. He located with his family on this tract of land, making a home in a rude log cabin, while he worked with persistence to place his land under cultivation and supply his home with comforts. By his marriage with Miss Nancy Wholf, he became the father of five children, of whom three are living, viz.: Mary J., the widow of John Welty; Margaret, the widow of Christian Kaylor, and our subject. The husband and father departed this life in 1863. His earnest character, benevolent disposition and kind heart endeared him to all whom he met, but his loss fell heaviest on her by whose side he had walked for many years, and to whose interests he was devoted.

Our subject can remember when Stark County was a sparsely settled wilderness and plenty of deer and wild game abounded. He attended the pioneer schools, where he obtained such an education as was offered, and was only a boy when he commenced to work with his father. September 1, 1861, on the outbreak of the late war, he enlisted in the Union army and became a member of Company F, Nineteenth Ohio Infantry, while his regiment became a part of the Army of the Cumberland. He participated in all the battles incident to the Atlanta campaign, and during the siege of that city received such injuries as occasioned his discharge, July 22, 1864. When he returned home at the close of a soldier's life, he resumed farming, and has been prospered in his operations, becoming the proprietor of two hundred and thirty-two acres of land. His estate is well developed, embellished with a good substantial farm house, barns, granaries, etc., and is supplied with farm machinery and stocked with domestic animals of good breeds and grades. In recognition of his services during the war, the Government awards to our subject a pension of $8 per month.

October 9, 1861, Miss Elizabeth Hall, daughter of Samuel and Susan Hall, became the wife of our subject. Her parents were early settlers of Sugar Creek Township, where they were representative citizens and well-to-do in this world's goods. By their union, Mr. and Mrs. McWhinney have become the parents of six children: Carrie E., Sterling J., Cullen H., Columbia V., Minnie H. and Jessie N. For four years, our subject served as Trustee of his township, and his military and civil record is highly honorable, and we are pleased to give this brief pen picture of it in this work.

The gentleman of whom we write has taken an active part in the meetings of the United Brethren Church, of which he is a member, and has served for some time as Trustee, Steward and Class-leader of that body. Socially, he is a Grand Army man, a prominent Mason and a member of the Knights of Pythias. He is a typical representative of the progressive agriculturists, and by his integrity and unimpeachable character enjoys the full confidence of the people. He carries on mixed farming and manages his affairs so well that, though he began life with limited means, he now occupies a front rank among the farmers of this county.

ROBERT ALAN MCDONALD, KATHIE EILEEN MCDONALD COURTNEY, RICHARD EDWIN MCDONALD, MARY JO MCDONALD HELFRICH

Farm Purchase

The Farm was purchased for $15,500 as shown on the agreements that follow:

```
                    Purchase Agreement      Feb 1st, 47.

    We  Carrie Mc Whinney              and  George  Stahl
   husband and wife  hereby agree to sell our    Farm
   located   Between Justus and Beach City
   to   Alpha Mc Donald                     for the sum of   $15,500
    $500.00   paid today, receipt of which is hereby acknowledged, and balance of  $15,000
   to be paid when deed and abstract, free of all encumbrances, is delivered. when possession
   is given
        It is further agreed that      we                  will pay the taxes due in

       june 1947       and taxes thereafter to be paid by   Mr Mc Donald
        Possession to be given on or before April 1st 1947
        ½ of the wheat now in the ground goes with the farm providing
        Mr Mc Donald pays for ½ of the ferterlizer, seed wheat, and threshing.
        Final payment to be made when possession is given.

                                    Signed  Geo. F. Stahl
                                            Jessie N. Stahl
                                            C Ethel Mc Whinney
                                            Alpha C. Mc Donald
```

THE MCDONALDS

Purchase Agreement Feb 1st, 47.

We Carrie Mc Whinney and Stahl

~~husband and wife~~, hereby agree to sell our Farm located Between Justus and Beach City

Alpha C. Mc Donald for the sum of $15,500.00

$500.00 paid today, receipt of which is hereby acknowledged, and balance of $15,000 be paid when deed and abstract, free of all encumbrances, is delivered. when possession is given.

It is further agreed that we will pay the taxes due in june 1947 and taxes thereafter to be paid by Mr Mc Donald possession to be given on or before April 1st 1947. of the wheat now in the ground goes with the farm providing Mc Donald pays ½ of the seed wheat and fertalizer and ½ of the ~~t~~hreshing. final payment to be made when possession is given

Signed R X Giffert
Realtor and agent for
Mc Whinney and Stahl

RALPH L. KINSEY   ATTORNEY-AT-LAW   NAVARRE, OHIO

*Paid in full
Ralph L Kinsey*

TO ALPHA C. McDONALD AND MARIAN P. McDONALD

```
Executing Mortgage and Note,
Bringing Abstract to date,
and certifying as to title.....$20.00

Recording Fees at Stark
County Court House for Deed
and Mortgage...................  3.55

Transfer Fee (Stark County
Auditor).......................    .10
                    Total......$23.65
```

ROBERT ALAN MCDONALD, KATHIE EILEEN MCDONALD COURTNEY, RICHARD EDWIN MCDONALD, MARY JO MCDONALD HELFRICH

McDonald Ancestry

The following information regarding our ancestry was taken from the web site: https://glenarmcastle.com/the-antrim-mcdonnell-heritage-centre/. The name Glenarm was derived from Gleann Arma, an Irish phrase which means "valley of the army."

Glenarm Castle

Glenarm Castle has been the ancestral seat of the McDonnell family, Earls of Antrim since it was first built by Randal, 1st Earl of Antrim in the 17th century.

In our Heritage Centre, you can discover the rollercoaster story of the Earls of Antrim full of adventure and intrigue, from the time when John Mor MacDonnell (Eoin Mor Mac Domnhaill) first arrived in Glenarm from Scotland in the 14th century, to the tumultuous wars of the 16th and 17th centuries when the family was based at Dunluce Castle, to the present day.

Glenarm is the family seat of the McDonnell (or MacDonnell) family, one of the oldest in these islands, which can trace its lineage back over 2,000 years. The Antrim McDonnells have played a key role in the story of the North Antrim coast, most notably in the 16th century under the leadership of famous warrior chief, Sorley Boy MacDonnell (Somhairle Buidhe Mac Domnhaill). It was Sorley's son Randal who became the first Earl of Antrim and built Glenarm Castle in 1636.

THE MCDONALDS

Translated from French "all days prepared" or Ever Ready

ROBERT ALAN MCDONALD, KATHIE EILEEN MCDONALD COURTNEY, RICHARD EDWIN MCDONALD, MARY JO MCDONALD HELFRICH

"Exploring the History and Mystery of Dunluce Castle"
By Colin
The following is a brief excerpt from the article:

"The MacDonnell Dynasty Takes Over:

In the mid-16th century, the powerful Scottish family, the MacDonnell clan, arrived in northern Ireland. Led by Sorley Boy MacDonnell, the clan quickly seized control of the area around Dunluce Castle, establishing themselves as the new Lords of the Route.

Under the MacDonnells, Dunluce Castle underwent a significant period of expansion and renovation. The castle's defenses were strengthened, and the living quarters were expanded and improved. The MacDonnell dynasty continued to hold the castle until the early 17th century when they were displaced by the invading forces of the English Commonwealth.

Despite the MacDonnells' eventual defeat, their legacy lives on at Dunluce Castle. Visitors to the castle today can still see the intricate carvings and decorations that the MacDonnells added to the castle, as well as the carefully tended gardens and grounds that they lovingly maintained.

Overall, Dunluce Castle is a testament to the rich and complex history of Northern Ireland. From its earliest beginnings as a simple stronghold to its lavish heyday as the seat of the MacQuillans and the MacDonnells, the castle has seen it all. Today, it stands as a proud symbol of Northern Ireland's past and a reminder of the enduring power of human ingenuity and creativity."

THE MCDONALDS

Falls House Tavern

Paul M. Smith authored an article entitled: "Beach City 1976 Bicentennial July 4, 1976, THE OLD FALLS HOUSE TAVERN, 1926 – 1936" which describes the tavern's history and disposition of the materials salvaged during the tear down. The article could not be reproduced here due to the possibility of copywrite infringement. It is suggested that the Beach City offices or the Brewster – Sugarcreek Township historical organization be contacted for further information.
https://www.brewster-sugarcreektwp-hist.org/history

50th Anniversary
The July 4th, 1969, Ohio Fireworks Derecho and Flooding Event

No one saw it coming

Authors and Contributors:
NWS Cleveland Summer Student Volunteers: Steven Weinstein (2019) and Michael Garberoglio (2018)
NWS Cleveland Hollings Student: Dallas McKinney
NWS Cleveland Meteorologists: Raelene Campbell and Zach Sefcovic
References: Thunder in The Heartland (Schmidlin J., Schmidlin T.), NOAA NWS Storm Prediction Center

Timing

Meteorology
July 4, 1969
The Unforeseen Aftermath
Loss, Images, and Personal Stories

ROBERT ALAN MCDONALD, KATHIE EILEEN MCDONALD COURTNEY, RICHARD EDWIN MCDONALD, MARY JO MCDONALD HELFRICH

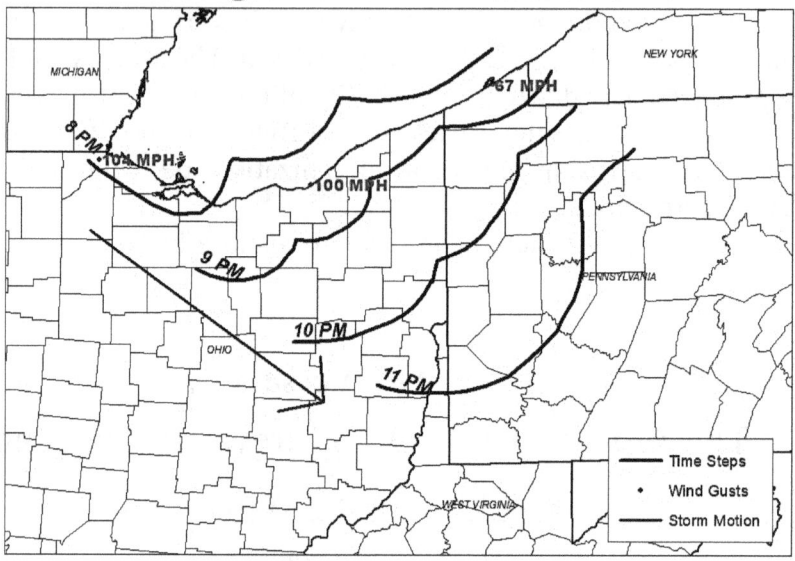

Areas affected by the July 4, 1969, derecho with the approximate hourly positions of the leading edge of the winds, and approximate wind gusts from the system. The red arrow represents the direction of the propagation of this storm system.

July 4th, 1969, started as a regular day of holiday fun. Families from all over the area gathered along the Lake Erie coastline for food and fireworks. However, unknown to the general public, a series of storms had developed over southeast Michigan. Several of these storms produced damaging winds, large hail, and several small tornadoes. Over the next few hours into the early evening, these storms evolved into a strong derecho as they moved southeast towards Lake Erie. These storms moved onshore very quickly before encountering a stationary boundary. The convection then slowed and stalled out for over 8 hours, causing catastrophic flooding. The derecho was responsible for millions in damages and several dozen fatalities.

Although forecasts early in the day pointed at the possibility for severe weather, when no storms turned up by late afternoon, the masses began to gather for what they thought would be a grand fireworks display. People along the lakeshore were completely unaware of the dangers brewing just some 50 to 75 miles to their northwest. Storms had fired over Lake Michigan and Lake Erie around 6 PM local time, but the masses carried on with the festivities, and were instructed to "think dry." Shortly after, the storms over the lake merged into a strong line, then into a bow echo before moving to the southeast.

Around 7:30 PM (local time here on), local forecasters from the National Weather Service (NWS) received their first alert that storms were approaching the area from the northwest. At 7:45 PM, the NWS informed the emergency broadcast system that an upgrade to a tornado warning was expected. This warning, however, was never issued. At Edgewater Beach, just west of downtown Cleveland where Independence Day festivities were in full swing, warnings were never relayed to the local public. According to a local account by Shirley Amster, a severe storm warning was issued and relayed by the Cleveland radio stations around 7:50 PM local time just before the derecho impacted the Lake Erie coastline but was not relayed over the marine channels. At the Edgewater Yacht Club, around 20,000 people had gathered to watch the fireworks. While police at the park had received the weather alert, it was not broadcasted over the P.A. because 'they didn't want the audience to panic.' Shortly after, and just before the storms moved into the Lake Erie coastline, the storms merged into a stronger line, and then into a bow echo, before moving off to the southeast.

The 1969 derecho, appropriately named the Ohio Fireworks Derecho, blasted on shore around 8 PM, right as holiday festivities were beginning in earnest all along the lakefront. Widespread winds wracked the entirety of the lakeshore, with a boater near Toledo recording a gust of 104 mph, and gusts of 100 mph reported in

ROBERT ALAN MCDONALD, KATHIE EILEEN MCDONALD COURTNEY, RICHARD EDWIN MCDONALD, MARY JO MCDONALD HELFRICH

Cleveland. The derecho continued its southeastern track reaching the Akron area between 9 and 10 PM and eventually into the Pittsburgh area between 10 and 11 PM. After 11 PM, the derecho began to dissipate and the strongest winds along the leading edge ceased. However, the danger was far from over as a stationary frontal boundary persisted. As a result of the wind damages, thousands of trees were uprooted and thrown, buildings and homes were damaged and destroyed, and boats were flipped and capsized, drowning 4 people in the process while also causing 100 others to need rescuing by the Coast Guard. People waiting outside for fireworks were offered a much different show than anticipated as rain, wind, and lightning ripped apart outdoor venues and caused mass power outages. One of the hardest hit areas was Toledo where the winds knocked down 5,000 trees and damaged several homes, leaving 75,000 homes without electricity. After the storms, according to the Cleveland Plain Dealer as reported by the Cleveland Electric Illuminating Company, 175,000 customers were without power. Another hard-hit area was Lakewood, located just to the west of Cleveland, where the damage and destruction was extensive.

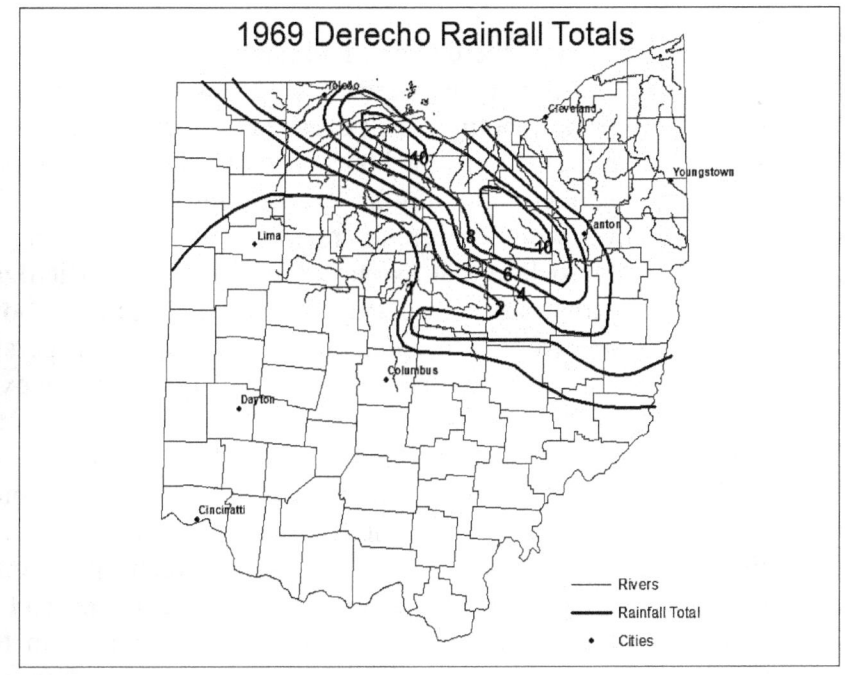

Reproduced image showing the rainfall (in inches) on July 4-5, 1969. The local area rivers and streams are also represented on this image in the blue outlines.

Despite the wind damages left behind from the powerful derecho, this was not the end of the storms reign in Northern Ohio. Most of the damages and fatalities associated with this event were to follow the derecho winds. Unfortunately, the fast-moving derecho, which should have moved on from the region rather quickly, left a strong pocket of instability and ample upper level and surface moisture behind. These ingredients resulted in additional storms firing overnight along the stationary front that evolved from the warm front seen on the 7 AM surface analysis.

The excessive rainfall that fell was the result of northwesterly winds across the surface in Northern Ohio that persisted after the main bowing segment of the derecho had passed. Specifically, it is these winds that brought in warm, moist air from the west throughout the overnight hours which caused the storms and rainfall to persist into the early morning hours on July 5th. Furthermore, these surface winds combined with the trailing regions of the derecho's outflow which became nearly stationary along a northwest-to-southeast line that extended from southern Michigan into northern Ohio to produce the deluge of rainfall seen in the above map. The stationary front also aided in causing storms to persist throughout the night of July 4th, and to continuously dump rain over the entire area for over 8 hours, causing widespread flooding and flash flooding. Ultimately, more than 10 inches of rain, with as much or more than 14 inches, fell over the duration of just 8 to 12 hours across portions of North-Central Ohio leading to disastrous impacts.

While the leading outflow associated with the derecho-producing convective system moved out of the Northern Ohio region by 10 PM local time, the persistence of the moisture and instability in the region continued to promote convection and storm development across the Northern Ohio with the "training" of the storms (rainfall persisting in a specific area) occurring. By 1 AM local time, after hours of heavy rains, flash floods were breaking out over a large swath of Ohio, along a line 20 miles wide that ran from the Toledo area clear into Wheeling, West Virginia. Rainfall rates exceeded a staggering 2 inches per hour in most areas, and rain accumulation totals were well into the double digits. In most of these areas, flooding was prominent as far as the eye could see. This was especially the case in Ottawa and Sandusky counties where fields, homes, and roads were all flooded. In the city of Toledo, an 8 million gallon water and oil storage basin overflowed, creating an oily pond in the area. In the city of Fremont along the Sandusky River, floodwaters were 4 feet deep, and further southeast in Norwalk the floodwaters pushed through the road network and the lower reservoir southeast of the city broke knocking out the power plant and leaving the city without power or clean drinking water for 5 days. Within the city of Norwalk, floodwaters were as deep as 7 feet inundating houses, buildings, and cars. Also in Huron County, the water remained 3 feet deep in the city of Bellevue a full week after the flooding began. Further southeast in Northern Ashland County, most areas were without power for two days after the floodwaters receded, and 30 bridges in Ashland County alone were damaged. All of Wayne County got more than 9 inches overnight, with Chester Township reporting a whopping 14.8 inches in just over 8 hours while observations at Marshallville and Wooster recorded 9.44 and 10.36 inches of rain. With 110 destroyed or damaged bridge structures and widespread flooding over major road networks, virtually every road leading in or out of Wooster was closed. The city's water plant wasn't operational until July 11th, while Orrville (also in Wayne County) suffered from a total power loss. They didn't manage to restore power to even 10 percent of the city until the 7th. Sixty-six bridges were damaged within Erie and Huron Counties with another sixty-five bridges damaged in Holmes County.

The worst of the flooding and its impacts, however, was associated with the flooding of the river basins, with several rivers reaching critical flood stage levels. Due to the suddenness of the heavy rain that fell as well as the excessive runoff into the local rivers and streams, several of the rivers reached into moderate or major flood stages. Some of the rivers even reached record flood levels. Some of those rivers still have the July 4th-5th, 1969, flooding event as the flood of record to this day. It is possible that even more rivers across Northern Ohio would have experienced record or near-record flooding if gauges and data had existed for the rivers at this time. The Killbuck Creek rose 20 feet from its usual levels, breaking an all-time record for the area and putting 95 percent of all standing structures in the town under water. On July 5th, 1969, the stage in Killbuck at the gauge KILO1 was reported as 26.4 feet, which is 7.9 feet above the present day major flood stage level. This resulted in hundreds of residents spending days living in the local elementary school. The Ashland Reservoir dam gave way the morning of the

ROBERT ALAN MCDONALD, KATHIE EILEEN MCDONALD COURTNEY, RICHARD EDWIN MCDONALD, MARY JO MCDONALD HELFRICH

5th, inundating the Jerome Fork Watershed with about 110 million gallons of water. This disaster cost the city of Killbuck a third of its entire water supply. The Vermilion and Elyria river site gauges along the Vermilion and Black Rivers also reached record flood stages from this event which still hold to this day. On July 6th, 1969, the stage at the VERO1 gauge along the Vermilion River just to the south of Vermilion reached 17.14 feet, 1.64 feet above the present day major flood stage level. Also on July 6th, the stage at the ELRO1 gauge along the Black River in Elyria reached 26.4 feet, 8.4 feet above the present day major flood stage level. As a result of both the flooding of the Vermilion and Black Rivers, 440 homes were evacuated within Lorain County. Further west, the Huron River in Milan at gauge location MILO1 also reached record flood level from this event. On July 5th, 1969, the river rose to a staggering 31.1 feet, a whole 8.6 feet above the present day major flood stage level. As a result, more than 4,800 people were evacuated from their homes in Erie County due to the excessive rainfall and flooding of the river. Other rivers that had this in the record books included the MLNO1 gauge along the Tuscarawas River in Massillon where the river crested to its second highest level ever on record, second only to the flooding caused by the Great Flood of 1913. On July 5th, 1969, the river reached a stage of 16.43 feet on, which is 0.43 feet above the present-day moderate flood stage level for the river gauge.

All, however, was not terrible, as there were a few bonding heroic moments from the disaster of the evening of July 4th. Major flooding was avoided in Massillon, where twelve men courageously worked together to close gates on the railroad opening between levees near the flooded Tuscarawas River. The river would have crested 10 feet above flood stage and would have caused millions more in damages. Additionally, in Ashland, two highway patrol officers, a gas station owner, and a truck driver were able to pull a family of four from their car after it got caught in flood waters and was swept right off of I-71. There were also other reports of heroic rescues across the state of Ohio.

THE MCDONALDS

In total, the floods killed 14 people in Wayne County alone with more deaths coming as people were swept off the roadways in their vehicles by the floodwaters or as they drowned trying to escape the floodwaters. A total of 25 to 30 people were killed by the flooding, mostly by drowning.

The National Weather Service describes The Great Blizzard of '78 as follows on its website:

The Great Blizzard of 1978 (weather.gov) Rain and fog were widespread across the region during the evening hours of January 25, 1978, with temperatures generally in the 30s and 40s. National Weather Service offices across the Great Lakes and Upper Ohio Valley had issued blizzard warnings for most of the region by late evening on January 25th. Early the next morning, an arctic airmass pushed into the area with bitter cold temperatures and howling winds. Blizzard conditions arrived in Cincinnati around 1 AM January 26 and reached Dayton and Columbus within the next couple hours. By 7 AM, blizzard conditions extended all the way to Cleveland. Visibilities were near zero for much of the day and even into the 27th. Temperatures rapidly plunged from the 30s to bitter-cold single digits in just a few hours. Wind gusts averaged 50 to 70 mph for much of the day on the 26th, reaching 69 mph at Dayton and Columbus and 82 mph in Cleveland. An ore carrier stranded in thick ice on Lake Erie just offshore from Sandusky reported sustained winds of 86 mph with gusts to 111 mph that morning! Extremely cold wind chills around minus 50 degrees or lower continued throughout the day, making it especially dangerous to venture outside. While snowfall was difficult to measure due to the strong winds, official storm-total snowfall amounts from January 25-27 ranged from 4.7 inches in Columbus to 6.9 inches in Cincinnati to 12.9 inches in Dayton. Other areas across the region saw well over a foot of snow from the storm.

ROBERT ALAN MCDONALD, KATHIE EILEEN MCDONALD COURTNEY, RICHARD EDWIN MCDONALD, MARY JO MCDONALD HELFRICH

From Wikipedia: Description of Hackney Ponies
General appearance

The Hackney pony may not be above 14.2 hands (58 inches, 147 cm) and usually range between 12 and 14 hh. It should have true pony characteristics and should not be a scaled down version of the Hackney Horse. The pony should have a small pony head, carried high, with alert and pricked ears and large, intelligent eyes. The neck should be muscular, arched, and carried proudly. Hackney ponies should have powerful shoulders, a compact back, and a light frame. The legs are strong with good joints, but the bone is usually fine. The feet are very hard and are usually allowed to grow long in the toe to accentuate the action of the pony. The tail is often set and is carried high. They usually have even more exaggerated action than the Hackney horse, knees rising as high as possible and hocks coming right under the body. The action should be fluid, spectacular, and energetic.

Colors

Hackney ponies may be black, bay (which includes brown), or chestnut. Bay is by far the most common color, but black is also relatively common. Chestnuts, on the other hand, are extremely rare; their color is usually particularly light, and chestnut ponies often possess flaxen manes and tails. Many hackneys also have some white markings. Due to the sabino gene, common in the breed, the Hackney Pony may have white markings on its body as well as on its legs and head. The sabino gene (possibly a gene complex), is generally unpredictable, so breeding solely for body white marks can be difficult.

Temperament

The Hackney Pony also has a reputation for being tenacious and fearless, qualities that are seen in top-tier show ponies. They are very brave, alert, and active, and possess great stamina. Generally, they have pony character. Hackneys have a reputation for being friendly toward humans and are suitable for both show and as companion animals.

ROBERT ALAN MCDONALD, KATHIE EILEEN MCDONALD COURTNEY, RICHARD EDWIN MCDONALD, MARY JO MCDONALD HELFRICH

THE MCDONALDS

Robert, Kathie, Richard, and Mary McDonald grew up on a northeast Ohio Farm near Amish Country. They wanted to share their experiences with their children and grandchildren so they decided to capture those stories in a book that would live on after they were no longer around. They found it took all four of them to record the various points of view. The stories were shared with friends and relatives who commented on how much they liked reading about their early lives. This is their first book.

All four are either retired or semi-retired, and none expected to write a book.

Robert was an internal auditor for several corporations finishing his career auditing major construction projects for project owners.

Kathie was a registered nurse, who completed her career as the charge nurse in a nursing home.

Richard is a carpenter and owner of a construction business.

Mary was a Speech Pathologist, certified to teach grades K through 12.

All of them credit their later success with upbringing and work ethic from those years on the farm.

www.ingramcontent.com/pod-product-compliance
Lightning Source LLC
Chambersburg PA
CBHW071235160426
43196CB00009B/1064